Letterla

PROGRAMME O

TEACHER'S GUIDE

by Lyn Wendon

I like

Clever Cat

Collins Educational

An imprint of HarperCollins*Publishers*

Contents

Foreword

The first edition of this guide in 1972 carried a Foreword by Peter Smith, a primary advisor and author of many books in the field. He described Letterland as:

'...straddling the ebb and flow of controversy concerning the best method for teaching literacy skills, and reading in particular.....bringing a fresh spirit of adventure into learning letters and a happy collaboration between teachers and children in the language built around this learning.'

I find it so good that this fresh spirit, which Peter Smith then detected in Letterland, is now active in more than 10,000 schools, continuing to spread its happy influence in the UK and to many English-speaking and English-teaching schools abroad.

I am grateful now to have the support of the leading English language publisher, HarperCollins, in developing the effectiveness of Letterland in accordance with best current professional practice. The present volume is just one fruit of this support.

I devised Letterland to rescue Special Needs children who had failed to respond to all conventional methods. Their successes with Letterland led teachers to think of using Letterland in classrooms with 6-7 year olds, to preclude failure rather than to cure it. Then the 5 year olds wanted to be involved in Letterland too. Clearly, they had no difficulty in picking up on its lore in reception classes. Pre-schoolers soon joined in as well, at home and in nurseries, and Letterland is now widespread as a very special way into print for all children.

At the World Congress of the International Reading Association in 1986, I drew attention to the dynamic triangle between children, parents and teachers in learning with Letterland. The nature of Letterland lore, explaining letter behaviour through stories, was eminently suited for sharing between children and parents, as well as between children and teachers. Anecdotes about the Quarrelsome Queen, who never goes anywhere without her umbrella (**qu**), or the Hairy Hat Man, who never speaks above a whisper (the voiceless sound of **h**), have carried Letterland into the home and have brought down the age level at which children want to tackle print. That is exciting.

Of course, the classroom is affected. 'Ownership' of Letterland, as a teaching tool, is now shared. Children's earlier familiarity with letters gives them confidence to control print as a tool of their own, and everyone, children, teachers and parents, have joy in a story-like language of instruction in which the power of metaphors – both visual metaphors (the pictogram designs which fuse Letterland characters into letters) and verbal metaphors (the story explanations) – is developed not only playfully, but in a way which enhances the children's sensitivity to language.

It is these metaphors which become the information carriers. Through them Letterland lore passes freely between teacher and child, teacher and parent, and child and parent. It is a happy equation, which I believe is the secret of Letterland's worldwide success.

Lyn Wendon

Introduction to Letterland

Letterland was devised to help teachers explain the complexities of written English, with its many rules and even more exceptions, in a child-friendly way. On one level, children will first perceive Letterland as simply fun, but beneath the surface, almost subliminally, there is a structured and systematic course for developing the following:

• listening and speaking skills
• phonic skills
• whole-word recognition
• reading for meaning
• early creative writing.

As with all Letterland teaching, the vehicle for learning about letters and how they combine in words is the telling of stories. Children are encouraged to listen carefully to the stories so that they can ask questions and speculate about letters, their shapes and their sounds. The discovery that all the letters' sounds can be found simply by starting to pronounce their characters' names* is strengthened when the children learn how to picture code each letter shape. This picture coding helps them to 'see' the letters' sounds. The effect is simultaneous reinforcement of both shape and sound in any given word.

The Early Years Programme provided guidance on how to introduce all the Letterland characters and focused predominantly on initial sounds. Programme One helps to take the teaching of Letterland many steps further. While consolidating skills already covered in the Early Years, it also shows children how to put letters together to form blends. They learn their first important digraphs, and above all, they come to understand how letters function in words, so that their reading and emergent writing progresses with real confidence.

Your story-like style of instruction gives the children a special initiative early on. Their curiosity about Letterland is stimulated, leading them to participate in the storytelling and to explore Letterland in their imaginations. They recount the stories and, as they do so, they reinforce their learning. You can encourage the children to decide which words apply to different characters. Is Hairy Hat Man handsome? Helpful? Handy with his hands? Is he quick to quarrel? Who is quick to quarrel? Quarrelsome Queen, of course. What hobbies might the Hat Man have? The children can decide. They may suggest hopscotch, hide and seek, hang-gliding, even hunting for hedgehogs! You can give them the confidence to speak up by making them realise that it is their ideas that count.

* The only exception to this is Max and Maxine's sound ('k-ss...'), which is found *inside* or at the *end* of words.

In teaching digraphs, you can maintain your storytelling style. Once the children are aware that **c** makes one sound and **h** another, they then need to know that **ch** together makes a completely different sound. With Letterland, children learn that whenever Clever Cat sits next to Hairy Hat Man, his hairy hat makes her nose tickle and so she sneezes, making the funny little 'ch...' sound we hear in words like **chips** and **much**. This story will stick in children's minds because it engages their curiosity and captures their imagination.

Some whole-word recognition is also encouraged from the start. The alliterative character names (Clever Cat, Eddy Elephant, Golden Girl, Poor Peter and so on) include no less than 40 common words which young readers will soon recognise as sight words in other contexts as well.

By the end of Programme One, your children should know:

- all the alphabet sounds and lower case and capital letter shapes
- how to blend and therefore read any regular word
- that letters may change their sound in specific sequences
- that words have recurring letter patterns within them
- that paying attention to these recurring letter patterns helps in developing a strong sight vocabulary
- how to alternate between 'sight' and 'sounding out' reading strategies, according to need
- that words carry messages, alone, in phrases and in sentences.

Above all, they will have discovered that reading, writing and spelling can be fun!

Why use Letterland?

The difficulties inherent in traditional phonic teaching lie in part in the language of instruction. Children have to learn it. They cannot speak it naturally, and they do not find it interesting. Letterland introduces a story-like instruction language where phonic facts ride home on memorable analogies which children readily understand. The stories enliven your teaching, making it more immediate for the children. Letterland also provides a way into print regardless of what other reading materials are being used in the school.

Below you can see a comparison between language spoken by a traditional teacher against that spoken by a Letterland teacher. The changes, though small in detail, are far-reaching in effect.

Traditional teaching	Teaching with Letterland
✰ Letters are called by their alphabet names: 'aee', 'bee', 'cee', etc. These are confusing for children, to say the least. In eight consonants the correct sound is at the start. In six it falls at the end, and in the remaining seven, at *neither* end! The five vowel names give no clue to the short vowel sounds. To add to the confusion, 15 letters actually begin with *another* letter's sound (**c, f, g, h, k, l, m, n, q, r, s, u, w, x** and **y**)!	✰ Letters are called by their Letterland names: 'Annie Apple', 'Bouncy Ben', 'Clever Cat', etc. All 26 letter names are made from descriptive and meaningful words, so children can learn them as readily as friends' names. Similarly, because letters are spoken about by their character names, they soon become 'friends' of the children. 
✰ The letter sounds 'ah', 'buh', 'cuh', etc. are meaningless to children and are difficult to remember. No logic in their letter names leads them to these sounds, or to their accurate pronunciation.	✰ Letter sounds are easy to learn, as a child *always* finds the correct sound just by starting to name the Letterland character.* Alliteration, built into each character name, reinforces the correct sound in every case.

* The only exception to this is Max and Maxine's sound ('k-ss...'), which is found *inside* or at the *end* of words.

Traditional teaching	Teaching with Letterland
✩ Position words when referring to letters can be ambiguous: 'before', 'after', 'followed by', 'in front of', 'behind', 'to the right of the', etc.	✩ Every letter has an unambiguous front and back, so all words describing letter position and orientation in a sequence are clear from the start.
✩ Technical phrases are hard to follow, such as 'short' or 'long' sounds, 'hard' or 'soft' sounds, 'this is a consonant', 'this is a vowel', 'it says its name', etc.	✩ Technical phrases are avoided where possible and more child-friendly phrases, such as 'he is a Vowel Man' and 'he says his name', are used instead.
✩ Digraphs are not logical. The teacher states a dry fact for the children to rote-learn, e.g. **sh**: 'When you see 'ess' next to 'aitch' in a word, the new sound will be 'sh'. (No reason available.) Children must suppress what they have already learnt about 'ess' and 'aitch' when learning the new sound. As a result, confusions between digraphs are common.	✩ Digraphs are made logical. The teacher tells a brief story, e.g. 'When you see Sammy Snake next to Hairy Hat Man, he hushes Sammy Snake up like this, 'sh!', because Hairy Hat Man hates noise.' Children use what they already know about the characters to understand a new development in their behaviour. As a result, confusions between digraphs are rare. 

SECTION 1

Be careful
Eddy Elephant!

Letterland for everyone

Letterland and the National Curriculum

Because Letterland approaches the teaching of phonics within a whole language context, it effortlessly combines speaking and listening, reading and writing, and is therefore entirely consistent with the National Curriculum at Key Stage 1 and Scottish 5-14 Guidelines.

As children listen to the stories explaining how letters behave, they naturally want to ask questions and speculate about letter shapes and sounds. This early phonological awareness leads them to recognise the letter sounds in words and helps them to decode the words for reading. By picture coding letter shapes, children begin to appreciate how letters combine to form words and this in turn informs their writing and spelling. In addition, the imaginative range of Letterland provides plenty of scope for creative writing as children explore the fantasy world and its inhabitants in their own stories, poems and plays.

Cross-curricular links

There are plenty of opportunities to incorporate Letterland into other areas of the curriculum. Art and craft is an obvious one. As a good starting point, you could organise a session where children make masks or puppets for all the Letterland characters out of card or papier maché. For children who still need hands on experience of letter shapes, you could provide modelling dough. Encourage them to make relatively thick letters in one colour and then to add all the characters' features in contrasting colours.

Large murals of Letterland can help to inspire children to consider how the imaginary world of Letterland might look. They could plan where each character might live and add appropriate alliterative landmarks or objects around them. You could re-create real life events in Letterland, such as the Olympics or a royal wedding, through artwork, crafts, puppetry, story-telling, etc.

Letterland can also be successfully incorporated into any Science and Technology teaching. On pages 176-80 you will find cross references to the Letterland book for teachers called *Ideas for Science and Technology*, where the Letterland characters and their characteristics are used as springboards for investigations across a wide range of scientific concepts.

Children with Special Needs

It was, in fact, children with Special Needs who, in the first instance, inspired the idea of Letterland stories to explain the behaviour of letters in words.

The fusing of a pictogram into each letter has also been shown to help the more severely handicapped child, the partially-sighted, the partially-deaf, the neurologically and the motor-handicapped child. The system reaches them not just through their eyes, ears or hands, but also by offering them a 'Letterland logic' to strengthen otherwise difficult rote-learning. Because the facts acquire reasons, they are easier to remember.

In any classroom there are children who will learn best if your first focus is on the initial letter and overall look of each new word they are learning. For them you will find simplified versions of the fully picture-coded *Programme One Flashcards* on pages 183-87, for all but the character name cards. These can be photocopied up to whatever size you wish and mounted on to card. For each flashcard, just the letter being taught has been picture-coded. At a later stage these children will make an easier transition to reading the fully picture-coded *Flashcards* and the sentences on the reverse sides.

English as a second language

By dispensing with the traditional alphabet names in the early stages of teaching phonics, the Letterland approach saves ESL (English as a Second Language) children from having to cope with the bewildering feature that no less than seven of the alphabet names are also high usage English words: **I, you, are, a, be, see** and **why,** not to mention **bee, sea, eye, oh, pea** and **tea.** Somehow, the non-English speaker must quickly gather whether the teacher is using them as common words or is referring to letter names.

The Letterland character names enable ESL children to learn useful words, for example, **g** is 'Golden Girl in her garden swing'. Before they know it, they have learnt six English words, the **g**-shape, and the 'g...' sound as well. The alliterative Letterland character names alone incorporate over forty common words.

Because the clues for learning the alphabet are not a miscellany of 26 separate pictures which a child must link to 26 foreign shapes, but rather 26 pictograms with the sound/symbol link already designed into them, the catch-up time for ESL children is achieved more swiftly than is normally possible.

While ESL children may not be able to keep up at first with the whole range of language activity contained in Programme One, they can share immediately in the play-acting, art, crafts and singing. Much of the story logic can be retold in their native language (a good opportunity for parent involvement). Meanwhile, the Letterland characters mediate between the ESL children and the undeciphered letters, motivating them to master all the new shapes and sounds.

Parental involvement

Research has highlighted the benefits of informed parental support at home as children progress in learning to read.

As soon as children start to learn the alphabet, parents can help by reading the *Letterland ABC Book* out loud to them. By exploring the illustrations together in search of objects beginning with the featured Letterland character's sound, parents can help to develop the letter shape/sound link in their children's minds. They can also pay special attention to Letterland artwork and any picture-coded words the children may bring home.

Some basic guidelines for parents are set out on page 191 in a 'Letter to parents'. This may be photocopied and distributed to parents, or used as a starting point for writing your own information sheet for them. Where some children in a class are receiving a lot of parental support but others are not, the school may like to provide time for parent volunteers to come into the school and work with those who lack help at home.

No matter what level of participation by parents becomes possible with any one class in any particular year or age group, the value of parents reading out loud to their child or children is important to stress. By letting this become a time of mutual pleasure, the parent will be providing for one of the most important long-term goals: a life-long appetite for reading.

Letterland Programme One

The materials

Essential

- ☆ *Letterland Programme One Teacher's Guide*
- ☆ *Letterland Programme One Picture Code Cards*
- ☆ *Letterland Programme One Flashcards*
- ☆ *Letterland Class Wall Frieze*
- ☆ *Letterland Handwriting Songs Cassette*
- ☆ *Letterland Alphabet Songs Cassette*
- ☆ *Letterland Programme One Songs Cassette*
- ☆ *Letterland Programme One Workbooks 1-4*
- ☆ *Letterland Programme One Copymasters*

Highly recommended

- ☆ *Letterland ABC Book*
- ☆ *Letterland Storybooks*
- ☆ *Letterland Links Books* (Groups 1-5)
- ☆ *Letterland Word Books*
- ☆ *Letterland Listen and Write Copymasters*
- ☆ *Letterland Code Sheet Copymasters*

Notes about the materials

Programme One Teacher's Guide

The *Programme One Teacher's Guide* has been specially written for teachers wishing to introduce Letterland to their children for the first time, as well as to those who have already met Letterland in the Early Years. It provides guidance on how to introduce all the Letterland characters including the Vowel Men (long vowels) and how to blend sounds into meaningful words (in Section 2). It covers all the consonant blends, some common endings and the most important digraphs with **n** (**-ng** and **-nk**) and **h** (**sh**, **th**, **wh**, **ch** and **-tch**) (in Section 3). In Section 3 it also introduces the major Magic **e** principle which enables children to predict the sound of the preceding vowel and therefore read countless previously unknown words.

Each lesson in Section 2 is called a 'Step' and there are 26 of them in this guide. The first page of each Step has detailed notes on preparing for the lesson and then guidance on how to introduce that particular Letterland character. This is followed by guidelines on how to teach writing the letter shape correctly, how to teach its sound and how to explain its capital letter shape. Finally, follow-up practice for that letter and suggestions on how to teach word building are provided.

What you will have achieved by the end of this Step

Letterland materials which are needed for teaching this particular Letterland character

What you will need to prepare before the lesson

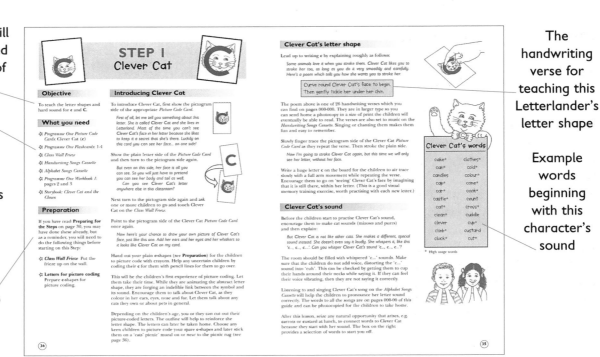

The handwriting verse for teaching this Letterlander's letter shape

Example words beginning with this character's sound

If some children are already familiar with the Letterland characters from pre-school, nursery or home, they will still enjoy the initial repetition and may even help other children. The major difference between their pre-school experience of Letterland and this Programme One will be the shift (from the third Step onwards) into creating words and learning not only how to read them, but also how to write them down with confidence, and to spell them accurately.

Programme One Picture Code Cards

The *Programme One Picture Code Cards* consist of 70 cards featuring all the lower case Letterland characters, as well as all the digraphs, endings and special characters covered in Programme One. In each case one side shows the pictogram letter and the reverse side shows the plain letter shape, so that you can, with a flick of the wrist, help with the transition to plain letter identification. It is particularly important that, even at the earliest stages, children link the Letterland character with its plain letter shape. Examples of words beginning with each letter sound are also provided on the backs of the cards. The purpose of the cards is for shape and sound recognition and word-building.

Programme One Flashcards

The *Programme One Flashcards* consist of 95 double-sided cards. For each letter of the alphabet there are one or two (if an alternative character exists) Letterland character name cards and three or four more cards showing fully picture-coded words. These words include the letter being taught, either at the beginning or within the word. The reverse side of each card shows a sentence presenting the featured word(s) in a meaningful context.

Initially, you may only wish to use the 31 main character names which draw attention to the **A-Z** capital letter shapes, introducing one character name as sight vocabulary at the start of each Step. The children can also seek out these names on the reverse sides of the cards as a skimming exercise, by running their eyes along the sentence.

For some children, learning to read the whole sentence can come later, as they become familiar with more and more letters of the alphabet, allowing more words in the sentence to become identifiable. Other children may be able to memorise the sentence and gradually learn all the words in it as 'sight vocabulary', simply by re-reading them often.

Simplified versions of all but the character name flashcards are also available at the back of this guide and may be photocopied up to an appropriate size and mounted on to card. On these flashcards, only the letter being taught in the Step has been picture-coded.

Class Wall Frieze

You will need to mount the frieze on the wall at a comfortable height so that the children can walk alongside it easily, talk about the letters, finger trace them, and match their *Picture Code Cards* to the frieze, using either the pictogram or plain letter sides. The frieze will also enable the children to become familiar with alphabetical order.

Handwriting Songs Cassette

The *Handwriting Songs Cassette* provides a memorable way of learning how to form all 26 letter shapes with the help of the Letterland characters. The words to these songs are given on the teaching pages for each letter. They are also laid out in full on pages 168-69 of this guide.

Alphabet Songs Cassette

The *Alphabet Songs Cassette* is intended to help children pronounce all the letter sounds correctly. Each song is sung to the tune of a well-known nursery rhyme. The words to these songs are on pages 170-71 of this guide.

Programme One Songs Cassette

The *Programme One Songs Cassette* is a collection of songs about the blends and digraphs covered in Section 3 of this guide, as well as any other special characters covered in Programme One. Also included on this cassette are songs about the vowel sounds and the Vowel Men.

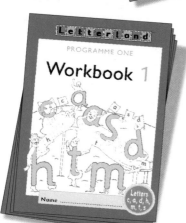

Programme One Workbooks 1-4

These workbooks follow the same teaching order as set out in this guide. Each workbook page provides opportunities for children to:
- identify the pictogram and compare it with the plain letter shape
- think about the Letterlanders' sound and pick out other objects beginning with the same sound
- practise writing the letter
- identify the featured letter in a short phrase by picture coding it
- use the letter to complete words.

Programme One Copymasters

These photocopiable sheets provide support material for Section 3 of this guide, that is, practice in common endings, all the consonant blends, the digraphs **ng**, **-nk**, **sh**, **th**, **wh**, **ch** and **-tch** and words containing the Magic **e**.

ABC Book

The *ABC Book* is strongly recommended for your Letterland teaching. All the Letterland characters are featured in language-stimulating scenes, where children can enjoy discovering numerous items beginning with their sounds.

Storybooks

These 20 storybooks provide hours of extra reading material. Each alphabet story features one or more of the Letterland characters.

Links Books (Groups 1-5)

The *Links* collection consists of five groups of eight readers, each group focusing on particular sound/symbol characteristics of individual letters and becoming progressively more difficult.

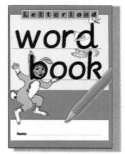

Word Books

These little *Word Books* enable children to create their own first personal dictionaries and to familiarise themselves with alphabetical order. Each letter page contains carefully chosen high usage words to start children off.

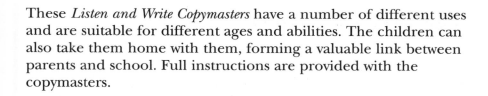

Listen and Write Copymasters

Photocopiable pages are available for all 26 letters of the alphabet, arranged in the Programme One teaching order. Their purpose is for linking letter shape with sound. Each Letterland pictogram is surrounded by various objects beginning with its letter sound, including one odd one out, which the children need to identify. They then colour in all but the odd one out.

These *Listen and Write Copymasters* have a number of different uses and are suitable for different ages and abilities. The children can also take them home with them, forming a valuable link between parents and school. Full instructions are provided with the copymasters.

Code Sheet Copymasters

Each of the 36 *Code Sheet Copymasters* is intended to be used many times. Their purpose is for handwriting practice, picture coding, reading practice and colouring in. They can also be taken home, either for further practice or to show how many words have been mastered so far. Full instructions are provided with the copymasters.

Teaching order

The teaching order of the letters in Programme One is as follows:

c, a, d, h, m, t, s, i, n, y, g, o, f, p, k, e, l, v, w, j, b, u, q, r, x, z.

The Steps begin with **c**, **a** and **d** to reinforce the same basic circular handwriting movement. Two of them (**d** and **a**) allow you and the children to create two useful words (**dad** and **add**) even before you teach any more of the alphabet. The letter **b** is deliberately introduced much later to avoid confusion with the letter **d**.

You then move on to **h**, **m** and **t** to keep the interest up and to allow the children to group letters into more meaningful words early on. The rest of the Steps' order is designed to keep potentially confusing letter shapes well apart (**d/b/p/q**, **n/u**, **m/w**, **s/z**, etc.), to introduce the vowels **a** and **i** first (because they occur in many essential words) and steadily to increase the number of words the children might sound out, spell and read for meaning.

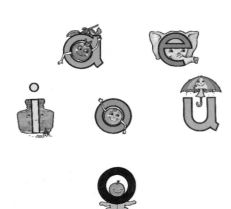

The first sounds that children will meet for the five vowels, **a**, **e**, **i**, **o** and **u**, are the short vowel sounds, represented in Letterland by Annie Apple, Eddy Elephant, Impy Ink, Oscar Orange and Uppy Umbrella. They will also meet the long vowels, in the form of the Vowel Men (see page 19). In addition, they will be meeting the irregular 'o...' sound as in **mother**, known in Letterland as Oscar's Bothersome Little Brother, the irregular 'e...' sound as in **they**, known as Mr Mean-E, and the silent **e**, as in the word **have.** The final part of this guide, Section 3, deals with the Magic **e**, some common endings, all the consonant blends and the most common consonant digraphs (see page 20 for further information). The contents of this section can either be taught after the 26 Steps, or referred to when appropriate. You could, for example, teach the letter **c** (Clever Cat) and then go on to teaching the **cl** blend (on pages 149-51).

The Steps all build on knowledge gained in the previous Steps, so the accumulative strengths of the teaching order could be lost by using, for example, an alphabetical order instead. The *Programme One Workbooks* also follow this teaching order. Feel free, however, to take advantage of events that give you a good reason to focus briefly on any Letterlander. For example, a safety event at school would be a very good reason to focus on Fireman Fred.

Nothing need be held back about 'who's who' in Letterland on account of the teaching order. Many children will, in any case, be gaining a growing familiarity with all the Letterland inhabitants at home from the *ABC Book* and other Letterland titles.

Long vowels (Vowel Men)

The Vowel Men are the only people in Letterland who ever say their names in words. This explanation makes it easier for children to understand that each of the five vowel letters has two different sounds: a long and a short sound.

The Vowel Men are called Mr A (the Apron Man), Mr E (the Easy Magic Man), Mr I (the Ice Cream Man), Mr O (the Old Man) and Mr U (the Uniform Man). By seeing and even dressing up as both the long and short vowels, and by comparing them on the *Class Wall Frieze*, children will improve their understanding of this dual function of the five vowels.

Some children will have long vowels in their names. Tell these children that their name is special 'because Mr A himself appears in it instead of Annie Apple', or 'Mr E himself...', etc.

Blending

The teaching of reading can get off to a very slow start unless the children learn the art of blending letters into words early on. By introducing a structured pattern of word building from the third letter learnt onwards, Letterland teaching provides many natural opportunities to work on blending: not just the consonant/vowel blends, but consonant/consonant blends as well. This early work on blending is an important key to good progress.

From the very first words you introduce (whether by constructing them from the *Picture Code Cards* or by getting the children to act out letter behaviour in live spelling) you will be teaching blending.

It is a good idea occasionally to slow down your voice so that you can emphasise each sound in a short word. For example, 'Do you think Hairy Hat Man is a nice mmmannn?' (Do not pause between sounds, distorting 'man' into 'muh/....a/...nnn'.)

Encourage the children to use this slow-speak technique as they start to write down words. Your aim is to ensure that children realise that they are capturing live speech, and that writing, in fact, is a way of keeping words after the talking is over. Good slow-speak words are those which you can pronounce slowly and continuously without distortion of their sound. You will find that dictating the words listed on pages 176-80 will do wonders for early emergent writing.

Consonant blends and digraphs

Programme One covers consonant-vowel blends, vowel-consonant blends and consonant-consonant blends (such as **bl**, **br**, **cl**, etc.). The latter are covered in more detail on pages 149-57.

For consonant digraphs (where both consonants represent a changed sound), new stories explain the sounds that single letters join to make, in this case, **-ng**, **-nk**, **sh**, **th**, **wh**, **ch** and also the trigraph **-tch** (see pages 135-48). The important feature in them is their logic. The storyline does not contradict the logic of the earlier stories, but extends it instead. Here the pictogram characters serve a vital function by enabling children to form a logical connection from the two single sounds (as in **s** and **h**) to the new otherwise contradictory sound (as in **sh**). While the digraph stories are placed at the back of this guide, be ready to explain, for example, the **sh** story as soon as the children stumble over common words like **she** or **shop** in their reading or emergent writing.

Pace

Before adopting Letterland, many teachers have considered it good practice to teach one letter a week. This all-out focus on single letter sounds spread over 26 weeks has often been the only way to ensure that all the class has known their **a-z** by the end of the year. Once Letterland has been adopted, however, teachers who continue this practice are not allowing the system to function at full strength.

If emergent writing is to begin early on, every letter of the alphabet is needed. Because Letterland characters can quickly be associated with the correct letter shapes, all the children then need is the trick of finding the letter's sound on their lips: simply by starting to say the character's name.

Most teachers find that their reception class pupils comfortably learn all the **aA-zZ** shapes and sounds, and the correct handwriting strokes for **a-z**, within two or three months. Each Step is intended to occupy one or two class sessions, workbooks included. Supportive art and craft work will take additional time. Aim to introduce three or four letters a week. Feel free to proceed more slowly in the beginning, but do not be surprised if the children increase the pace for you by asking for more stories, unaware perhaps that they are asking to learn more about reading and spelling.

Section 3 of this guide, the *Programme One Flashcards* and *Copymasters* (covering the Magic **e**, common endings, consonant blends and consonant digraphs) will help your children to move well beyond **a-z** before the school year is over.

Teaching with Letterland

Introducing each alphabet letter

Having 'arrived in Letterland' (see page 32), you will be ready to introduce the first Letterland character to the children, with the help of the appropriate *Programme One Picture Code Card*.

In each Step, the text printed in blue provides you with a model for the story-like style which will make your teaching both interesting and memorable. Do not feel that you have to stick to this wording rigidly: use your own wording and your own story-telling manner. Don't worry if you leave points out. Letterland is intended to be flexible.

At this stage, always refer to letters by their Letterland names, for example, 'Clever Cat' and not 'cee'. Traditional names like 'cee, aitch, em, cue, are, double-u, why' are confusing because they do not match the sounds that letters make in words (see page 7) or help with emergent writing. (See also **From alphabet names to Letterland names** on page 32.)

Picture coding

Picture coding is the process of adding Letterland pictogram details to a letter shape. By doing this, the children become the animators of lifeless letters. The drawing process is fun. As the children bring the letter shapes to life, they make the letters their own. It also greatly increases attention to the shape, sound and orientation of each letter.

After introducing each Letterland character, you may like to give each child the appropriate plain black letter shape for picture coding (see **Preparing for the Steps** on page 31). Both you and the children will be animating specific letters from time to time on children's names, art and craftwork, and workbook pages throughout the Steps.

When you meet irregular parts of a word you wish to animate, draw a wiggly line beneath those letters to signal that they are not representing the sound(s) taught so far. This wiggly line signals to the children that they should look at the word as a whole and if necessary ask for help if they cannot read it. While you will want to keep irregular words to a minimum at first, the wiggly line will enable you to bring in any high interest words as and

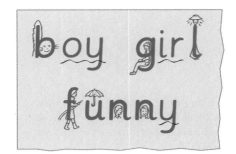

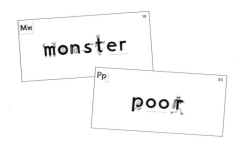

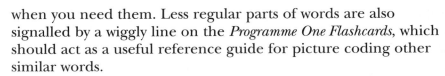 when you need them. Less regular parts of words are also signalled by a wiggly line on the *Programme One Flashcards*, which should act as a useful reference guide for picture coding other similar words.

Many words also contain silent letters. In these instances, when you want to add picture coding, simply show these letters by using a grey-coloured pen, or by writing them in dotted lines.

Use the special animating process only as long as the children need its support. By the time the novelty of drawing heads, feet, etc. on the letters has worn off, the picture coding will have served its purpose, until you introduce more advanced picture coding in Programme Two.

Letter shapes

The pictogram designs turn letter shapes into body parts. This makes it possible to teach correct letter formation in a memorable way, using the Letterland handwriting verses. They are set out in each Step and also at the back of this guide (see pages 168-69) and can be photocopied and sent home with the children for parental support. The verses are also set to music on the *Handwriting Songs Cassette*.

Each Letterland pictogram acts as a signpost orientating the children's eyes in the 'Reading Direction' (to the right) through parallels to their own bodies and actions (swimming, jumping, kicking, etc.). Whenever you are demonstrating the Reading Direction, be careful that you do not point to your right when you are facing the children. It is always safest to turn round, so that both you and the children are facing the same way. Most children find the term 'Reading Direction' easy enough to follow.

The children can practise letter formation by finger tracing letter shapes on the appropriate *Picture Code Card* or on the *Class Wall Frieze*, and by tracing them in the air. Handwriting practice for each letter shape is provided in the *Programme One Workbooks* and also on the *Code Sheet Copymasters*.

Letter sounds

By starting to say any Letterland character's name, a child can rely on having just said that letter's correct sound.*

The Letterland *Alphabet Songs* are useful for ensuring that all the letter sounds are pronounced correctly. As these songs are sung to the tunes of well-known nursery rhymes, they are easy to pick up and remember. The lyrics for them are printed in larger type on pages 170-71 and can be photocopied for taking home.

* The only exception to this is the letter **x** (Max and Maxine), whose sound is found *inside* or at the *end* of words.

For each Letterland character, including the Vowel Men, a list is provided of words beginning with that character's sound.* This should be helpful when you need suitable examples, and ensure, in the case of the vowels in particular, that you are choosing words starting with the correct sound. Word lists are also provided for the word endings, consonant digraphs and trigraphs, consonant blends, Magic **e** and other word groups covered in Programme One (see pages 130-66).

Capital letters

Letterland presents both lower case and capital letter shapes on the *Class Wall Frieze*. The character name *Flashcards* also feature picture-coded capital letters. Since the pictograms make the link to capital letters easy to learn, there is no need, for example, to write days of the week like this: **monday** or **tuesday**, or to limit early reading to sentences with no capital letters. Instead, you can let the children see words from the outset just as they appear in the world outside the classroom.

Children's names provide excellent teaching opportunities for capital letters, because children greatly enjoy discovering 'who' from Letterland helps them to start their name. Throughout the Steps, children can be shown how to picture code their names (see **Picture coding names** on page 26).

Live spelling

'Live spelling' is when children 'become' letters themselves and stand together in a row to form a word in 3-D. If the term 'letter' was meaningless at first, it will become more meaningful now because the children will mime being letters themselves. Then by grouping together, they will gain first-hand experience of being a 'word'.

To 'become' the Letterland characters themselves, the children simply hold or wear a *Picture Code Card*. While there is no need to add props or dress up appropriately, doing so adds to the fun of building words and makes 'live spelling' a popular activity (see **Costume box** on page 27). Play-acting the Letterland characters and copying their 'behaviour' enables children to remember each letter more easily. It also provides you with valuable opportunities for discussing letter sounds, working on blending sounds and, later on, for talking about silent or interacting letters (digraphs) exactly when they occur in a particular word.

To ensure that children are facing in the right direction as they create words, ask them to stand next to arrows on the wall and/or floor which point in the Reading Direction (see **Reading Direction sign** on page 31).

While children are making a word in 'live spelling', the other children can copy the word down from their standing friends. This is a very effective way to start learning to spell.

Revising letters ('Quick dash')

Before starting on a new letter, it is always a good idea to begin with a quick revision of the letters learnt so far. More detailed revision sessions are also provided throughout this guide.

Ideally, conduct your revision in a game-like atmosphere. Call it your 'Quick dash' routine and make it just that! Naturally you will want to begin slowly, but the aim of the game will be to develop speedy responses.

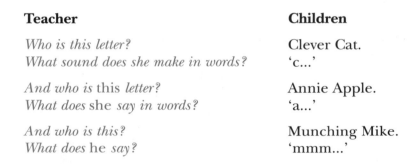

Hold up each *Picture Code Card* in turn, asking for the Letterland character's name, and then for its sound, as follows:

Teacher	Children
Who is this letter?	Clever Cat.
What sound does she make in words?	'c...'
And who is this *letter?*	Annie Apple.
What does she say in words?	'a...'
And who is this?	Munching Mike.
What does he say?	'mmm...'

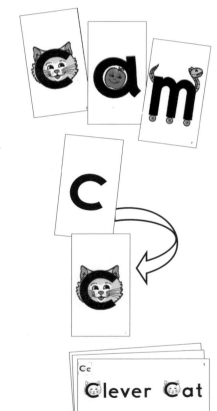

Next hold up the plain sides of each card and repeat your questions. Turn to the pictogram side only to confirm the children's answers.

Add each new letter you teach to the 'Quick dash' routine. Soon you can drop the questions. Just hold up the cards, plain sides only, and challenge the children to give you *just* the sounds. Follow on with a quick revision of the character name *Flashcards* (**Clever Cat**, etc). This will reinforce the capital letter shapes and whole-word recognition at the same time.

Developing your own style

The Steps are not intended to be taught word for word. Suggested teacher dialogue is printed in blue. If you feel it will help to read this out loud until you are familiar with it, then do so. Your aim, however, should be to find your own wording as soon as possible. Eye contact with the children is more important. You will also feel freer to enjoy the spontaneity in your classroom which will spring from the mix of Letterland fact and fantasy.

The pictogram system offers great flexibility. There is room in it for you to develop your own ideas and stories around the characters and encourage the children to contribute their own ideas, too. Letterland simply becomes a natural part of your language curriculum.

When to introduce the traditional alphabet names

Most children will get to know all the Letterland character names, such as Annie Apple and Bouncy Ben, long before you have completed all the Steps in this guide.

Ideally, you should progress to the conventional 'aee, bee, cee' letter names *only* when:

- the children have learned the letter sounds from the reliable Letterland character names, and are confidently sounding out 3, 4, 5 and 6-letter short vowel words in their reading
- their early writing shows that the children have learned to pay attention to the sounds in their own speech
- the children are able to write down the words they speak with reasonable approximation to their actual spelling.

Many spelling mistakes can appear to be careless omissions of letters, e.g. **bgan** (**be**gan), **rember** (rem**em**ber), **emt** (empt**y**), **yous** (**us**e), **prt** (pa**r**t), etc. In fact, such mistakes arise out of a confusion in the child's mind: which alphabet name, which is its sound, which to use in this word? Letterland teaching saves children from the burden of an ancient labelling system which, in the initial stages, is actually counterproductive to early reading and to confident early writing. By temporarily bypassing the traditional alphabet names, Letterland ensures that literally thousands of spelling errors need never occur.

So when should the traditional alphabet names be introduced and how? Many teachers find no need to introduce them at all, because children acquire such information informally or pick it up simply by singing a traditional alphabet song. Alternatively, once you are satisfied that the children have achieved the decoding and encoding skills described above, simply make temporary use of the 'Quick dash' routine (see page 24) to practise alphabet naming instead of practising the letter sounds. It will not take long. See also **The Traditional Alphabet Names Verses** on page 174-76 of this guide, which you may like to present in the form of a rap. Where a child cannot come up with a particular alphabet name easily, you can simply select the appropriate verse. Pause just before the alphabet name so that the child can supply it with the aid of the rhyme.

Further ideas

First dictionary

Give each child an exercise book containing a minimum of 26 pages and number the pages. As children learn a new letter, ask them to draw the appropriate Letterland character at the top of the correct alphabetical page, e.g. Clever Cat on page 3. They can then write in any new words they have learnt on the correct pages. Initially, they can also use it as a place for practising the new letter shape.

Picture coding names

Children's names provide excellent opportunities for picture coding both lower case and capital letters, because children greatly enjoy discovering 'who' in Letterland helps to spell their name. Names, however, often include silent letters and exceptions which will contradict the first letters you teach. By sign-posting these silent letters and exceptions, you can ensure that the children do not have to flounder among the contradictions (see **Picture coding** on page 21). A list of picture-coded children's names has been provided for you on pages 188-89 to help you with this task.

Throughout the Steps use the names of children in your class for highlighting any particular letters. You can either picture code them yourself on the board, or you can write out any names with a thick black felt-tip pen for children to picture code themselves, allowing plenty of space around the letters. Initially, you or the children will probably only be picture coding the first letter and each recurrence of this letter within their names. Display any picture-coded names in the classroom.

NOTE Children who have already met Letterland at the pre-school stage or at home may wish to picture code every letter in their names right away. If so, do not discourage them, but you may wish to draw a wiggly line under any irregular letters (see page 21).

Spelling pictures

A spelling picture is a vivid way of emphasising both the phonic features of a word and its whole-word meaning.

To begin with, you will need to write out a word using a thick black felt-tip pen. Choose concrete words which can be illustrated. Allow plenty of space around the word for the pictures illustrating its meaning. The letters of the word itself must also allow space for any picture coding. Different children can illustrate different words. Displayed on the wall, they quickly become words which every child wants to and *can* read.

Costume box

Create a costume box and collect any Letterland props in it. You might like to name it 'Clever Cat's Costume Box'. The props can be bought, borrowed or made. Headgear is especially useful for 'Live spelling' (see page 23), since hats, helmets, etc. only take a moment to put on. Any props will make demonstrations of words more lively and effective. Specific suggestions for all the Letterland characters are given below.

Annie Apple Make an apple leaf collar or hat.

Mr A Add a red and white striped apron.

Bouncy Ben Make ears or a mask for Bouncy Ben.

Clever Cat Make a Clever Cat mask.

Dippy Duck Enlarge the template of Dippy's head on page 183. Use two to make a duck headband. You could also collect any spare yellow clothing.

Eddy Elephant Make an elephant mask.

Mr E A magic wand should be an easy prop to make or find.

Fireman Fred Add one or two toy fireman's helmets.

Golden Girl Bring in a couple of old pairs of (sun)glasses and green items of clothing. Include some gardening gloves for Golden Girl and and some green gloves for her Granny, if possible.

Hairy Hat Man Make one or two hairy hats. They will be useful both now and later when the children play-act the digraph stories with **h** (see pages 138-48).

Impy Ink Make a black lid-like hat from stiff card or simply use a black hat or beret to serve as Impy Ink's bottle top.

Mr I Make one or two realistic ice cream cones.

Jumping Jim Add some juggling balls or thread three onto a wire.

Kicking King The children will enjoy helping you to make and decorate one or more crowns. In addition, you could try making Kicking King's cape using red crepe paper edged with cotton wool (the best kind is the type available on a roll).

Lucy Lamp Lady Add old lampshades or yellow clothing.

Munching Mike Make two monster masks, using cereal boxes covered in tin foil or painted.

Naughty Nick Add a toy hammer and a large nail made from stiff card.

Oscar Orange Add any orange clothing, such as an old T-shirt.

Mr O It should be quite easy to make a fluffy white beard from a roll of cotton wool or using white fur.

Poor Peter The children may like to make droopy ears out of paper, with pale brown patches painted on them. These can then be attached to headbands for wearing.

Quarrelsome Queen You will probably already have a crown in the Costume box for Kicking King, but it is useful for Quarrelsome Queen to have her own crown for words such as **quick**, where both characters are needed together in a word!

Robber Red Add any red clothing and make a mask.

Sammy Snake You may like to make a Sammy Snake glove puppet (using a large sock) or mask.

Ticking Tess Include one or two telescopes for Ticking Tess and Tom, made out of long cardboard tubes from tin foil or kitchen roll.

Uppy Umbrella Any old umbrellas would be very useful, but child-sized ones will be easier for the children to hold.

Mr U Add gold buttons or braid to a jacket and find or make a toy cap similar to Mr U's.

Vase of Violets Make a Vase of Violets headdress.

Wicked Water Witch It should be very easy to get hold of a witch's hat (especially around Halloween) and almost as easy to make one yourself!

Max and Maxine Make a large red cardboard **x**.

Yellow Yo-yo Man Make or buy yellow caps with yellow visors. If you haven't got any yellow or other coloured yo-yos, make some pretend ones out of cardboard discs attached to string.

Zig Zag Zebra Add some black and white striped clothing.

Actions to accompany the Letterlanders

As the children learn the Letterland *Alphabet Songs*, they can also, at the same time, mime the particular character's behaviour. They will consolidate both the letter shapes and their sounds through associations.

If the children are doing these actions in front of other children, make sure that their orientation is in the Reading Direction for their audience. To do this, they will need to think of the wall behind them as a large imaginary page. Opposite are some ideas for all the Letterland characters. You may also have ideas of your own.

a — Bob up and down like an apple on a branch.

Mr A — Mime picking apples and putting them into an apron pocket.

b — Bounce with arms outstretched.

c — Stroke imaginary whiskers, or go on all fours.

d — Flap elbows and waddle.

e — Two children can make the front and back of the elephant. The front child can swing an arm to make the trunk.

Mr E — Take off an imaginary hat and bow.

f — Hold an imaginary hose, with arms close to the chest.

g — Pretend to swing your feet as if on a swing.

h — Hop along with arms at sides.

i — Dip an imaginary pen into some imaginary ink and pretend to write.

Mr I — Lick an imaginary ice cream cone and wave.

j — Jump with both knees bending and elbows out.

k — Kick a leg and raise an arm repeatedly.

l — Walk stiffly in tiny steps, smiling brightly.

m — Three children can become a monster, moving and munching.

n — Bang in imaginary nails.

o — Cup hands in an **o**-shape, or do some forward rolls.

Mr O — Hobble like an old man and wave with the right hand.

p — Walk sadly, drooping both head and arms (ears).

q — Stomp about, followed by an umbrella child.

r — Run or prowl about, with an imaginary sack over the shoulder.

s — Slither on the floor in an **s**-shape.

t — Turn on tiptoe, with arms outstretched.

u — Carry an imaginary or real umbrella.

Mr U — March proudly, as if in uniform.

v — Make a **v**-shape with elbows together, hands apart.

w — Pretend to be a witch flying on a broomstick.

x — One or two children can blow kisses, and cross their arms.

y — Pretend to play with a yo-yo.

z — Pretend to canter, in an anti-clockwise direction. Try to look shy.

Stand next to me.

Hide one hand
under the other.

Action sentences

Action sentences such as 'Lift your little finger', written out on pieces of paper or card, give excellent practice in silent reading. If a child has understood the sentence correctly, he or she will prove it by doing the action stated.

A number of action sentences are provided on the backs of the *Flashcards* and will be referred to throughout this guide. Feel free to supplement these with your own cards.

In a group children can take it in turns to read the sentences silently and then to respond with the appropriate action. The other children will benefit from reading the words to themselves and watching/checking the actions made by the child having the turn. This also works well in pairs.

Preparing for the Steps

Before starting on Step 1, it is a good idea to have done the following things.

Things to do

☆ **Letterland materials** For each Step, you will need to gather the Letterland materials described under **The materials** on page 13. The **What you need** section in each Step tells you the precise cards or pages to have to hand.

☆ *Class Wall Frieze* You will also need to have put up the entire *Class Wall Frieze* on the wall. Place it at an accessible height for the children so that they can easily touch or finger trace the Letterland pictograms. Be prepared to tell the children any character names they ask to know!

Things to make

☆ **Reading Direction sign** You will need to prepare a Reading Direction sign and a number of paper arrows. Attach the sign somewhere prominent on the wall and put the arrows beneath it pointing to the right. You could also put some arrows on the floor to help the children when they are building words using 'Live spelling' (see page 23).

☆ **Letters for picture coding** One of the best ways for a child to 'get to know' a letter is by picture coding it (see **Picture coding** on page 21).

To do this, prepare thick black lower case letter shapes on pieces of card or paper for each child. For Step 1, you will only need to make these for the letter **c**: the other letters can be prepared as you work through the Steps. For the letter **c**, you may like to prepare a few extra ones in varying sizes for use on the 'cats' picnic' mural (see page 34).

As you progress through the Steps and the children become more confident, you may find that they are ready to draw or paint their own large letters to animate during an art period.

The 'journey to Letterland'

You may like to begin your teaching with a short 'Going to Letterland' routine which can be used before any Letterland session. You can all pretend to climb onto a magic Letterland carpet, flying on it to 'the special place called Letterland where all the letter people and alphabet animals live'. Alternatively, you and the children can ask each other 'How do you get to Letterland?' Then you might answer each other with 'Just open a book!' One of you can slowly and dramatically open a book, with large print, and peer into it. To leave Letterland you ceremoniously close the book. Later on you can ask the children to invent new ways of getting to Letterland.

From alphabet names to Letterland names

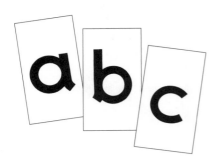

It is very likely that some children will come to school already knowing some of the traditional alphabet names. Many of these terms are misleading (as described on pages 7-8), so while showing the plain sides of the *Programme One Picture Code Cards* for Annie Apple, Bouncy Ben and Clever Cat to the children, explain how you will be talking about the letters, roughly as follows:

> *Some of you may be used to calling these letters by the names 'aee', 'bee' and 'cee'. Those are alphabet names. Your mothers and fathers may talk about them that way too.*

Now show the picture sides of the same three *Picture Code Cards*.

> *But the Letterland people and animals you see on these cards don't call each other by their alphabet names. They call each other by their Letterland names instead, names like Annie Apple, Bouncy Ben and Clever Cat.*

The reason for stressing the Letterland character names at this vital early stage is to ensure that the correct sound will be on the child's lips the moment he or she starts to say any Letterland character's name. By developing this reliable connection, all the confusions inevitably caused by overlearning the unreliable traditional alphabet names can be avoided.

Remember to develop your own presentation of the letters as the scheme progresses. Some children in your class may already be familiar with Letterland. Use your own judgement to decide how many of the stages to go through for each letter.

The initial Steps in this guide are set out in considerable detail. The later Steps are set out more briefly, since by then you will have acquired confidence in the storytelling style of teaching Letterland and seen how it strengthens communication between you and your children.

SECTION 2

STEP 1
Clever Cat

Objective

To teach the letter shapes and hard sound for **c** and **C**.

What you need

☆ *Programme One Picture Code Cards*: Clever Cat (**c**)

☆ *Programme One Flashcards*: 1-4

☆ *Class Wall Frieze*

☆ *Handwriting Songs Cassette*

☆ *Alphabet Songs Cassette*

☆ *Programme One Workbook 1*: pages 2 and 3

☆ *Storybook: Clever Cat and the Clown*

Preparation

If you have read **Preparing for the Steps** on page 31, you may have done these already, but as a reminder, you will need to do the following things before starting on this Step:

☆ *Class Wall Frieze* Put the frieze up on the wall.

☆ **Letters for picture coding** Prepare **c**-shapes for picture coding.

Introducing Clever Cat

To introduce Clever Cat, first show the pictogram side of the appropriate *Picture Code Card*.

*First of all, let me tell you something about this letter. She is called **C**lever **C**at and she lives in Letterland. Most of the time you can't see **C**lever **C**at's face in her letter because she likes to keep it a secret that she's there. Luckily on this card you can see her face... on one side!*

Show the plain letter side of the *Picture Code Card* and then turn to the pictogram side again.

But even on this side, her face is all you can see. So you will just have to pretend you can see her body and tail as well.
  *Can you see **C**lever **C**at's letter anywhere else in this classroom?*

Next turn to the pictogram side again and ask one or more children to go and touch Clever Cat on the *Class Wall Frieze*.

Point to the pictogram side of the Clever Cat *Picture Code Card* once again.

*Now here's your chance to draw your own picture of **C**lever **C**at's face, just like this one. Add her ears and her eyes and her whiskers so it looks like **C**lever **C**at on my card.*

Hand out your plain **c**-shapes (see **Preparation**) for the children to picture code with crayons. Help any uncertain children by coding their **c** for them with pencil lines for them to go over.

This will be the children's first experience of picture coding. Let them take their time. While they are animating the abstract letter shape, they are forging an indelible link between the symbol and its sound. Encourage them to talk about Clever Cat, as they colour in her ears, eyes, nose and fur. Let them talk about any cats they own or about pets in general.

Depending on the children's age, you or they can cut out their picture-coded letters. The outline will help to reinforce the letter shape. The letters can later be taken home. Choose any keen children to picture code your spare **c**-shapes and later stick them on a 'cats' picnic' mural on or near to the picnic rug (see page 36).

Clever Cat's letter shape

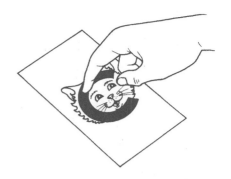

Lead up to writing **c** by explaining roughly as follows:

*Some animals love it when you stroke them. **C**lever **C**at likes you to stroke her too, as long as you do it very smoothly and **c**arefully. Here's a poem which tells you how she wants you to stroke her:*

> Curve round Clever Cat's face to begin.
> Then gently tickle her under her chin.

The poem above is one of 26 handwriting verses which you can find on pages 168-69. They are in larger type so you can send home a photocopy in a size of print the children will eventually be able to read. The verses are also set to music on the *Handwriting Songs Cassette*. Singing or chanting them makes them fun and easy to remember.

Slowly finger trace the pictogram side of the Clever Cat *Picture Code Card* as they repeat the verse. Then stroke the plain side.

*Now I'm going to stroke **C**lever **C**at again, but this time we will only see her letter, without her face.*

Write a huge letter **c** on the board for the children to air trace slowly with a full arm movement while repeating the verse. Encourage them to go on 'seeing' Clever Cat's face by imagining that it is still there, within her letter. (This is a good visual memory training exercise, worth practising with each new letter.)

Clever Cat's sound

Before the children start to practise Clever Cat's sound, encourage them to make cat sounds (miaows and purrs) and then explain:

*But **C**lever **C**at is not like other cats. She makes a different, special sound instead. She doesn't even say it loudly. She whispers it, like this '**c**..., **c**..., **c**....'. Can you whisper **C**lever **C**at's sound '**c**..., **c**..., **c**...'?*

The room should be filled with whispered 'c...' sounds. Make sure that the children do not add voice, distorting the 'c...' sound into 'cuh'. This can be checked by getting them to cup their hands around their necks while saying it. If they can feel their voice vibrating, then they are not saying it correctly.

Listening to and singing Clever Cat's song on the *Alphabet Songs Cassette* will help the children to pronounce her letter sound correctly. The words to all the songs are on pages 170-71 of this guide and can be photocopied for the children to take home.

After this lesson, seize any natural opportunity that arises, e.g. **c**arrots or **c**ustard at lunch, to connect words to Clever Cat because they start with her sound. The box on the right provides a selection of words to start you off.

Clever Cat's words

cake*	clothes*
can*	cold*
candles	colour*
cap*	come*
car*	cook*
castle*	count
cat*	cross*
clean*	cuddle
clever	cup*
climb*	custard
clock*	cut*

* High usage words

Explaining the capital C shape

Many children come to school having been taught only capital letters at home, whereas you will want to limit capitals to the beginning of their names and sentences. The story explanation for the difference between small **c** and capital **C** is as follows:

One exciting thing about Letterland animals and people is that they can change size whenever they want to. All they have to do is take a deep breath and they become bigger.

Point to the capital version of Clever Cat on the *Class Wall Frieze*.

This getting bigger trick is how Letterland animals and people like to show us that they are starting an important word. Names are important, so you will always see them looking bigger than the other letters at the beginning of a name.

Introduce the **Clever Cat** *Flashcard* (1) and point out how she appears twice in her own name. Show how she also appears twice, only smaller, on the **picnic** *Flashcard* (2) or use the simpler version on page 183. Talk about the **Clever Cat** *Flashcard* as follows:

Look, the two words on this card are Clever Cat's own name. They say Clever Cat. The word on the other card says picnic. Can you see and hear Clever Cat saying 'c...' twice in picnic? See how much smaller she is in words like picnic than when she starts her name? She knows names are important, so she takes a deep breath and makes herself bigger to start her name – and yours [Calum and Catherine] – because she knows your names are important, too!

Treat all the character names as sight words from the start. Encourage the children to look out for the recurring capital letters. These are the hallmark of every character name, so they all provide good capital letter practice as well as sight word practice.

Practising Clever Cat's shape and sound

Cats' picnic mural

An attractive way of displaying the children's first attempts at picture coding is to stick some of their **c**-shapes on to a 'cats' picnic' mural. The children will enjoy helping you to paint or make a country scene, showing a picnic laid out on a rug.

Clever Cat in words

Have your **cat** and **cats** *Flashcards* (3 and 4) ready. Show the **cat** *Flashcard* and point to **at** while you explain:

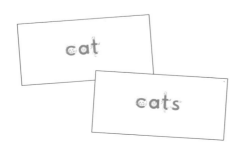

Clever Cat has found two other letters to help her make this word. Of course the word she likes to make best is cat, because she is a cat. So here she is, making her 'c...' sound at the beginning of the word cat. I'm going to whisper the word cat and I want you to listen for her 'c...' sound at the beginning of the word: ca...t, ca...t, cat. The next word is cats: a good word to label the cats on our mural!

Clever Cat in names

Take advantage of capital **C** shapes in children's names. If there is a **C**laire, **C**atherine or **C**raig in the class, make that an exciting discovery. Give those children plain versions of their names so they can picture code Clever Cat's face. Display their efforts on the wall.

You may, however, also have children in your class called **C**harles, **C**harlotte, etc., where **c** is not a 'hard' sound. For the time being, let these children add the cat's face as usual to their capital **C**'s, but add a wiggly line under any **ch**'s or 'soft' **c**'s. Explain that the wiggly line shows that Clever Cat is making another sound in these names. (The story explanations for the two **ch** sounds are on pages 145 and 146. The soft **c** sound will be explained in Programme Two.)

Clever Cat on signs

This is a good time to put up picture-coded labels on objects beginning with the hard 'c...' sound. Hopefully the children will now start to spot the **c**-shape in words about the school, and outside. Remind them that Clever Cat can be in lots of places at the same time, so they should be on the lookout everywhere!

Costume box

Now is a good time to start a costume box specifically for Letterland props. You might like to call it 'Clever Cat's Costume Box', and picture code the capital **C**'s to highlight the alliterative words. (See pages 27-8 for more information.)

Clever Cat in blends and digraphs

Some of your children may be ready to practise the blends and digraphs with **c**. In Section 3, you will find information on **-ck** (page 130), **ch** (page 145), **cl** (page 150) and **cr** (page 152).

Consolidation

Workbooks

Guide the children through the exercises on pages 2 and 3 of *Programme One Workbook 1* to consolidate learning of Clever Cat's letter shape and sound. Draw special attention to her name and to the word **Colour** in the instruction text.

Storybooks

For further listening practice, read the *Letterland Storybook: Clever Cat and the Clown* aloud and draw the children's attention to the recurring 'c...' sound. See also the *Letterland Links* titles, listed on pages 176-80.

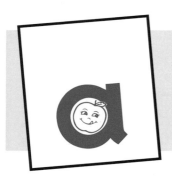

STEP 2a
Annie Apple

Objective

To teach the letter shapes for **a** and **A** and the short vowel sound 'ă...'.

What you need

☆ *Programme One Picture Code Cards*: Annie Apple (ă)

☆ *Programme One Flashcards*: 5-7

☆ *Class Wall Frieze*

☆ *Handwriting Songs Cassette*

☆ *Alphabet Songs Cassette*

☆ *Programme One Songs Cassette*

☆ *Programme One Workbook 1*: pages 4, 5 and 7

☆ *Storybook: Annie Apple's Adventure*

☆ *Links Group 1: Annie Apple*

Preparation

☆ **Letters for picture coding**
Prepare thick black **a**-shapes on pieces of card or paper for each child to picture code. Make six or seven extra ones in varying sizes for use on the apple tree mural (see top right).

☆ **Applestand** Make an **A**-shaped paper Applestand for adding to the apple tree mural later on. You can either draw your own one or use the template on page 187.

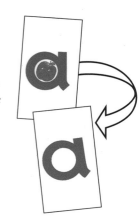

☆ **Apple tree mural**
Make or paint a simple apple tree mural, showing one or more large apple trees. Leave space for Mr A and his Applestand to be added later on. The trees should be bare of apples at this stage and large enough to take the children's picture-coded **a**'s. Mount your mural in a prominent place on the wall.

☆ **Further flashcards**
Prepare two flashcards reading **apples** and **add an apple**: templates are provided on pages 183 and 187.

Introducing Annie Apple

Point to an apple tree on your apple tree mural (see **Preparation**) and introduce Annie Apple's apple tree:

*This is an **a**pple tree growing in Letterland. We are going to help it to grow lots of **a**pples.*

Distribute your prepared **a**-shapes and let the children draw and colour in red apples inside them. Let them add faces on them if they wish. While they are colouring in, hold up the Annie Apple *Picture Code Card* and explain:

*Now don't forget that all these **a**pples which you are making are Letterland **a**pples, growing inside a letter, this **a**pple letter shape.*

Now show the plain side.

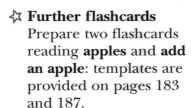

Annie Apple's letter shape

Introduce Annie Apple's handwriting verse (set to music on the *Handwriting Songs Cassette*) to teach the correct stroke for **a**:

> At the leaf begin. Go round the apple this way.
> Then add a line down, so Annie won't roll away.

Choose children to demonstrate the stroke on the *Class Wall Frieze* or *Picture Code Card*. Write a huge **a** on the board for them to air trace while they sing or chant the verse again.

The words to all of the songs are also on pages 168-69. They are set out in larger print, so that you can send home a photocopy which the children will eventually be able to read.

Annie Apple's sound

Holding up the pictogram side of the Annie Apple *Picture Code Card*, explain Annie Apple's sound along these lines:

*Letterland **a**pples are very special. Not all of them are eating **a**pples. Some of them are talking **a**pples, like the one here called **A**nnie **A**pple. Let's pretend you have a real, very big **a**pple in front of you and you are about to take a big bite. At the same time you start to say '**a**pple', like this 'ă…'!*

Let the children mime biting an apple and saying 'ă…'.

*That is exactly what **A**nnie **A**pple and all the other talking **a**pples say. They say 'ă…'! Whoever heard of **a**pples that can say 'ă…'? It is rather fantastic and it can only happen in Letterland.*

*The **a**pples which you have drawn are all talking **a**pples. Let's hear all of you talk like Letterland **a**pples. Say 'ă…, ă…, ă…', like that.*

Annie Apple's song on the *Alphabet Songs Cassette* is another enjoyable way to help the children achieve the correct sound. The words to all the songs are on pages 170-71. These may be photocopied for the children to take home. The children could bob up and down like apples on a branch as they sing the song. (Actions for all the letters are suggested on page 29.)

Next hold up and read out your **add an apple** flashcard. Point to the words each time as you ask a child to come up to the mural with their 'apple' (picture-coded **a**).

*Now let's see each of you come in turn and **add an apple** to the **a**pple tree. As you do this, let's hear you say 'ă…, ă…, ă…' again, just like a Letterland **a**pple.*

When all the apples have been added to the trees, compare *Flashcards* 6 (**apple**) and 7 (**apples**) and help the children to decide that **apples** is the best word to label so many apples. Use your prepared **apples** card to place on the mural, so that you can keep *Flashcard* 7 in circulation.

Annie Apple's words

add*	animal*
address	ant
adventure	apple*
alligator	arrow
alphabet	as*
ambulance	at*
an*	avenue
and*	axe

* High usage words

add an apple

apples

Explaining the capital A shape

Explain the capital **A** shape along these lines:

Mr A likes to make neat little Applestands for his talking apples. You can often see these Applestands at the beginning of words.

Point out a few capital **A**'s in a large print book. As you add your paper Applestand to the mural, you can say:

*You will also see these Applestands at the beginning of names which Mr A has given to his talking apples, names like: **A**nnie **A**pple, **A**ndy **A**pple, **A**lison **A**pple **a**nd **A**dam **A**pple.*

Show the **Annie Apple** *Flashcard* (5) and point to each capital **A**.

Here is Annie Apple's name and here is Annie Apple herself with some of her apple friends, right in the middle of the Applestand!

Practising Annie Apple's shape and sound

Annie Apple in names

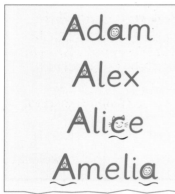

Distribute any children's names starting with **A** (**A**lexander, **A**shish, etc.), writing them out boldly so they can become wall display items. Show those children how to picture code the 'Applestands' with one or more big red apples. If the **a** sound is not short (e.g. in **A**melia and **A**isha), ask them to draw a wiggly line under it, so that everyone can see that Annie Apple is not making her usual sound in their names. Save any names beginning with the long **ā**, such as **A**my, **A**idan, etc., for another lesson (see page 42). Display the name pictures on the wall.

Consolidation

Workbooks

Guide the children through the exercises on pages 4 and 5 of *Programme One Workbook 1* to consolidate learning of Annie Apple's letter shape and her short 'ǎ...' sound. Draw special attention to her name and to her 'ǎ...' sound in the word **that** in the instruction text.

Storybooks

For further listening practice, read the *Letterland Storybook: Annie Apple's Adventure* or *Letterland Links Group 1: Annie Apple* aloud and draw the children's attention to the recurring short 'ǎ...' sound.

Cassette

Sing or listen to **Annie Apple** and Annie Apple's verse (in particular) of the **Vowel Sounds Song** on the *Programme One Songs Cassette*.

STEP 2b
Mr A, the Apron Man

Objective

To teach the long vowel ā.

What you need

☆ *Programme One Picture Code Cards*: Annie Apple (ă) and Mr A (ā)

☆ *Programme One Flashcards*: 8

☆ *Class Wall Frieze*

☆ *Programme One Songs Cassette*

☆ *Programme One Workbook 1*: pages 6 and 7

☆ *Storybook: The Vowel Street Party*

☆ *Links Group 1: Five Vowel Men*

Preparation

☆ **Mr A** Draw or paint a picture of Mr A for adding to the apple tree mural. Alternatively, photocopy the template of Mr A on page 187, asking a child to colour it in for you.

Introducing Mr A, the Apron Man

Make sure the children are confident of Annie Apple's sound (the short 'ă...' sound) before formally introducing Mr A, representing the alphabet name **a**. Up till now they will have seen this Vowel Man on the *Class Wall Frieze* and sung about him in the last line of the Annie Apple song on the *Alphabet Songs Cassette*. You may also have decided to explain to one or two children how to picture code any long ā's in their names. Continue stressing the 'apple' sound in words, but start to talk about Mr A, the Apron Man (from Asia).

Traditionally we tend to speak of ā as a 'long vowel sound'. In fact, it is both a *sound* and the vowel *name*. It can, therefore, be confusing for children if you talk about 'Mr A's sound'. Instead, refer to 'Annie Apple's *sound*', but 'Mr A's *name*' in words.

While showing the pictogram side of the Mr A *Picture Code Card*, talk along these lines:

All the apples in Letterland belong to a Vowel Man called Mr A. You can tell that his talking apples must be very special because Mr A has come from a faraway place called Asia, especially to grow these apples and look after them.

Mr A collects all his apples in his apron. That is why everyone calls him Mr A, the Apron Man. Mr A has a shop where he sells lots of eating apples, but he puts the special talking apples into words which need an 'ă...' sound in them.

No explanation of the term 'vowel' is needed at this stage. Just let the children become used to hearing the word. (See also page 20.)

Mr A is a very busy man, but he loves being in words. So when he is not busy putting apples into words, you may find Mr A himself appearing in a word. Then you will hear him saying his name 'Ā!' loud and clear. Can you hear Mr A saying his name right at the beginning of the word apron? You say it: apron, a-pron, apron.

Look together at Mr A on the frieze and at *Flashcard 8* (**Mr A**). Write the sentence on its reverse side on the board. Decide together how to picture code it.

> Mr A has apples in his apron.

Mr A has apples in his apron.

You can now add your picture of Mr A (see **Preparation**) to the apple tree mural.

Practising Mr A saying his name

Mr A in names

Pick out any children whose names begin with the long ā, e.g. **A**idan or **A**my. Write out their names for them using a thick black felt-tip pen and show them how to draw a stick man right through their apple letters to signal Mr A's presence. If these names also contain another long ā, let them picture code it with Mr A as well. Any short 'ǎ...' sounds can be picture-coded with Annie Apple. Display names with Mr A on the wall and treat them as special 'because Mr A always manages to find time to appear in them, even though he is such a busy man!'

Mr A in the word a

It is useful from the start to draw attention to Mr A's presence in one of the 12 most used words in the English language: **a**. When we speak, we tend to pronounce this word as 'uh', but to write it, a child must think **a**, and not **u**. So now (or later if you are teaching complete beginners or children with Special Needs), it is a good idea to introduce a stick man into the word **a** in *some* phrases and sentences. This will accustom children to seeing two alternative picture codings for this one letter. It will also make their early writing free from contradiction over the sound of this extremely high usage word.

By using a stick man to picture code the word **a**, you also prepare the way for the concept that every Vowel Man regularly appears in a few much used little words to say his name: Mr E in **be**, **he**, **me**, **she** and **we**; Mr I in **I**; Mr O in **go**, **no** and **so**; and Mr U at the end of **you**.

Consolidation

Workbooks

Guide the children through the exercises on pages 6 and 7 of *Programme One Workbook 1* to consolidate learning of the long ā in words. Draw special attention to Mr A's name and the word **name** in the instruction text.

Storybooks

For further listening practice, read the *Letterland Storybook: The Vowel Street Party* or *Letterland Links Group 1: Five Vowel Men* aloud and draw the children's attention to Mr A's name in words.

Cassette

Sing or listen to Mr A's verse (in particular) of the **Vowel Men Song** on the *Programme One Songs Cassette*.

STEP 3
Dippy Duck

Objectives

To teach the letter shapes and sound for **d** and **D**, and to start building the first words.

What you need

- ☆ *Programme One Picture Code Cards*: Dippy Duck (**d**), Diana Duck (**d**) and Annie Apple (**ă**)

- ☆ *Programme One Flashcards*: 9-13

- ☆ *Class Wall Frieze*

- ☆ *Handwriting Songs Cassette*

- ☆ *Alphabet Songs Cassette*

- ☆ *Programme One Workbook 1*: pages 8 and 9

- ☆ *Storybook: Dippy Duck Dresses up*

- ☆ Yellow tissue paper (see **Dippy Duck display** on page 45)

Preparation

- ☆ **Letters for picture coding** Prepare thick black **d**-shapes on pieces of card or paper for each child to picture code.

- ☆ **Picture coding signs** Make and display your own versions of signs around the school with the **d**'s and **D**'s picture-coded.

☆ **Reading Direction sign** Prepare a Reading Direction sign and a number of paper arrows if you haven't already done so. Attach the sign somewhere prominent on the wall and put the arrows beneath it pointing to the right. You could also put some arrows on the floor to help the children when they are doing live spelling (see pages 46-7).

Introducing Dippy Duck

With the introduction of the letter **d**, you can give the children four new words to treat as sight words: **duck**, **ducks** and **Dippy Duck** (which you will find on *Flashcards* 11, 12 and 9), and two words based on sounds which they now know: **dad** and **add** (on *Flashcard* 13). The latter two words are worthy of considerable attention as they may be the children's first experience of word building, as they learn to mime being letters and setting themselves up as a word (see **Live spelling:** *dad* **and** *add* on page 46).

Take care to refer to Dippy Duck as *she* when you show the children how to picture code her. Later, when you compare the **d** and **b** shapes, you will naturally be talking about *her* and *him* (Bouncy Ben), so that even your pronouns help to make your instructions totally clear.

To introduce Dippy Duck, show the pictogram side of the appropriate *Picture Code Card* and say:

*Meet **D**ippy **D**uck. She is quite a young **d**uck, so she is covered with yellow **d**own.*

Explain what down is, i.e. the soft, fluffy pre-feather stage. Then turn to the plain side.

Can you see where her head goes when I only show you her letter? And where her body is? Where will her tail feathers be?

You can now distribute your prepared **d**-shapes for the children to picture code with crayons.

Dippy Duck's letter shape

Introduce Dippy Duck's handwriting verse (set to music on the *Handwriting Songs Cassette*) to teach the correct stroke for **d**:

> Draw Dippy Duck's back. Go round her tum.
> Go up to her head. Then down you come!

Choose children to demonstrate the stroke on the *Class Wall Frieze* or *Picture Code Card*. Write a huge **d** on the board for them to air trace while they sing or chant the verse again.

Now let the children discover Dippy Duck's letter shape in their own right hands.

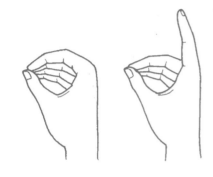

Curl all the fingers of your right hand towards your thumb. Lift up your first finger. Then imagine Dippy Duck's head on it, and you will see Dippy Duck's letter, right there in your own right hand!

Use Dippy Duck's rightward orientation as a pointer for the children's eyes. Like her, they should always look ahead as they read. Point to your Reading Direction sign and arrows on the wall and explain:

Dippy Duck always swims in the Reading Direction in words, because in Letterland it is very important to know who is going to be next to you in a word. That is why she always looks ahead as she swims along.

Stress that Dippy Duck *never* turns round. She feels that if she *did*, something *dreadful* would happen!

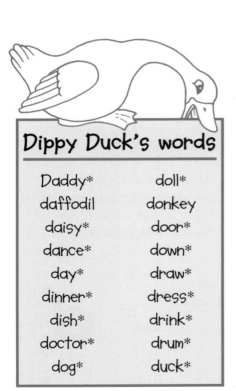

Dippy Duck's words

Daddy*	doll*
daffodil	donkey
daisy*	door*
dance*	down*
day*	draw*
dinner*	dress*
dish*	drink*
doctor*	drum*
dog*	duck*

* High usage words

Dippy Duck's sound

What kind of sound does Dippy Duck make? Well, remember she is a Letterland duck, so she doesn't quack like other ducks you may have heard. She makes the sound that you can hear at the beginning of her name instead. If you start to say 'Dippy', you can make her sound too. It's like this: 'd..., d..., d...'.

Make sure you clip your voice immediately following this sound. Tell the children to keep their mouths nearly shut. It must not sound like 'duh', as this will make blending difficult later. Avoiding a big 'uh' sound is very important when they practise singing Dippy Duck's song on the *Alphabet Songs Cassette*. They can also mime waddling, wing flapping, etc.

Introducing Diana Duck

Dippy Duck has a best friend called Diana Duck. (She has a closed beak.) Introduce her, using the appropriate *Picture Code Card*, when children want to spell not only **Dad**, but **Daddy** and other words containing **dd**. Diana Duck can be used for the *second* **d** of the pair.

Explaining the capital D shape

Although you will not be focusing on writing capital **D** at this stage, you will be talking about it in some detail as an essential shape to recognise in reading. On the *Class Wall Frieze*, point out how straight one side of Dippy Duck's door is. This is the door to her duck den in the river bank. Show how the door opens in the Reading Direction.

Now is also a good time, while all the children watch, to picture code the capital **D** on your Reading Direction sign, and colour it in yellow.

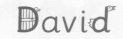

Use your **Dippy Duck**, **Diana Duck** and **duck** *Flashcards* (9, 10 and 11) to compare the two ways of writing the word **duck/Duck**. Explain that the Duck Door 'opens' important words like Dippy and Diana Duck's names and other names, such as **David**.

Practising Dippy Duck's shape and sound

Dippy Duck heads

Using the template on page 187, photocopy Dippy's head and duplicate it on to thick paper, making enough for all your class. Let the children colour them in and take their paper ducks home. The duck's head is small, so it is best if a parent cuts it out for them. A parent will also need to bend and fix it so that it fits on to their child's right index finger.

The next day, wearing their duck heads, the children can practise moving their index fingers so that Dippy Duck puts her head under her wing, then makes her head pop up again. (Add a paper tail or real feather tail to make it even more fun.) Call their right hand their 'duck hand'. It will always be there to remind them of Dippy Duck's shape. (It will be especially useful later when you introduce **b**, in preventing **b/d** confusions.)

Dippy Duck on signs

Take the children on a walk around the school and encourage them to whisper: 'Do I see Dippy Duck in the distance?' as you search the hall, notices, etc. for **d**'s and **D**'s, some picture-coded by hand, and other plain ones.

Dippy Duck display

You may like to feature Dippy Duck's pond and her Duck Door on its own, or as part of a larger Letterland mural. Choose four or five children to picture code some extra **d**'s and a **D** for it. Add **Dippy Duck** and **ducks** labels, introducing **ducks** on *Flashcard* 12. Alternatively, make a huge picture-coded **d** for the children to cover with crumpled up yellow tissue paper for down. Let either display become a collecting place for words and objects beginning with **d**.

Word building with Dippy Duck

Blending letters into words

The children should now be ready to create their first word: **dad**. Lead into blending **d** with **a** by introducing a Letterland secret, shared by all the consonants. Present this blending verse now as 'Dippy Duck's secret':

> I always sound better beside another letter,
> so don't make my sound all alone.
> Put a nice round apple right beside me,
> so I don't have to be on my own.

This 'secret' is especially useful for blends with **b**, **d**, **g** and **r**. (See also page 54, where the 'store up and release' technique is explained.) You should now be ready to move on to 'live spelling', first described on page 23.

Live spelling: dad and add

Choose three children to create the word **dad** in 'live spelling'. They will need to hold or wear (e.g. on headbands) the *Picture Code Cards* for Dippy Duck, Annie Apple and Diana Duck. Tell any boys taking part that they can be Daniel Duck or Adam Apple, or any other alliterative boy's names. They will enjoy wearing or holding any suitable props you have had time to make or collect. (See **Costume box** on pages 27-8.)

Place the three children on the class' left, near a wall. Then ask the Dippy Duck child to come towards you making her sound.

> *Now **D**ippy **D**uck, let's see you swim along in the Reading Direction until you reach me. Say '**d**..., **d**..., **d**...' as you come, because '**d**...' is your sound.*

When 'Dippy Duck' reaches the centre, make sure she stands with her feet still pointing to the right while looking towards the class.

> *Can everyone see **D**ippy **D**uck here? Now I want you to think of this wall behind **D**ippy **D**uck as a great big page in a book. **D**ippy **D**uck has just walked on to that page.*
> *Remember **D**ippy **D**uck's secret. She doesn't like to make her sound all alone, does she? No. So let's give her an apple for company. Come on, Annie Apple. Say 'ă..., ă..., ă...' as you come over to join **D**ippy **D**uck.*

Show 'Annie Apple' where to stand to make '**da**...'.

> *Let's say **D**ippy **D**uck and **A**nnie **A**pple's sound together now: '**da**...'! When you were little, you probably said '**da-da**' for '**dad**', but now you can say '**dad**' easily, can't you! Say '**dad**'. Say it again very slowly, '**da**...**d**'. Did I hear you make a '**d**...' sound at the end, '**da**...**d**', as well as at the beginning? Listen: '**da**...**d**'!*

Diana Duck, you swim over here on to the other side of Annie Apple now and make your 'd...' sound. Let's see whether together you have made the word dad! 'Da...d', 'da...d', 'da...d'! Yes, you have!

Send your three children back to the left-hand side of the 'page' to wait while you go over this new achievement. Write **da**, **da-da** and **dad** on the board, and read these words together.

Let's see if you can make the word dad again.

This time involve the others to help get the children into the right sequence. Remember, they can't see themselves, and they may not be very clear yet about thinking of the wall behind them as a big page.

You can then move on to building the word **add**. With the same three children, say:

But dad is not the only word these three friends can make. Annie Apple, come to the middle. Now you two ducks hold hands and say 'd..., d..., d...' together while you come over here beside her. In Letterland when you see two ducks together in a word they both make the same sound at exactly the same time so they sound more like one sound.

Encourage the other children to discover what word they have made. Compare it with **add** on *Flashcard* 13. You can also see if anyone can spot the same word, **add**, on the sentence side.

Leave the **a**, **d** and **d** *Picture Code Cards* out where the children can handle them and sequence them to match the **add** *Flashcard*. (First use the pictogram sides, and then the plain letter sides.)

Consolidation

Workbooks

Guide the children through the exercises on pages 8 and 9 of *Programme One Workbook 1* to consolidate learning of Dippy Duck's letter shape and sound. Draw special attention to her name and to the word **sound** in the instruction text.

Storybooks

For further listening practice, read the *Letterland Storybook: Dippy Duck Dresses up* aloud and draw the children's attention to the recurring 'd...' sound.

STEP 4
Hairy Hat Man

Objectives

To teach the letter shapes and sound for **h** and **H**, and word building.

What you need

- ☆ *Programme One Picture Code Cards*: Hairy Hat Man (**h**), Annie Apple (**ă**), Dippy Duck (**d**) and Diana Duck (**d**)

- ☆ *Programme One Flashcards*: 14-16

- ☆ *Class Wall Frieze*

- ☆ *Handwriting Songs Cassette*

- ☆ *Alphabet Songs Cassette*

- ☆ *Programme One Workbook 1*: pages 10 and 11

- ☆ *Storybook: The Hairy Hat Man's House*

Preparation

- ☆ **Letters for picture coding**
  Prepare thick black **h**-shapes on pieces of card or paper for each child to picture code.

Introducing Hairy Hat Man

If you have started gradually, teaching one letter a week, you should now consider introducing the next few Steps at an increased pace, especially if you have a number of children who have met Letterland at pre-school. You will be surprised how quickly the others catch them up.

Now that the children are accustomed to expect a pictogram design in each letter, you can change your approach. Present the *Picture Code Card* for the letter **h** as a plain letter first and then ask the children to tell you how the shape can be turned into a man *before* showing the pictogram side.

Where will his head be? His feet? What part of the letter becomes his back? His legs? Which way will he be going? [The Reading Direction.]

Show the pictogram side as you go on to discuss the Hairy Hat Man's name.

*So now **h**ere is the man. Is that **h**ow you thought he might look? Do you know what his name is? He is **H**arry, the **H**airy **H**at Man. Why do you think the people in Letterland call him 'the **H**airy **H**at Man'? Because his **h**at is **h**airy? Or maybe because he has a **h**airy **h**ead?*

*I do know that everyone in Letterland thinks very **h**ighly of the **H**airy **H**at Man, because he is a good friend. He is always **h**elpful. He never **h**arms anyone. He enjoys making other people feel **h**appy.*

You can now distribute your prepared **h**-shapes for the children to picture code with crayons. Give help if need be.

Hairy Hat Man's letter shape

Introduce Hairy Hat Man's handwriting verse (set to music on the *Handwriting Songs Cassette*) to teach the correct stroke for **h**:

> Hurry from the Hat Man's head
> down to his heel on the ground.
> Go up and bend his knee over,
> so he'll hop while he makes his sound.

Choose children to demonstrate the stroke on the *Class Wall Frieze* or *Picture Code Card*. Write a huge **h** on the board for them to air trace while they sing or chant the verse again.

Hairy Hat Man's sound

*There is a special thing you need to know about the **H**airy **H**at Man, and it is important. He **h**ates noise. That is why he never speaks above a whisper. He can be quite **h**ard to **h**ear, so you'll have to be very quiet while I tell you what he says in words. He says '**hhh**…'. Just like that, '**hhh**…'. You whisper '**hhh**…' too. '**Hhh**…, **hhh**…, **hhh**…'.*

Let the children look closely at the Hairy Hat Man *Picture Code Card*, while you discuss why the Hairy Hat Man does not wear shoes.

*There is another funny thing about the **H**airy **H**at Man. Have you noticed? He has no shoes on, has he? I wonder why? If you wanted to keep things as quiet as possible, would you wear shoes? The **H**airy **H**at Man never wears shoes. You see he doesn't even want to **h**ear the sound of his own footsteps, because that makes it **h**arder for him to **h**ear **h**imself whispering '**hhh**…'!*

Hairy Hat Man's song on the *Alphabet Songs Cassette* is a popular way for children to practise making his sound correctly. Make sure the children whisper '**hhh**…' (a quick sigh, not 'huh' with voice) when they reach that point in the song.

Explaining the capital H shape

Introduce the capital H along these lines:

*You can always tell when the **H**airy **H**at Man is feeling particularly **h**appy, because he does his special trick. He does a **h**andstand with his **h**at on!*

Point to the capital **H** on the *Class Wall Frieze*, on the **Hairy Hat Man** *Flashcard* (14) and, if possible, in the names of any children in the class (Helen, Henry, Hassan, etc.), or a surname known to them.

*Look! **H**ere he is doing his **h**andstand in [**H**elen's] name! Why do you think he is particularly **h**appy at the beginning of her name? Names are important, so the **H**at Man always feels particularly **h**appy when he is **h**elping out with something important like starting a name. See, he clearly thinks **h**is name is important!*

Practising the Hat Man's shape and sound

Hairy Hat Man in words

Help the children to associate as many alliterative words as possible with the Hat Man character by speculating together about him. Accept all answers with 'You could be right,' but the best answers will start with **h**. Here are some possible points for discussion:

- What might Hairy Hat Man's house look like? Will it have hairy carpets inside? Will it be cold inside or…? (Hot.) What does he make in his house? (Hundreds of hats. This is a good moment to introduce the **hat** and **hats** *Flashcards* (15 and 16)).

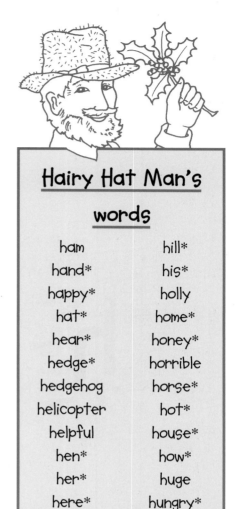

Hairy Hat Man's words

ham	hill*
hand*	his*
happy*	holly
hat*	home*
hear*	honey*
hedge*	horrible
hedgehog	horse*
helicopter	hot*
helpful	house*
hen*	how*
her*	huge
here*	hungry*

* High usage words

Hairy Hat Man

- What hobbies might he have? (Possible answers could be hang-gliding, playing hopscotch or making people happy.)

- What would he most like to eat when he is hungry? (Honey, ham, hamburgers, hot-dogs, hazelnuts, hard-boiled eggs, etc.)

- How might he like to travel on holiday? (By helicopter, hovercraft, horseback, hot air balloon, etc.)

You may like to follow up this language work by letting the children paint pictures of him, including some of the images arising from your discussion.

Hat Man display

Help the children to make a huge Hat Man display. Paint a large picture of Hairy Hat Man and add labels for his hat, hair, hands and heels. Let the children decide where the labels should go. Include pictures of objects beginning with his sound: hedgehogs, hamsters, hamburgers, etc. Mount the picture on the wall beside a table or shelf and encourage the children to make a collection of items there beginning with Hairy Hat Man's sound.

Hairy Hat Man in digraphs

Some of your children may be ready to practise the digraphs with **h**. In Section 3, you will find information on **sh**, **th**, **wh**, **ch** and **-tch** (see pages 138-48).

Word building with Hairy Hat Man

Live spelling: had

Choose three children to revise the word **dad** in live spelling (see page 46) and then create a new word: **had**. Afterwards leave the *Picture Code Cards* out so the children can reconstruct **add**, **dad** and **had** for themselves.

Consolidation

Workbooks

Guide the children through the exercises on pages 10 and 11 of *Programme One Workbook 1* to consolidate learning of Hairy Hat Man's letter shape and sound. Draw special attention to his name and to the word **his** in the instruction text.

Storybooks

For further listening practice, read the *Letterland Storybook: The Hairy Hat Man's House* aloud and draw the children's attention to the recurring 'hhh...' sound.

STEP 5
Munching Mike

Objectives

To teach the letter shapes and sound for **m** and **M**, and word building.

What you need

☆ *Programme One Picture Code Cards*: Munching Mike (**m**), Munching Maria (**m**) and all the cards covered so far

☆ *Programme One Flashcards*: 17-19 and all the character name cards covered so far

☆ *Class Wall Frieze*

☆ *Handwriting Songs Cassette*

☆ *Alphabet Songs Cassette*

☆ *Programme One Workbook 1*: pages 12 and 13

☆ *Storybook: Munching Mike's Mistake*

Preparation

☆ **Letters for picture coding** Prepare thick black **m**-shapes on pieces of card or paper for each child to picture code.

Quick revision

From now on, begin each Letterland session with a 'Quick dash' revision routine (see **Revising letters** on page 24 for more information). Use the *Picture Code Cards* for ă, ā, c, d and h to revise sounds. Then use the character name *Flashcards* (1, 5, 9 and 14) to reinforce capital letter recognition and rapid whole-word recognition.

Introducing Munching Mike

You can now develop Munching Mike's character. He is a merry little monster. He is also mischievous, makes mistakes and has a mighty appetite. As monsters go, however, he is a mild one, because he is still only little: just a mini-monster compared to his big, sharp-looking Mum (the capital **M**).

Draw rough mountains on the board similar to the capital **M** shape and talk about his home:

In Letterland there are some Mighty Mountains which look a bit like this. These Mighty Mountains are the home of Munching Mike, the Metal Monster.

Show the plain side first of the Munching Mike *Picture Code Card* this time and encourage the children to imagine how he might look before they see the pictogram side:

On this card you can only see parts of this monster. His head and neck and tail are invisible, but can you tell me how many legs he has? [Three.] Yes, three legs. And instead of feet he has three wheels! Because he is a metal monster, his legs, head, tail, wheels and everything are made of metal.
    Don't forget Munching Mike is a Letterland monster, so which way will he be looking? Which way is the Reading Direction?

Point to your Reading Direction sign on the wall.

Yes, that way. So where will Munching Mike's head be? And where will his tail be?

Let several children touch where the head, tail, and wheels will be on the plain side of the *Picture Code Card*.

Finally show the pictogram side.

*So now let's take a good look at **M**unching **M**ike, the **M**etal **M**onster. Here he is! Let's count his legs again. How do you think he **m**oves? Yes, he rolls along on his three **m**etal wheels!*

Go on to discuss what things in the classroom are made of metal: tables, chairs, trolley legs, pencil sharpener, magnets, etc.

Distribute your prepared **m**-shapes for the children to picture code with crayons.

Munching Mike's letter shape

Introduce Munching Mike's handwriting verse (set to music on the *Handwriting Songs Cassette*) to teach the correct stroke for **m**:

> Make Munching Mike's back leg first,
> then his second leg, and third,
> so he can go munch–munching in a word.

Choose children to demonstrate the stroke on the *Class Wall Frieze* or *Picture Code Card*. Write a huge **m** on the board for them to air trace while they sing or chant the verse again.

Munching Mike's sound

*You can tell that **M**unching **M**ike loves his food, because he keeps on saying '**Mmm**...! **Mmm**...! **Mmm**...!' with every **m**outhful. Can you be a **m**unching **m**onster and say '**Mmm**...!'?*

Make sure everyone keeps their lips closed until they have finished the 'Mmm...' sound. Do not allow a 'muh' sound. Munching Mike's song on the *Alphabet Songs Cassette* will help the children to achieve the correct sound. While they are singing it, they can also mime being Munching Mike (using either one or three children to make a monster).

Introducing Munching Maria

Munching Mike's best friend is a second mini-monster called Munching Maria. (The differences are just the mouth and the eyelashes.) Introduce her, using the appropriate *Picture Code Card*, when children want to spell not only **Mum,** but **Mummy** and other words containing **mm**. Munching Maria can be used for the *second* **m** of the pair.

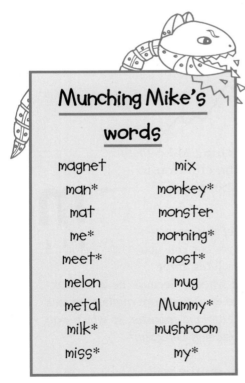

Munching Mike's words

magnet	mix
man*	monkey*
mat	monster
me*	morning*
meet*	most*
melon	mug
metal	Mummy*
milk*	mushroom
miss*	my*

* High usage words

Explaining the capital M shape

Write **Munching Mike** on the board. Then start by getting the children to tell and show you how Clever Cat makes herself look bigger (by breathing in deeply). Then go on:

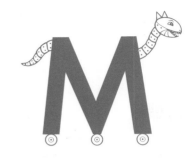

*Well, **M**unching **M**ike would like to make himself bigger too. But he is not quite old enough to do it properly yet! So for the time being, **M**unching **M**ike just leaves the job of starting important words to his **M**um. Since **M**unching **M**ike's **M**um is much bigger than him, she **m**unches **m**uch **m**ore than her son and says '**MMM**...' even louder as she **m**unches.*

Point to Munching Mike's name on the board.

*This is **M**unching **M**ike's name. See his **M**um looking big and sharp, twice, to start the two words of his name for him? Names are important words. Now who do we have in our classroom whose names begin with **M**unching **M**ike's **M**um? Yes, yours, [**M**artin and **M**atthew], because your names are important, too!*

Write any children's names beginning with **M**, and **Munching Maria** on the board. Show the **Munching Mike** and **Munching Maria** *Flashcards* (17 and 18), and also the sentence side of *Flashcard* 17, at this stage just to look at the plain words **Munching Mike** for comparison. On *Flashcard* 19, point out how little Munching Mike loves to start the word **monster**, because he *is* a monster!

Practising Mike's shape and sound

Munching Mike's foods

Have a discussion about what Munching Mike likes to eat.

*Munching Mike has an amazing appetite. He **m**unches and **m**unches, but he **m**ostly eats things that begin with his sound. So he **m**unches **m**ints by the **m**outhful. He also **m**unches **m**ats, **m**ushrooms and **m**acaroni, **m**aps and **m**agazines, **m**ops, **m**etal **m**agnets and **m**achines. And he has even been known to eat a whole **m**otorbike! All these things just **m**elt in his **m**etal **m**outh and slip down his **m**etal throat like **m**ilk.*

Encourage the children to expand on what Mike might eat, the more far-fetched, the more fun and the more memorable, the better, but exclude people, e.g. men or mums, because Munching Mike thinks they taste 'monstrous'!

Munching Mike in names

In this and future Steps continue to draw attention to capital letters in children's names. Display their names on the wall, picture-coded by the children. They can picture code just the initial capital letters, and/or some or all of the letters. Don't forget to add wiggly lines under any letters not representing their normal, single letter sounds.

Word building with Munching Mike

Live spelling: ham

Munching Mike is now going to help us to discover the Hat Man's favourite food.

Choose three children to be the Hat Man, Annie Apple and Munching Mike. Start with the **h** and **a** children standing, holding or wearing the appropriate *Picture Code Cards*.

Remember the Letterland secret:
I always sound better beside another letter,
so don't make my sound all alone.
Well, Hairy Hat Man wants you to know that secret, too, so let's see how he sounds together with this nice round apple beside him.

Stand behind the two children pointing to the **h** child as you prolong the 'hhh...' sound and then to the **a** child as you demonstrate the blend: 'hhha...'.

Next send your **m** child from the left (as in writing) to join them and add Munching Mike's 'mmm...' sound. Help the children to discover that the sounds, put together, equal the word **ham.** Confirm that **ham** *is* the Hat Man's favourite food: ham with honey on it, to be exact!

The Letterland 'secret' is really a store-up-and-release technique. Demonstrate it by setting out the **ha** *Picture Code Cards* and guiding the children as follows:

– *Be ready to whisper the Hat Man's 'hhh...' sound (without saying it)*
– *Be ready to make Annie Apple's 'ă...' sound (again without saying it)*
– *Now let both sounds burst out of your mouths together: 'ha...!'*

Quickly add the **m** card while they chorus 'mmm...'. Check if the store-up-and-release concept has been understood by doing the same with '**da...d**'.

Consolidation

Workbooks

Guide the children through the exercises on pages 12 and 13 of *Programme One Workbook 1* to consolidate learning of Munching Mike's letter shape and sound. Draw special attention to his name and to the word **missing** in the instruction text.

Storybooks

For further listening practice, read the *Letterland Storybook: Munching Mike's Mistake* aloud and draw the children's attention to the recurring 'mmm...' sound.

STEP 6
Ticking Tess

Objectives

To teach the letter shapes and sound for **t** and **T**, and word building.

What you need

☆ *Programme One Picture Code Cards*: Ticking Tess (**t**), Ticking Tom (**t**) and all the cards covered so far

☆ *Programme One Flashcards*: 20-22, also 15 (**hat**) and 3 (**cat**) and all the character name cards covered so far

☆ *Class Wall Frieze*

☆ *Handwriting Songs Cassette*

☆ *Alphabet Songs Cassette*

☆ *Programme One Workbook 1*: pages 14 and 15

☆ *Storybook: Ticking Tess and the Tiger*

Preparation

☆ **Letters for picture coding** Prepare thick black **t**-shapes on pieces of card or paper for each child to picture code.

☆ **Spelling pictures** Write out the words **cat**, **hat** and **mat** on separate large sheets of paper, using a thick black felt-tip pen, so each child can picture code and illustrate the meaning of one of the words.

Quick revision

Start with a 'Quick dash' through the character name *Flashcards* first this time and then the sounds learnt so far, using the relevant *Picture Code Cards*. (For more information, see **Revising letters** on page 24.) Hold up two cards to read **ca**, **da**, **ha** and **ma** as well, for practice in storing up both sounds, then at a signal from you, releasing them together.

Introducing Ticking Tess

Next introduce Ticking Tess and tell her story:

*Now meet **T**icking **T**ess who works in the Letterland **T**eletouch **T**ower. She is a **t**all letter. She lives in a **t**all **t**ower, surrounded by **t**elephones, **t**ape recorders and **t**elevision sets. When people want to get in **t**ouch with each other in Letterland, they just **t**ell **T**icking **T**ess to start **t**icking. In no **t**ime at all she sends messages in all directions! How does she do it? Just by **t**alking into her machines in **t**iny, **t**iny **t**icks!*

Distribute your prepared **t**-shapes for picture coding.

Ticking Tess' letter shape

Introduce Ticking Tess' handwriting verse (set to music on the *Handwriting Songs Cassette*) to teach the correct stroke for **t**:

> Tall as a tower make Ticking Tess stand.
> Go from head to toe, and then from hand to hand.

Choose children to demonstrate the stroke on the *Class Wall Frieze* or *Picture Code Card*. Write a huge **t** on the board for them to air trace while they sing or chant the verse again.

Ticking Tess' sound

*I am going to whisper the **t**iny **t**icking sound that **T**icking **T**ess makes. It's like this: '**t**..., **t**..., **t**..., **t**..., **t**...'. Can you whisper **T**icking **T**ess' sound? Let me hear you.*

*Now listen again while I whisper some more. I **t**ick with the **t**ip of my **t**ongue, '**t**..., **t**..., **t**...'. Can you whisper that with me?*

telephone

Hold up the **telephone** *Flashcard* (22) and ask everyone not to say, but to whisper the word several times so that they really listen to the 't...' sound at the beginning.

The children can practise Ticking Tess' sound further on the *Alphabet Songs Cassette*. They can also act out her shape and sound by stretching out their arms, softly ticking, and turning on their tiptoes.

Introducing Ticking Tom

Ticking Tess has a best friend called Ticking Tom, who also works in Teletouch Tower. Introduce him, using the appropriate *Picture Code Card*, when children want to spell words like **tent** and words containing **tt**. Ticking Tom can be used for the *second* **t** of the pair.

Explaining the capital T shape

Talk about the capital T shape along these lines:

To start important words, Ticking Tess quickly changes into her trousers, takes a deep breath and makes herself even taller, so tall, that her head disappears in the clouds! Then all you can see is her tall, straight body, her arms, and if you are lucky, maybe a telephone in her hand! Her best friend Tom can do that, too!

Introduce *Flashcards* 20 and 21 (**Ticking Tess** and **Ticking Tom**). Discuss them, including the 'mmm...' sound in **Tom**. Make these cards available both now and again later, when more of the letters in them have been introduced.

Practising Ticking Tess' shape and sound

Ticking Tess in blends and digraphs

Some of your children may be ready to practise the blends and digraphs with **t**. In Section 3, you will find information on **th** (page 140), **tr** (page 152) and **tw** (page 157).

Word building with Ticking Tess

Live spelling: hat, cat, at and mat

Appoint five children to hold the **h**, **a**, **t**, **c** and **m** *Picture Code Cards*. They should always enter into the word they are building from the class' left.

*Today Hairy Hat Man and Annie Apple feel like making a word. Here they come, and what will they say together? 'Ha... ' Right! But that isn't a word, is it? So they call Ticking Tess to come over and add her sound. You call her. Here she comes ticking along, getting ready to tick next to them. Let's see if they have made a word now. 'Ha...t, ha...t, hat.' Yes, **hat** is a word! One of Hairy Hat Man's favourite words!*

Ticking Tess' words

table*	tiny
tall*	tomatoes
tap	top*
tea*	toy*
teddy	tractor
telephone*	train*
telescope	tree*
tell*	trousers
ten*	true
tent	turn*
tiger	twice

* High usage words

Go over this again, helping the children to discover **ha...t**. It helps to have a real hat available and the **hat** *Flashcard* (15) to confirm meaning.

Next, organise the children to make **cat**, as follows:

Now the Hairy Hat Man sees Clever Cat. He knows she loves being in words, so he says, 'Here, Clever Cat. You can have my place.' He hops off in the Reading Direction while in comes Clever Cat. So now which word have these three friends made together?

As 'Clever Cat' leaves, go on to discover **at**, and then also to make **mat**.

Spelling pictures

Distribute the words **cat**, **hat** and **mat** written on large sheets of paper for the children to picture code and illustrate.

Then hold up different children's pictures and ask them to point to the objects while naming them, e.g. '**hat, hat, hat, hat**' and then to read '**hat**' as they slide their finger across the word. Help them to end with their finger at the **t** as they pronounce this sound at the end. Do a similar routine with the **cat** and **mat** spelling pictures, giving the children practice with each others' words.

Encourage the children to construct **cat**, **hat** and **mat** in *Picture Code Cards* as well, using the pictogram sides first, then the plain sides. If they make non-words, let them try to pronounce them to you and treat them as fun.

Slow speak dictation

Ask various children to come to the board. Slow speak **hat** ('hhha...t') for them to write on the board, then **ham**, **mat**, **dad**, **add** and **cat**. Hold up the relevant *Picture Code Cards* to help any uncertain children.

Consolidation

Workbooks

Guide the children through the exercises on pages 14 and 15 of *Programme One Workbook 1* to consolidate learning of Ticking Tess' letter shape and sound. Draw special attention to her name and to the word **Trace** in the instruction text.

Storybooks

For further listening practice, read the *Letterland Storybook: Ticking Tess and the Tiger* aloud and draw the children's attention to the recurring 't...' sound.

STEP 7
Sammy Snake

Objectives

To teach the letter shapes and sounds for **s** and **S** (including **s** sounding like **z**), and word building.

What you need

☆ *Programme One Picture Code Cards*: Sammy Snake (**s**), Sally Snake (**s**), Sammy and Sally Snake together (**ss**), Sleepy Sammy (**s**) and all the cards covered so far

☆ *Programme One Flashcards*: 3, 6, 11, 15, 23-26 and all the character name cards covered so far

☆ *Class Wall Frieze*

☆ *Handwriting Songs Cassette*

☆ *Alphabet Songs Cassette*

☆ *Programme One Workbook 1*: pages 16 and 17

☆ *Storybook: Sammy Snake and the Snow*

☆ Old magazines and comics in large print for cutting up

Preparation

☆ **Letters for picture coding** Prepare thick black **s**-shapes on pieces of card or paper for each child to picture code.

☆ **Hissing and snoozing Sammy lists** Prepare two lists: one for 'hissing' Sammy Snake and another for Sleepy Sammy (see page 60), using the templates on page 187.

Quick revision

Start with the usual 'Quick dash' revision routine. You can judge best whether to revise only the principle character name *Flashcards*, or to include the best friends' names as well. Let the children handle, discuss and identify the single word *Flashcards*: **cat** (3), **apple** (6), **duck** (11) and **hat** (15). See if they can spot the **ca** and **ha** blends in **cat** and **hat**.

Introducing Sammy Snake

If, like **s**, every alphabet letter shape were as instantly evocative of a creature that actually makes that letter's sound, there would have been no need for Letterland! Make the most of Sammy Snake. He will help you to teach shape and sound and to explain the function of **s** as a plural signal.

Introduce him as follows:

> *Sammy Snake is a sweet little smiling snake, not a scary snake at all. He is happy as long as you stroke him properly. Start at the top of his head and smooth down his scales to his tail and he will smile all day long.*

Distribute your prepared **s**-shapes for the children to picture code. They may like to add some sand and sea behind him.

Sammy Snake's letter shape

Ask a child to kneel in a snake-like **s** position and let some other children stroke 'Sammy' the way he likes it. Emphasise that they should stroke from the top of his head and never ruffle his scales up the wrong way. (This should help to motivate children to drop the common habit of writing the letter **s** from the bottom upwards.)

The children can then chant or sing Sammy Snake's handwriting song from the *Handwriting Songs Cassette*, while air tracing his letter:

> Start at Sam's head where he can see.
> Stroke down to his tail, oh so care-ful-ly!

Write a huge **s** on the board for them to air trace while they sing or chant the verse again. Choose children to finger trace the letter on the *Class Wall Frieze* or *Picture Code Card*.

Sammy Snake's sound

Talk about Sammy's voiceless hissing sound like this:

Sammy Snake spends most of his time in words hissing away like this, 'sss..., sss..., sss...'. He hisses as he slips and slides and slithers along in the Reading Direction. If you lisssten carefully, you will hear him hisssing in lotsss and lotsss of words.

Now let's hear you say this sentence after me:
'*SSSammy SSSnake likes to sssit bessside the sssea.*'

Pause halfway through to allow time for the children to repeat it after you. Encourage them to exaggerate the 'sss...' sound so that they really feel it escaping from between their teeth. This is a sound to enjoy! Tactfully correct any child who has mistakenly learned the **s** sound as 'suh' (with voice) by explaining that Sammy always whispers his hisses.

Sammy Snake's song on the *Alphabet Songs Cassette* is a lively way to practise his sound. (Make sure that no-one sings 'suh'.)

Introducing Sally Snake

Hold up the pictogram side of the Sally Snake *Picture Code Card*. (She has eyelashes.)

Sammy Snake has a sister called Sally Snake who loves hissing just as much as he does, and you will often see them hissing together.

Explain that **ss** is a 'shared' sound. Sammy and his sister Sally both hiss at exactly the same time in some words, because these words need them both, e.g. **his** but **hiss**. Sally Snake can be used for the *second* **s** of the pair. She can also be used when children want to spell words like **sister**.

Ask the children to go 'snake spotting', i.e. looking out for words where Sammy and Sally occur side by side. They can make a collection of words, cutting them from magazines and newspaper headlines. The box on page 132 should give you some ideas.

Explaining the capital S shape

Ask the children what Clever Cat does to start important words.

Yes, she takes a deep breath and gets bigger. Sammy Snake takes a deep breath and gets bigger, too. He says, 'Now I'm a super-size snake!'

Compare the small and super-size Sammy on the *Class Wall Frieze* and show how much bigger Sammy has made himself than all the other letters on the **Sammy Snake** *Flashcard* (23). Ask if Sally Snake can do the same. (Look at *Flashcard* 24 together to find out.) Compare with the small **s**'s on *Flashcards* 25 and 26, too.

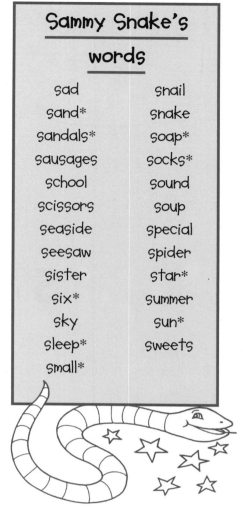

Sammy Snake's words

sad	snail
sand*	snake
sandals*	soap*
sausages	socks*
school	sound
scissors	soup
seaside	special
seesaw	spider
sister	star*
six*	summer
sky	sun*
sleep*	sweets
small*	

* High usage words

Sammy Snake sounding like z (Sleepy Sammy)

You have taught the voiceless hissing sound, but a close analysis of the sound of **s** in common words shows that six out of ten contain not a hissing sound, but a voiced **s** sound exactly like **z**, as in **is**, **his**, **has**, **was**, **comes**, **goes**, **lives**, **plays**, **these**, **boys**, **girls** and **cars**. You will need, therefore, to present Sammy as having two kinds of hiss: his wide awake hiss ('sss...'), and his sleepy hiss ('zzz...'). Since **z** is used far less often to spell the 'zzz...' sound than **s**, it is important for children to link both sounds to **s** first.

Hold up the Sleepy Sammy *Picture Code Card* and introduce him like this:

> *One reason everyone likes Sammy Snake is because he works hard. He has to work hard because so many words need his hissing sound. He has to dash about and be in so many places that he doesn't have time to sleep all night, so instead he has lots of very quick snoozes in the daytime, just for a few seconds each time. In some words you can hear him snoozing because his hisses don't sound like 'sss....' any more. Instead they sound like this: 'zzz...'.*
>
> *Listen for his snoozing sound while I say these words slowly: boys, girls, eyes, hands, ears, nose. And now here is a word with two quick snoozes: noses. Did you hear Sammy's two snoozes?*

Write **nose** and **noses** on the board and picture code each **s**. Ask the children to mime Sammy hissing, then snoozing, and then swiftly waking up again: 'sss..., zzz..., sss...'!

Display your prepared lists, one showing Sammy Snake wide awake and the other showing him snoozing. Let the children collect suitable words on them. Searching for examples will sharpen their listening skills and their attention to their own speech sounds. Leave the lists up so they can add new words as they find them. It should emerge that Sammy is prone to a snooze beside certain letters (the voiced ones) and never beside certain other ones (the whispered or unvoiced letters).

Sammy at the end of words (plurals)

Re-use the children's **cat**, **hat** and **mat** spelling pictures (see page 57) to draw attention to the ends of words and to plurals.

Let the children re-read their words, e.g. **cat**, and then hold up the Sammy Snake *Picture Code Card* at the end as they make Sammy's hissing sound: 'cat**sss**' (meaning more than one cat, as in their pictures). Encourage them to show you and tell you in their own words what Sammy is doing (adding his hiss to change the meaning of the word from one to 'ssseveral of sssomething').

Now look together at *Flashcards* 3 (**cat**), 4 (**cats**), 6 (**apple**), 7 (**apples**), 11 (**duck**), 12 (**ducks**), 15 (**hat**) and 16 (**hats**), and notice where Sammy Snake hisses, and where he is having a quick snooze (**apples**).

Practising Sammy's shape and sound

Sammy Snake in blends and digraphs

Some of your children may be ready to practise a few of the blends and digraphs with **s**. In Section 3, you will find information on -**ss** (page 131), **sh** (page 138), **sl** (page 150), **sc**, **sk**, **sp** and **st** (page 153), **sm**, **sn** and **sw** (page 155) and **scr**, **spl**, **spr** and **str** (page 156).

Word building with Sammy Snake

Live spelling: sad, sat, mat and mats

Give out out the *Picture Code Cards* for **a**, **d**, **h**, **m**, **t** and **s**. Ask those children to come up who think they are needed to make the word **sad**. The others then read this word, and decide who must come up to change **sad** into **sat**. Ask which word they will have made if Munching Mike then takes Sammy Snake's place. Finally, let the children build and read the word **mats**, reminding them how Sammy can change the meaning from one to 'several of something' by appearing at the end.

Consolidation

Workbooks

Guide the children through the exercises on pages 16 and 17 of *Programme One Workbook 1* to consolidate learning of Sammy Snake's letter shape and sound. Draw special attention to his name and to the words **sound** and **missing** in the instruction text.

Storybooks

For further listening practice, read the *Letterland Storybook: Sammy Snake and the Snow* aloud and draw the children's attention to the recurring 'sss...' sound.

Revision of
STEPS 1–7

Quick revision

Start with your usual 'Quick dash' routine for all the letters learnt so far, using the appropriate *Picture Code Cards*. Don't forget to include both the short **ă** and long **ā** (Annie Apple and Mr A), the 'best friends', as well as **s** making the 'zzz...' sound (Sleepy Sammy).

Match the sound game

This game practises auditory discrimination of initial sounds. Ask each child to write **dD** and **hH** on both sides of two separate cards, and then to picture code one side only. (Write the letters for them if necessary.)

Say the following words clearly, while the children hold up the card for whichever initial sound they hear. (It doesn't matter which side they show you: in each case they will benefit from the reinforcement on the reverse side of the card.)

1 dreary day	4 hillside house	7 delicious dessert	10 digging
2 heavy hammer	5 hole	8 diving	11 dancing
3 dozing donkey	6 dusty desk	9 hopping	12 hippopotamus

At another convenient time, the children can make and use **cC** and **aA** cards to hold up when they hear the initial sound. They can also do the same with **dD/cC, mM/dD** and **mM/hH**.
Take note of any children who frequently make mistakes. Arrange to play the game with them again on a one-to-one basis later. This game may help you to identify children with hearing loss or poor auditory perception.

cC/aA	dD/cC	mM/dD	mM/hH
1 cold cabbage	1 dandelion	1 marshmallows	1 moonlight
2 appetising apple	2 clean cups	2 dry doughnuts	2 haystack
3 crazy costume	3 damp dog	3 merry music	3 medicine
4 angry alligator	4 deep ditch	4 misty mountains	4 head over heels
5 caravan	5 cosy cushions	5 dizzy dancers	5 helicopter
6 ant	6 copy cats	6 magazines	6 meadow
7 camera	7 danger	7 marmalade	7 heated house
8 caravan	8 coconut	8 different	8 headache
9 arrow	9 dinner	9 my mother	9 magic mark
10 candle	10 caterpillar	10 dirty dishes	10 more meat

Frieze game

Use the *Class Wall Frieze* with the *Picture Code Cards* for revising the letters learnt so far.

Hand out the *Picture Code Cards* for Clever Cat, Annie Apple, Dippy Duck, Hairy Hat Man, Munching Mike, Ticking Tess and Sammy Snake to seven children. Appoint other children to call out one of these character names. The child holding the card called out must run to the frieze and match his or her letter either to the same lower case letter, or to its corresponding capital letter, as you have specified.

The same game can be repeated using the letter sounds instead of the character names.

Spelling pictures

You may like to prepare further spelling pictures (see page 26) for the children to picture code and illustrate, using the phrases **duck hat**, **cat hat**, **cat hats** and **apple hats**.

Slow speak dictation

The value of this activity is worth stressing again. Showing children how to take the sounds from their own mouths into written speech is your best technique for consolidating the good work done in live spelling. Other strategies will help them to manage less regular words later on. Meanwhile this will equip them to cope with all regular words and all the regular parts of thousands more!

Make this slow speak dictation a group activity at this stage, using the board as you did in Step 6 (page 57) or, if you think the age group you are teaching is ready to try to capture their own spoken words on paper without the group support, provide exercise books to use regularly for this activity.

Say each word several times, both normally and in slow speak. Make sure the children do the same. They need to hear their own voices, role-modelling their pronunciation on yours. Use some or all of the following words:

had	hat	mat	sad	cat	has
ham	hats	mats	dad	cats	add

It will help to give some words a context, e.g. 'lots of door mmma...tsss'.

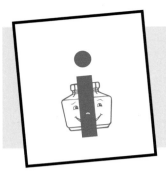

STEP 8a
Impy Ink

Objectives

To teach the letter shapes for **i** and **I** and the short vowel sound '**ĭ**..', and word building.

What you need

- ☆ *Programme One Picture Code Cards*: Impy Ink (**ĭ**) and all the cards covered so far
- ☆ *Programme One Flashcards*: 27 and 28 and all the character name cards covered so far
- ☆ *Class Wall Frieze*
- ☆ *Handwriting Songs Cassette*
- ☆ *Alphabet Songs Cassette*
- ☆ *Programme One Songs Cassette*
- ☆ *Programme One Workbook 2*: pages 2-4
- ☆ *Storybook: Impy Ink's Invisible Ink*
- ☆ *Links Group 1: Impy Ink*

Preparation

- ☆ **Ink and ice cream mural** You may like to create an 'ink and ice cream' mural. It should show Mr I with a vendor's cart which has two sections: one for ink and one for ice cream.

- ☆ **Letters for picture coding** Prepare thick black i-shapes on pieces of card or paper for each child to picture code.

- ☆ **Further flashcards** Prepare a double-sided flashcard reading **it is**: a template is provided for this on page 187.

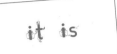

- ☆ **Important words sign** Prepare a sign reading **Important Words**: picture code just the letters covered so far.

- ☆ **Spelling pictures** Write out the words **it is** reasonably large on pieces of paper, using a thick black felt-tip pen. As the children cannot illustrate the meaning of these two words, no extra space is needed around them. Make enough copies for each child.

Quick revision

Start the lesson as usual with your 'Quick dash' revision routine, covering all the letters learnt so far. Use the *Picture Code Cards* to revise initial sounds and the character name *Flashcards* to revise the character names.

Introducing Impy Ink

Three words beginning with **i** are among the 12 most used words in the English language: **in**, **is** and **it**. Both **is** and **it** are taught in this Step (see Step 9 for **in**). In Step 8b you will be talking about the Vowel Man 'Mr I' (the alphabet name **i**). Some attention to the long **ī** is essential as **I** is another of the 12 most used English words. Your pack of *Picture Code Cards* includes the word **I** so that you can work with such phrases as **I am**, **I can**, etc.

When introducing Impy Ink, it may be useful to bring a real ink pen and bottle of ink into school. The fact that ink is not sold everywhere these days should not deter you. It is still available in numerous colours in art shops. Ink also remains an essential material in printing books, newspapers, etc., so children still need to know what ink is, even if they only see it these days flowing from the tips of their felt-tip pens. You can then go on to present a very special bottle of ink called 'Impy Ink', a friendly and sometimes mischievous little fellow who plays an important part in everyone's life in Letterland.

In Letterland, ink is important, because every child in every school in Letterland writes with an ink pen. You see, there are no pencils in Letterland, and no felt-tip pens. You can buy crayons, but they are too thick to write with. So everyone who wants to write anything down needs an ink pen and some ink to put in it.

Luckily in Letterland there is a nice man called Mr I who sells lots of ink, and ink pens. He sells ink in many different colours: he sells red ink, blue ink, green ink, pink ink and lots of other colours too, all in little ink bottles.

There are some ink bottles though, which Mr I will not sell. They are his very special talking ink bottles. Who ever heard of an ink bottle that could talk? Impossible you might think, but not in Letterland. Let me tell you about one of them, Impy Ink!

Hold up the Impy Ink *Picture Code Card*.

Does he look as though he is about to wink? He has an impish face, and he does have a habit of winking every few minutes. Can any of you wink like Impy Ink?

Let the children try, while you distribute your prepared **i**-shapes for the children to picture code.

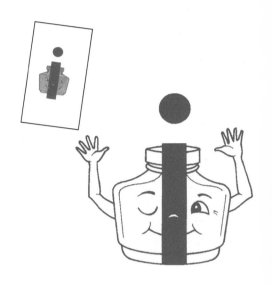

Impy Ink's letter shape

Can you think why people call this talking ink bottle 'Impy Ink'? It might just be because he likes to play tricks. Shall I tell you Impy Ink's favourite trick? He spills ink! Just a spot, mind you. But every time you see him in a word you will see a little spot of ink over his head. Why do you think he does it?

Discuss possible reasons. Lead the children to decide that maybe this is Impy Ink's way of helping children to recognise him quickly in words, because his letter is so thin and little without a dot above it.

Introduce Impy Ink's handwriting verse (set to music on the *Handwriting Songs Cassette*) to teach the correct stroke for **i**:

> Inside the ink bottle draw a line.
> Add an inky dot. That's fine!

Choose children to demonstrate the stroke on the *Class Wall Frieze* or *Picture Code Card*. Write a huge **i** on the board for them to air trace while they sing or chant the verse again.

* High usage words

Impy Ink's words

if*	insect*
ill*	inside*
important*	interesting*
in*	into*
infants*	invitation
ink*	itch

Impy Ink's sound

Impy Ink has lots of talking friends. We don't know all their names, but one is called 'Isobel Ink' and another is 'Ingrid Ink'. What sound do you think Impy Ink and his friends make in words?

Help the children to isolate the '**ĭ**...' sound at the start of his name and then chorus it. Use Impy Ink's song on the *Alphabet Songs Cassette* to confirm this important short vowel sound.

Explaining the capital I shape

Remember how some Letterland people and animals tell us that they are starting an important word by taking a deep breath and getting bigger? Well, when Impy Ink takes a deep breath, his letter gets so tall and thin that you can't see his ink spot anymore. His letter looks long and thin like an ink pen instead of a short little line with a dot. If you are lucky, you may see an ink pen in it...

Point to the capital I on the *Class Wall Frieze*, and let the children examine the Impy Ink *Flashcard* (27) showing the ink pens.

Or...you may see Impy Ink himself, looking just a little bigger and ever so important - just like on this sign which says 'Important Words'.

While the ink pen picture coding stresses the thin **i**-shape in printed Letterland materials, the ink bottle coding is more practical for use in handwritten words, where the pen cannot be drawn within the narrow stroke of the capital **I** (see left).

Practising Impy Ink's shape and sound

Impy Ink in names

Many children will have an **i** in their names, but in quite a few cases the **i** will be irregular, e.g. **I**an, Mar**i**a, Lou**i**sa and Kulv**i**r. Do not worry at this stage if they picture code these **i**'s as Impy Ink. Simply tell them to draw a wiggly line beneath the **i** to show that Impy Ink is not making his usual sound there. For names beginning with the long **ī**, such as **I**sla, see page 69.

Word building with Impy Ink

The important little words it and is

These two little words (and also **in**) rank among the 12 most used words in the English language.

Hold up your prepared **it is** flashcard and say:

*You will often hear Impy Ink making his little 'ĭ...' sound right at the beginning of these two little words: **it is**.*

Sound out the words together. Then draw an animated ink bottle on the board and put your **it is** flashcard beside it. Elicit 'It is Impy Ink'.

*Yes, it is Impy Ink. Can you hear Impy's little 'ĭ...' sound in the word **it**? Can you hear it again in **is**? And in Impy's own name: Impy Ink?*

Do not show the Impy Ink *Flashcard* (27) yet.

Discuss how often we need these two little words to say, for example, the following:

It is raining.   It is interesting.
It is time to play.   It is an insect.
It is late.   It is an ink pen.
It is silly.   It is an ink bottle.
It is important.

Decide together that it is *important* to be able to read and write little words which we use very often.

(Save *Flashcard* 28 (**in**) to introduce in Step 9: Naughty Nick.)

Spelling pictures

Hand out your prepared spelling pictures for the phrase **it is**. This time the children will only be able to picture code the letters. Explain that many words help us to name things which we *can* draw, but other words like these two are different. They help us to talk about hundreds of things that we cannot draw.

Live spelling: sentence building

Use your **it is** flashcard with the character name *Flashcards* (27, 9 and 20) to make little sentences, and listen together to the 'ĭ...' sounds in all three of these Letterland names:

it is Impy Ink
it is Ticking Tess
it is Dippy Duck

You can also make 'living' sentences by placing the **it is** phrase, or a child's hand-coded **it is** spelling picture, beside any other child holding their own name.

Consolidation

Workbooks

Guide the children through the exercises on pages 2-4 of *Programme One Workbook 2* to consolidate learning of Impy Ink's letter shape and his short 'ĭ...' sound. Draw special attention to his name and to the word **in** in the instruction text.

Storybooks

For further listening practice, read the *Letterland Storybook: Impy Ink's Invisible Ink* or *Letterland Links Group 1: Impy Ink* aloud and draw the children's attention to the recurring short 'ĭ...' sound.

Cassette

Sing or listen to **Impy Ink** and Impy Ink's verse (in particular) of the **Vowel Sounds Song** on the *Programme One Songs Cassette*.

STEP 8b
Mr I, the Ice Cream Man

Objectives

To teach the long vowel ī and word building.

What you need

☆ *Programme One Picture Code Cards*: Mr I (capital and lower case ī) and Impy Ink (ĭ)

☆ *Programme One Flashcards*: 29-31 and any of the character and plural noun *Flashcards* met so far

☆ *Class Wall Frieze*

☆ *Programme One Songs Cassette*

☆ *Programme One Workbook 2*: page 5

☆ *Storybook: The Vowel Street Party*

☆ *Links Group 1: Five Vowel Men*

Preparation

☆ **Ice cream cone** Make a simple ice cream cone out of paper.

Introducing Mr I, the Ice Cream Man

As the Impy Ink song on the *Alphabet Songs Cassette* points out, Impy Ink belongs to Mr I. Mr I looks after him and all the other ink bottles in Letterland.

Since the word **I** is such a high-usage word, and will be needed for the writing under children's pictures, etc., you will want to give the long ī a fair amount of attention. By introducing Mr I as selling two products, ink and ice cream, you can immediately use the essential word **I** and follow on with another high-usage word, **like**, without contradicting your short ĭ teaching.

Mr I, the Ice Cream Man, is everyone's friend because he supplies nice tasty ice cream in Letterland. Any child can play-act being Mr I by handing out lots of imaginary ice creams. (Others can mime at receiving and licking them.)

Using the paper ice cream cone that you have made, talk about Mr I roughly as follows:

Do you like ice cream? Well then, if you went to Letterland, who is the first person you might like to meet?

Elicit the answer 'Mr I' and show his capital letter *Picture Code Card*.

Yes! Mr I, the Ice Cream Man! Everyone says that his ice cream tastes very, very nice. He has all kinds of tasty ice creams for you to buy. Mr I is a Vowel Man just like... Who else do we know who is a Vowel Man?

Elicit Mr A, the Apron Man from Asia.

So now we have met two Vowel Men, Mr A and Mr I.

Choose the right moment to introduce your small **i** card showing Mr I on it as well. The *Picture Code Cards* themselves will do more than anything you can say, explaining visually that Impy Ink and Mr I share both the **i** and **I** shapes.

Mr I's presence on the *Class Wall Frieze* also serves to confirm in the children's minds the fact that the letter **i** can represent either its sound or its alphabet name.

Practising Mr I saying his name

Mr I in names

If any children's names begin with the long ī, e.g. **Isla** or **Ivor**, show them how to draw a stick man right beside the capital **I** to signal Mr I saying his name. Treat their names as special 'because Mr I always manages to find time to appear in them'. Any short 'ĭ...' sounds can be picture-coded with Impy Ink. Add a wiggly line if any **i**'s are irregular.

Mr I in the word I

Hold up the **I am** and **Mr I** *Flashcards* (31 and 29) for everyone to read. Give your paper cone to a child to hold up while reading this sentence. Give others a turn, too. Point to the words as they read.

Give other children the character name *Flashcards* 14, 17 and 23 (**Hairy Hat Man**, **Munching Mike** and **Sammy Snake**) to hold up beside the **I am** *Flashcard*. The others can read them and then everyone can make that character's sound. Follow on with the **I like** *Flashcard* (30) and use the same name cards again.

Many already familiar *Flashcards* can now be combined to make new sentences, e.g. **I like cats/ducks/apples/hats**, or other character names. You could also hold up the **I like** *Flashcard* (30) next to any child holding their own picture-coded name painting.

cats

i like

ducks

apples

Consolidation

Workbooks

Guide the children through the exercises on page 5 of *Programme One Workbook 2* to consolidate learning of the long ī in words. Draw special attention to Mr I's name in the instruction text.

Storybooks

For further listening practice, read the *Letterland Storybook: The Vowel Street Party* or *Letterland Links Group 1: Five Vowel Men* aloud and draw the children's attention to Mr I's name in words.

Cassette

Sing or listen to Mr I's verse (in particular) of the **Vowel Men Song** on the *Programme One Songs Cassette*.

Mr I's words	
I*	iron*
ice cream*	island*
idea*	ivy

* High usage words

STEP 9
Naughty Nick

Objectives

To teach the letter shapes and sound for **n** and **N**, and word building.

What you need

☆ *Programme One Picture Code Cards*: Naughty Nick (**n**), Naughty Nicola (**n**) and all the cards covered so far

☆ *Programme One Flashcards*: 28, 32-35 and all the character name cards covered so far

☆ *Class Wall Frieze*

☆ *Handwriting Songs Cassette.*

☆ *Alphabet Songs Cassette*

☆ *Programme One Workbook 2*: pages 6 and 7

☆ *Storybook: Naughty Nick and the Nettle Nibbler*

Preparation

☆ **Letters for picture coding**
Prepare thick black **n**-shapes on pieces of card or paper for each child to picture code.

* If any problem arises using Nick's nickname 'Naughty Nick', feel free to use one of his other nicknames: 'Noisy Nick' or even 'Nice Nick'.

Quick revision

Take a 'Quick dash' through the character names and sounds for all the letters learnt so far. Then ask for the sounds only as you hold up the cards for **ca**, **da**, **ha**, **ma**, **ta** and **sa**. You could also add **st** (whispered) and **sta** in preparation for the word **stand** on page 72.

Introducing Naughty Nick

By introducing Naughty Nick now, you can focus on the word **no** well in advance of the word **on**, helping to avoid typical early confusions between **on** and **no**.

There is a naughty boy who lives in Letterland. His name is Naughty Nick.* Naughty Nick is a nice boy really, but unfortunately he does like to be naughty quite often. He can also be very nosy, which is a nuisance. And he is noisy. He loves hammering nails, which grown-ups especially find very annoying. See how he always has at least one nail with him?

Point to the nail in the **n**.

Another annoying habit of Nick's is saying 'No!' He likes saying 'No', even when he knows he should be saying 'Yes'! When his mother says it's bedtime, Naughty Nick always says 'No! Not yet!' Sometimes he shouts so loudly, he disturbs all the neighbours.
Once Naughty Nick did something so naughty with some nails, that people nicknamed him 'Naughty Nick Nails'. And that has been his nickname ever since!*

Distribute your prepared **n**-shapes for picture coding while you allow discussion. Leave the children to wonder what very naughty thing Naughty Nick did to earn his nickname. Meanwhile, the topic of naughtiness is likely to elicit a good deal of language from children, based on their own experience!

Naughty Nick's letter shape

Naughty Nick's letter starts with a straight line, just like a nail. The rest of it looks like another nail which is bent over. Try making his letter shape with your left hand, holding your thumb and fingers like this.

Demonstrate making an **n**-shape with your left hand turned towards the children (see right) and introduce Naughty Nick's handwriting verse (set to music on the *Handwriting Songs Cassette*) to teach the correct stroke for **n**:

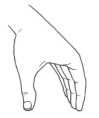

> 'Now bang my nail,' Naughty Nick said.
> 'Go up and over around my head.'

Choose children to demonstrate the **n** stroke on the *Class Wall Frieze* or *Picture Code Card* and with their own left hands. Write a huge **n** on the board for them to air trace while they sing or chant the verse again.

Naughty Nick's sound

*Now put your hand over your nose and press it against your face and say "**Nn**naughty **Nn**ick' a few times, slowly, until you can feel Naughty Nick's funny '**nnn**...' sound going through your nose. This is the sound Naughty Nick makes in words.*

Make sure everyone keeps their mouths almost shut when practising the 'nnn...' sound in Naughty Nick's song on the *Alphabet Songs Cassette*.

Introducing Naughty Nicola

Naughty Nick has a best friend and next-door neighbour called Naughty Nicola, who is just as naughty and noisy as Nick! Introduce her, using the appropriate *Picture Code Card*, when children want to spell words like **nine** and words containing **nn**. Naughty Nicola can be used for the *second* **n** of the pair.

Explaining the capital N shape

Explain the capital N shape as follows:

Remember how lots of Letterland people and animals begin important words by taking a deep breath and becoming bigger? Naughty Nick should do the same too, but the naughty fellow says 'No, I won't!' Instead, he does his own special trick. He starts important words with three big nails. You can see them here in his own name, Naughty Nick.

Introduce the **Naughty Nick** and **Naughty Nicola** *Flashcards* (32 and 33).

Practising Nick's shape and sound

Naughty Nick in blends and digraphs

Some of your children may be ready to practise the blends and digraphs with **n**. In Section 3, you will find information on **-nd** and **-nt** (page 133), **-ng** (page 135) and **-nk** (page 137).

Naughty Nick's words

nails	nice*
name*	night*
nap	nine*
near*	no*
neck*	noise*
need*	nose*
needle	not*
nest*	now*
net	number*
never*	nurse*
new*	nursery
next*	nuts

* High usage words

Word building with Naughty Nick

Live spelling: an, can, man, and, hand, stand and handstand

Hand out the **c**, **a**, **d**, **m** and **n** *Picture Code Cards* to five children. Slow speak **an** ('annn') twice and let the other children decide which two should come up to make **an**, as in **an apple**.

Now who will help us to turn the word an into can?

When the **c** child has joined the **a** and **n** children, go on to build **man** ('mmmannn') and **and**. Then ask which word they can make if they put the Hat Man next to Annie Apple (**hand**).

With two more children as Sammy Snake and Ticking Tess, you can also go on to combine the whispered 'ssst' sound with **and** to form **stand**. Even more exciting, try building **handstand** (using the reverse side of the Mr A card and four more children). The other children will be surprised they can read such a long word!

The important little word no

Write **no** on the board. Ask two children to write **no** again twice.

no, no, no

What does Naughty Nick like to say when he should be saying 'yes'?

Point to the words on the board for all the children to read. You can now introduce the **no** *Flashcard* (34). The children will probably now be able to read both sides of *Flashcards* 34 and 35.

The important little word in

Next look at the word **in** on *Flashcard* 28. Point out how Naughty Nick likes making his funny 'nnn...' sound in **in**.

Consolidation

Workbooks

Guide the children through the exercises on pages 6 and 7 of *Programme One Workbook 2* to consolidate learning of Naughty Nick's letter shape and sound. Draw special attention to his name and to the word **in** in the instruction text.

Storybooks

For further listening practice, read the *Letterland Storybook: Naughty Nick and the Nettle Nibbler* aloud and draw the children's attention to the recurring 'nnn...' sound.

STEP 10
Yellow Yo-yo Man

Objectives

To teach the letter shapes and the first sound for **y** and **Y**, and word building.

What you need

☆ *Programme One Picture Code Cards*: Yellow Yo-yo Man (**y**), Eddy Elephant (**ĕ**) and all the cards covered so far

☆ *Programme One Flashcards*: 34, 36-39 and all the character name cards covered so far

☆ *Class Wall Frieze*

☆ *Handwriting Songs Cassette*

☆ *Alphabet Songs Cassette*

☆ *Programme One Workbook 2*: pages 8 and 9

☆ *Storybook: Zig Zag Zebra Saves the Day*

Preparation

☆ **Letters for picture coding** Prepare thick black **y**-shapes on pieces of card or paper for each child to picture code.

☆ **Yo-yo Man display** Make a large Yo-yo Man display, making his sack out of real cloth or plastic. Cut out some yo-yos from yellow card and write a variety of Yo-yo Man's words on the backs of them (see page 74 for ideas).

Quick revision

Give priority in your revision this time to Impy Ink's sound, alone, and in the blends **di**, **hi**, **mi**, **ni**, **si** and **ti**. By now, the children will, hopefully, be growing more confident at reading the character names on the *Flashcards* and spotting them in the *Programme One Workbooks*, as well.

Introducing Yellow Yo-yo Man

The words listed under **Yo-yo Man's words** (see page 74) represent Yellow Yo-yo Man's few chances to make his own sound in common words. As soon as the letter **y** moves into a medial or final position (e.g. in **my**, **bicycle** or **baby**) this semi-vowel sounds quite different. (In Letterland terms, he puts down his yo-yos to make other letters' sounds for them instead.)

The best place to find Yellow Yo-yo Man is in the words **yes**, **yellow** and **yo-yos**.

*The next person for **y**ou to meet in Letterland is a good friend of Mr I's called the **Y**ellow **Y**o-**y**o Man. The children in Letterland can always tell when the **Y**o-**y**o Man is coming, because the first thing he does is **y**ell out:*
*'**Y**o-**y**os for sale. **Y**ellow **y**o-**y**os, **y**es, **y**es, **yyy**es!'*

Hold up the plain side of the Yellow Yo-yo Man *Picture Code Card*.

*Can **y**ou picture the **Y**o-**y**o Man's head here, and his feet here? Which way will he be going? **Y**es, in the Reading Direction. What colour will the **Y**ellow **Y**o-**y**o Man's **y**o-**y**os be? **Y**es, **y**ellow!*

Turn to the pictogram side.

*Can **y**ou see where he carries his **y**ellow **y**o-**y**os in his sack on his back?*

Elicit 'Yes.'

*Yes! And 'yes' is just what the **Y**ellow **Y**o-**y**o Man **y**ells. '**Y**o-**y**os for sale. **Y**ellow **y**o-**y**os, **y**es, **y**es, **yyy**es!'*

Distribute your prepared **y**-shapes for picture coding.

Yo-yo Man's letter shape

Introduce Yo-yo Man's handwriting verse (set to music on the *Handwriting Songs Cassette*) to teach the correct stroke for **y**:

> You first make the yo-yo sack on the Yo-yo Man's back, and then go down to his toes so he can sell his yo-yos.

Point out that his straight letter shape is used more in books and his curved shape more for handwriting. Choose children to demonstrate the stroke on the *Class Wall Frieze* or *Picture Code Card*. Write a huge **y** on the board for them to air trace while they sing or chant the verse again.

Yo-yo Man's sound

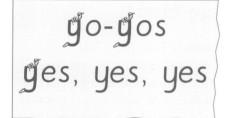

Write **yo-yos** and **yes, yes, yes** on the board. Picture code only the **y** in the first **yes**.

> Here **y**ou can see the **Y**o-**y**o Man's letter twice in the word **yo-y**os. And here he is again at the beginning of **y**es.
> If **y**ou want to discover what sound the **Y**o-**y**o Man makes in these words, start to say '**Y**o-**y**o Man'. '**Y**yyyy…'

Encourage the children to prolong the 'yyy…' sound, then let them read **yes** very slowly and repeat 'Yyyyes, yyyyes, yyyyes'.

Now call for quick responses to the **yes** and **no** *Flashcards* (37 and 34). Try hiding both *Flashcards* behind your back and bringing them out one at a time for the children to identify swiftly.

For further practice in Yo-yo Man's sound, sing his song on the *Alphabet Songs Cassette*.

Yo-yo Man's words

yacht	yet*
yawn	yo-yo
year*	yogurt
yell	yolk
yellow*	you*
yes*	young*
yesterday*	your*

* High usage words

Explaining the capital Y shape

While the children look at both the lower and upper case **y**'s on the *Class Wall Frieze*, explain as follows:

> Many letters take a deep breath and get bigger to start an important word or name. Well, so does the **Y**ellow **Y**o-**y**o Man. But he also does something else as well. **Y**ou've seen how full his **yo-y**o sack usually is, haven't **y**ou? All those **yo-y**os make quite a heavy load. This is why in most words **y**ou will see the **Y**ellow **Y**o-**y**o Man resting his sack on the line. This makes him rather low down.
> So when he is going to start an important word - like his own name - he quickly empties some **yo-y**os out so he can step lightly up on to the line!

Point to the lighter load in the capital letter on the wall frieze and study and compare the **y** and **Y** positions on *Flashcards* 36, 38 and 39 (**Yellow Yo-yo Man**, **you** and **yellow**).

Practising Yo-yo Man's shape and sound

Play-acting the Yo-yo Man

Let the children play act being the Yo-yo Man out of doors so that they can all yell out, 'Yyyellow yyyo-yyyos for sale! Yyyes, yyyes, yyyes.' Some can take turns being 'youngsters' coming to buy the yo-yos, saying 'Yes, please' and 'A yellow one, please.'

Yo-yo Man in names

Names beginning with the Yo-yo Man's sound are rare. Celebrate it if you do have, say, a **Y**asmin in your class. More children will, however, find that they do have 'the Yo-yo Man's letter' in their names, but not his usual sound (e.g. the **y** in K**y**lie or at the end of names such as Jenn**y**). These children should draw a yellow sack but with *no* yo-yos in it *and* draw a wiggly line beneath their **y**. (The story explanations for these changes in sound are available in Programme Two.)

Yo-yo Man display

Make a large Yo-yo Man display (see **Preparation**). The children can help you to fill up the Yo-yo Man's cloth sack by playing the following game. Ask them to read the words on your prepared yo-yos (e.g. **yes**, **yet**, **yell**, **yo-yo** and **you**). If they read a word correctly, they can then put it into the sack. Gradually you can add harder words to the game, such as **yesterday**, **year** and **young**.

Word building with Yellow Yo-yo Man

Live spelling: yes and yet

Even though the letter **e** is taught later (in Step 15), feel free to use the Eddy Elephant *Picture Code Card* now and help the children to build the words **yes** and **yet**.

Consolidation

Workbooks

Guide the children through the exercises on pages 8 and 9 of *Programme One Workbook 2* to consolidate learning of Yo-yo Man's letter shape and sound. Draw special attention to his name and to the word **yellow** in the instruction text.

Storybooks

For further listening practice, read the *Letterland Storybook: Zig Zag Zebra Saves the Day* aloud and draw the children's attention to the recurring 'yyy...' sound.

STEP 11
Golden Girl

Objectives

To teach the letter shapes and hard sound for **g** and **G**, and word building.

What you need

☆ *Programme One Picture Code Cards*: Golden Girl (**g**), Golden Granny (**g**) and all the cards covered so far

☆ *Programme One Flashcards*: 40-43 and all the character name cards covered so far

☆ *Class Wall Frieze*

☆ *Handwriting Songs Cassette*

☆ *Alphabet Songs Cassette*

☆ *Programme One Workbook 2*: pages 10 and 11

Preparation

☆ **Letters for picture coding**
Prepare thick black **g**-shapes on pieces of card or paper for each child to picture code.

☆ **Gardening with Golden Girl**
You may wish to prepare the basis for a miniature garden beforehand (see page 78).

Quick revision

Once again give priority to revision first. Begin by practising Impy Ink's sound. Then practise **d**, **h**, **m**, **t**, **s** and **n** in a blend with **i**. Carry on practising the character name *Flashcards* as they will strengthen capital letter recognition.

Introducing Golden Girl

All the pictograms emphasise the Reading Direction in one way or another except three: **g**, **q** and **z**. These all face *against* the Reading Direction. Each one has its own special explanation. This Step features Golden Girl, also nicknamed 'Green Girl' by her grandad, because she is such a good gardener.

*There is a **g**arden in Letterland where the **g**rass is as **g**reen as **g**reen can be. This **g**arden is full of flowers, and in it there is also a **g**arden swing. The swing looks quite different from other **g**arden swings you may have seen. This swing looks like this.*

Show the plain side of Golden Girl's *Picture Code Card*.

*It belongs to a **g**irl called **G**olden **G**irl. Here is how she looks when she sits in it.*

Show the pictogram side of the card. Then show both the plain and the picture sides again. Ask several children to identify on the plain letter where they saw the girl's head, body, legs and ask which part is the swing where she sits. Did they notice which way she faces? Elicit 'Not in the Reading Direction.'

Explain that Golden Girl knows it's important for everyone in Letterland to face in the Reading Direction, so they can see what letter is going to come next in a word. Yet whenever she gets into her garden swing she faces the wrong way! Why? Accept possible explanations. Then discuss how the movement of a swing can make your stomach feel funny.

*Well, **G**olden **G**irl's stomach never feels funny when she's in her **g**arden swing. Instead, her head feels funny. As soon as she starts to swing she **g**ets **g**iddy. So she swings round and faces the wrong way. That is why she is looking back instead of looking ahead in the Reading Direction. What a problem!*

Distribute your prepared **g**-shapes for picture coding.

Golden Girl's letter shape

Introduce Golden Girl's handwriting verse (set to music on the *Handwriting Songs Cassette*) to teach the correct stroke for **g**:

> Go round Golden Girl's head. Go down her golden hair.
> Then curve to make her swing, so she can sit there.

Choose children to demonstrate the stroke on the *Class Wall Frieze* or *Picture Code Card*. Write a huge **g** on the board for them to air trace while they sing or chant the verse again.

Golden Girl's sound (hard g)

Maybe getting giddy explains too why Golden Girl makes a funny gurgling sound when she is sitting in her garden swing. This is the sound she makes: 'g..., g..., g..., g..., g...' She looks quite happy, though. Maybe she is just giggling.

Ask everyone to make her 'g..., g..., g....' sound. Avoid 'guh', but do not whisper, as that will produce Clever Cat's sound instead!

Golden Girl's song on the *Alphabet Songs Cassette* provides practice in making the 'g...' sound, and also prepares children to expect a soft **g** in some words, made by 'her girlfriend' (Gentle Ginger, who they will meet in Programme Two).

Introducing Golden Granny

Introduce Golden Girl's best friend, her very own grandmother, Golden Granny, using the appropriate *Picture Code Card*, when children want to spell words containing **gg**. Golden Granny can be used for the *second* **g** of the pair.

Explaining the capital G shape

The very different shape of capital G needs special attention. In Letterland terms it is Golden Girl's Go-cart.

Right next to Golden Girl's garden gate there is a garage. In it Golden Girl keeps her Go-cart. Her Go-cart is special because it doesn't have to go on roads, like cars in our land. In Letterland, her Go-cart glides along just above the ground. This means that she can even drive round her garden over the green, green grass without spoiling it.

Her Go-cart makes a gurgling 'g..., g..., g...' sound as it glides. It sounds just like Golden Girl's 'g..., g..., g...' sound. But it could be the green gas inside it gurgling instead, because green gas is what makes her Go-cart go!

Ask everyone to make the 'g..., g..., g...' sound of her Go-cart. Examine Golden Girl's name on *Flashcard* 40. Compare it with

Golden Girl's words

game*	golden*
garden*	goldfish
get*	good*
giggle	grandfather*
girl*	grandmother*
give*	grapes
glad*	great*
glass*	grass*
glasses*	greedy*
glove*	green*
glue	ground*
go*	group*
goat*	grow*
gold*	guess*

* High usage words

Flashcard 41, where the children will discover that Golden Granny enjoys gliding into important words in Golden Girl's Go-cart just as much as her granddaughter! This may also be a good time to introduce *Flashcards* 42 (**green**) and 43 (**going**) too.

Practising Golden Girl's shape and sound

George
Gemma

Golden Girl in names

You may well have at least one child with a soft **g** in his or her name, e.g. **G**eorge or **G**emma. If so, they should draw a wiggly line under any soft **g**'s to show that they are not Golden Girl making her usual 'g...' sound (but her girlfriend, Gentle Ginger, who they will meet in Programme Two).

Gardening with Golden Girl

You may like to create a miniature garden in your classroom. You could also try growing cress in a **g**-shape or displaying different kinds of grasses.

Golden Girl in blends and digraphs

Some of your children may be ready to practise the blends and digraphs with **g**. In Section 3, you will find information on **-ng** (page 135), **gl** (page 150) and **gr** (page 152).

Word building with Golden Girl

Live spelling: gas, did and dig

Ask the children what Golden Girl uses to make her Go-cart go and elicit '**green gas**'. Then see who would like to help make the word **gas**. Hand the appropriate *Picture Code Cards* to three children and ask a fourth to help them stand in the right order. Do the same with three more children to create **did**. Ask which word they will have made if Golden Girl takes Diana Duck's place, and go on to create **dig** (what Golden Girl likes to do in her garden).

Consolidation

Workbooks

Guide the children through the exercises on pages 10 and 11 of *Programme One Workbook 2* to consolidate learning of Golden Girl's letter shape and sound. Draw special attention to her name and to the words **garden** and **begin** in the instruction text.

STEP 12a
Oscar Orange

Objectives

To teach the letter shapes for **o** and **O**, the short vowel sound 'ŏ...', the irregular **o** sound as in **brother**, and word building.

What you need

☆ *Programme One Picture Code Cards*: Oscar Orange (ŏ), Oscar's Bothersome Little Brother (o) and all the cards covered so far

☆ *Programme One Flashcards*: 44-46 and all the character name cards covered so far

☆ *Class Wall Frieze*

☆ *Handwriting Songs Cassette*

☆ *Alphabet Songs Cassette*

☆ *Programme One Songs Cassette*

☆ *Programme One Workbook 2*: pages 12-15

☆ *Storybook: Oscar Orange and the Octopus*

☆ *Links Group 1: Oscar Orange*

Preparation

☆ **Orange tree mural** Prepare an orange tree mural. Include Mr O on the mural: a template of him can be found on page 187.

☆ **Letters for picture coding** Prepare thick black **o**-shapes on pieces of card or paper for each child.

Quick revision

This is a good time to practise handling both the short vowel sounds learnt so far, 'ă...' and 'ĭ...', by dictating some or all of the words below. You may like to do the first group of words together on the board, helping different children who come up and write them. Place a special emphasis on prolonging each vowel as you say it.

| at | as | has | hiss | man | sad | sat | did | ham | hit | and |
| it | is | his | miss | mat | mad | sit | dad | him | hat | hand |

Introducing Oscar Orange

Show the children the Oscar Orange *Picture Code Card* and your orange tree mural (see **Preparation**). Hand out your prepared **o**-shapes for picture coding and while they are doing this, explain that, just as there are special apples in Letterland, there are also special juicy oranges to eat...and special talking oranges. The *talking* oranges say 'ŏ...' in words.

*Not all **o**ranges grow in Letterland, because Letterland is n**o**t very h**o**t, and **o**ranges need l**o**ts and l**o**ts of h**o**t sun to grow properly. So most of them are brought to Letterland by boat from other lands where there is l**o**ts of h**o**t sunshine.*

*The **o**range tree we have here is one of the very few **o**range trees that grow in Letterland, even though Letterland is n**o**t h**o**t. The only **o**ranges that can talk are the **o**ranges that grow **o**n it. Have you coloured in your talking **o**ranges? Let's hear them say 'ŏ...' then.*

Choose children to place their oranges on the top of the tree. If possible, choose those children with clear 'ŏ...' sounds in their names.

*P**o**p your **o**range **o**n the tree, [**O**liver]. P**o**p it on t**o**p, where it will get as much h**o**t sun as possible. Now p**o**p yours on t**o**p, [Holly].*

When there are no children's names left with a short 'ŏ...' sound, say to all the rest of the group:

*Come on, let's p**o**p l**o**ts and l**o**ts of **o**ranges on the tree - right on the t**o**p.*

Show the Oscar Orange *Picture Code Card* once again and say:

We don't know the names of all the Letterland oranges, but we do know the name of this one. He is Oscar Orange, and he says 'ŏ...' in lots and lots of words.

Introduce *Flashcard* 44 (**Oscar Orange**) and practise reading his name.

Oscar Orange's letter shape

Introduce Oscar Orange's handwriting verse (set to music on the *Handwriting Songs Cassette*) to teach the correct stroke for **o**:

> On Oscar Orange start at the top.
> Go all the way round him, and...then stop.

Choose children to demonstrate the stroke on the *Class Wall Frieze* or *Picture Code Card*. Write a huge **o** on the board for them to air trace while they sing or chant the verse again.

Oscar Orange's sound

Now what sound did we just learn that Oscar Orange makes? Oscar Orange says 'ŏ...' in lots and lots of words.

Hold up *Flashcards* 45 and 46 (**lots** and **hot**).

Oscar Orange says 'ŏ...' in lots and 'ŏ...' in hot. And, of course, he says 'ŏ...' in the word orange!

The children can practise making Oscar's sound in his song on on the *Alphabet Songs Cassette*. While they are doing this, let them make **o**-shapes with their hands by placing all the fingertips of both hands together.

Explaining the capital O shape

Explain the capital **O** shape roughly along these lines:

To start an important word Oscar Orange uses the same trick as quite a few other letters. He just takes a deep breath and becomes bigger. Who else uses this trick among those we have met so far?

The deep breath trick so far applies to **c**, **t**, **s** and in a special way to **y**. Revise *all* the capital letters already covered.

Oscar's Bothersome Little Brother

Your pack of *Picture Code Cards* includes a card for Oscar's Bothersome Little Brother. Use it to introduce Letterland's version of the irregular 'o...' sound, as in the words **brother**, **mother**, **other**, etc. This **o** crops up early in reading and writing

* High usage words

Oscar Orange's words

object	often*
October*	on*
octopus	opposite
odd	or*
of*	orange*
off*	ostrich
office*	otter

because it occurs in so many high usage words, but introduce this 'bothersome but loveable' little brother as you see fit.

Oscar's Bothersome Little Brother is always willing to try and say 'ŏ...' just like Oscar, but no matter how hard he tries, his sound always comes out as 'uh' instead! He's just too little. Luckily, everyone still loves him just the same. Keep a look out for him in words, so we can make a collection of them.

Words for your collection will present themselves as children misspell words like **come**. Thank such children for discovering one of the 'Little Brother's' words!

Practising Oscar's shape and sound

Oscar Orange in names

Let the children picture code all the short 'ŏ...' sounds in their names with crayons. For names containing the long ō, such as **O**wen, see page 82. Use a wiggly line for other irregular **o**'s, such as in Vict**o**ria.

Word building with Oscar Orange

Live spelling: hot, hat, hit, in and on

Revise the short vowel sounds 'ă...', 'ĭ...' and 'ŏ...' by asking different children to build the word **hot**. Let them discover what happens when Oscar Orange swaps places with Annie Apple (**hat**) or Impy Ink (**hit**). Then let them make **in** and **on**.

Oscar's Bothersome Little Brother's words

above*	money*
among*	monkey*
another*	mother*
become*	nothing*
brother*	onion
come*	other*
cover*	some*
does*	somebody*
done*	something*
front*	sometimes*
glove*	son*
honey*	won*
love*	wonderful*
Monday*	

* High usage words

Consolidation

Workbooks

Guide the children through the exercises on pages 12-14 of *Programme One Workbook 2* to consolidate learning of Oscar Orange's letter shape and his short 'ŏ...' sound. Page 15 practises Oscar's Bothersome Little Brother's 'o..' sound. Draw special attention to their names and to the word **Colour** in the instruction text.

Storybooks

For further listening practice, read the *Letterland Storybook: Oscar Orange and the Octopus* or *Letterland Links Group 1: Oscar Orange* aloud and draw the children's attention to the recurring short 'ŏ...' sound.

Cassette

Sing or listen to **Oscar Orange, Oscar's Brother** and Oscar Orange's verse (in particular) of the **Vowel Sounds Song** on the *Programme One Songs Cassette*.

STEP 12b
Mr O, the Old Man

Objectives

To teach the long vowel ō and word building.

What you need

☆ *Programme One Picture Code Cards*: Mr O (ō), Golden Girl (g), Sammy Snake (s) and Naughty Nick (n)

☆ *Programme One Flashcards*: 47

☆ *Class Wall Frieze*

☆ *Programme One Songs Cassette*

☆ *Programme One Workbook 2*: pages 16 and 17

☆ *Storybook: The Vowel Street Party*

☆ *Links Group 1: Five Vowel Men*

Introducing Mr O, the Old Man

If the children seem quite happy coping with the presence of Mr A and Mr I in a limited number of words, they should be able to handle the idea of another Vowel Man who also pops into words sometimes to say his name. Ask which Vowel Men they have met so far. Briefly discuss Mr A, owner of the apples, and Mr I who sells ice cream and ink. Then introduce Mr O.

Mr O, the Old Man is a good friend of Mr A and Mr I. He is also the oldest Vowel Man of all. Everyone is glad that Mr O lives in Letterland, because without him, there would hardly be any oranges at all. Remember, Letterland is too cold for most oranges to grow there. That is why Mr O, the Old Man, brings whole boat loads of oranges from over the ocean to Letterland.

He sells quite a few of them, but he does not sell the talking oranges like Oscar. Instead, he spends most of his time popping oranges like Oscar into lots and lots and lots of words which need an 'ŏ...' sound in them.

This job keeps him so busy that he only has time to appear in words himself at special times. Let's keep a sharp look out in case we come across him in some words. He particularly likes turning up in quite small words, like go, and no and so, and of course, in his own name, Mr O!

Introduce *Flashcard 47* (**Mr O**).

Practising Mr O saying his name

Mr O in names

Pick out any children whose names begin with or contain the long ō, e.g. **O**mar or S**o**phie. Show them how to draw a stick man right through their letters to signal Mr O's presence. Treat these children's names as special 'because Mr O always manages to find time to appear in them, even though he is such a busy man!' Examine all the character name *Flashcards* learnt so far to see if Mr O appears in any of them, too. (He does, in Naughty Nic**o**la, Yellow Y**o**-yo Man, G**o**lden Girl, G**o**lden Granny and later, Z**o**e Zebra.)

Any irregular **o**'s will need wiggly lines under them. Any short 'ŏ...' sounds can be picture-coded with Oscar Orange.

Mr O's words	
ocean*	open*
old*	over*
only*	own*

* High usage words

Word building with Mr O

Live spelling: go, so and no

Reinforce the spelling of the words **go**, **so** and **no** with four different children holding or wearing the appropriate *Picture Code Cards*. It's also a good idea to prepare a poster listing these three small high-usage words. Read through it together regularly until they become easy sight vocabulary.

Choose a good time, later on, to compare **on** and **no** in live spelling with the *Picture Code Cards* and by making spelling pictures of both words, which the children can then copy.

Consolidation

Workbooks

Guide the children through the exercises on page 20 of *Programme One Workbook 2* to consolidate learning of the long ō in words. Draw special attention to Mr O's name and the words **over** and **ocean** in the instruction text.

Storybooks

For further listening practice, read the *Letterland Storybook: The Vowel Street Party* or *Letterland Links Group 1: Five Vowel Men* aloud and draw the children's attention to Mr O's name in words.

Cassette

Sing or listen to Mr O's verse (in particular) of the **Vowel Men Song** on the *Programme One Songs Cassette*.

STEP 13
Fireman Fred

Objectives

To teach the letter shapes and sound for **f** and **F**, and word building.

What you need

☆ *Programme One Picture Code Cards*: Fireman Fred (**f**), Fireman Frank (**f**), Fireman Fred and Frank together (**ff**), and all the cards covered so far

☆ *Programme One Flashcards*: 48-51 and all the character name cards covered so far

☆ *Class Wall Frieze*

☆ *Handwriting Songs Cassette*

☆ *Alphabet Songs Cassette*

☆ *Programme One Workbook 2*: pages 18 and 19

☆ *Storybook: Eddy Elephant and the Forest Fire*

Preparation

☆ **Letters for picture coding** Prepare thick black **f**-shapes on pieces of card or paper for each child to picture code.

☆ **Spelling pictures** Write out the words **fat cat(s)**, **on/off**, **sad cat** and **sad Sam**, allowing enough space for the children both to picture code and illustrate the words' meanings. Make enough copies for each child.

Quick revision

Before introducing Fireman Fred, do a 'Quick dash' through the character names and sounds learnt so far. Then practise just these blends with Oscar Orange: **co**, **ho** and **mo**, and revise the following short vowel blends: **da**, **di**, **ma**, **mi**, **na** and **ni**.

Introducing Fireman Fred

Fireman Fred is a character who is both fierce, when he is fighting fires, and friendly in his free time. He is fond of children, fond of fishing and fond of food.

Hold up your Fireman Fred *Picture Code Card*, showing the pictogram side, and introduce him along these lines:

> *Here's Fireman Fred who runs the fire station in Letterland. He and his fellow firemen are the fastest firefighters you can find anywhere.*
> *What is Fireman Fred wearing? Look, he has a fine fire helmet. He has a fine fire-proof coat, and he has fine fire-proof boots.*
> *What do you think Fireman Fred uses in his hose for putting out fires? It's not water - it's frothy foam!*

Discuss the meaning of foam if necessary and distribute your prepared **f**-shapes for the children to picture code.

Fireman Fred's letter shape

Introduce Fireman Fred's handwriting verse (set to music on the *Handwriting Songs Cassette*) to teach the correct stroke for **f**:

> First draw Fred's helmet.
> Then go down his clothes.
> Give him some arms
> so he can hold his hose.

Choose children to demonstrate the stroke on the *Class Wall Frieze* or *Picture Code Card*. Write a huge **f** on the board for them to air trace while they sing or chant the verse again.

Fireman Fred's sound

As Fireman Fred's foam flows out of the hose, it makes a funny, fizzy sort of sound like this: 'fff...'. Whenever you see Fireman Fred in a word you will hear that fizzy 'fff...' sound as the foam flows from the firehose.

This is a voiceless sound, so make sure that the children do not produce it with voice ('fffuh'). Using Fireman Fred's song on the *Alphabet Songs Cassette*, make sure they break into a whisper for the 'fff...' sounds.

Introducing Fireman Frank

Fireman Fred's best friend is his fellow fireman, Fireman Frank. Introduce him, using the appropriate *Picture Code Card*, when children want to spell words containing **ff**. Fireman Frank can be used for the *second* **f** of the pair.

*Fireman Fred has lots of fellow firefighters who can help him to put out fires. Often they work in two's. Whenever Fireman Fred sets off to fight a fire, he always sets off with his best friend Fireman Frank. This is why you will always see them together in the word **off**.*

Off is an important word, as it is on switches, controls, etc. It is also easily confused with the word **of** (which the children can see on *Flashcard* 51). Find some examples of the word **off** with the children. Can they find **Staff** on the staffroom door? For other words with double **ff** in them, see page 131.

Fireman Fred's words

face*	five*
fall*	fix*
farm*	flag*
fast*	flame
favourite*	flower*
feel*	fly*
feet*	fork*
fence*	four*
fetch*	fox*
field*	friend*
fill*	fruit*
fireworks	fun*
fish*	funny*

* High usage words

Explaining the capital F shape

Point to the lower half or the *Class Wall Frieze* and explain:

Like some letters you have met so far, Fireman Fred takes a deep breath to start an important word. In this case, his letter becomes a bit bigger and sharper as well. Fireman Frank does the same.

Introduce both firemen's names on *Flashcards* 48 and 49.

Practising Fireman Fred's shape and sound

Talking about Fireman Fred

Encourage the children to build up their own image of Fireman Fred by associating alliterative words. You can help by offering choices. As they learn to pick words beginning with Fred's sound, they will discover they already 'know' much more about Fireman Fred than they thought. Soon, instead of you asking them, they will be telling you!

Fire prevention

Discuss fire-fighting and fire prevention, and generally involve the figure of Fireman Fred in any safety work. Explain that Fireman Fred likes children to know about safety. That way he makes sure there are very few fires to fight in Letterland.

Fireman Fred in blends

Some of your children may be ready to practise the blends with **f**. In Section 3, you will find information on **-ff** (page 131), **fl** (page 150) and **fr** (page 152).

Word building with Fireman Fred

Live spelling: fit, fat, cat, cats, if, gift, gifts

Help seven children to build the words **fit**, **fat**, **cat**, **cats**, **if**, **gift** and **gifts**, holding or wearing the appropriate *Picture Code Cards*. The remaining children can write down the words as they are made, and then read them out to you or to each other.

Slow speak dictation

Try slowly dictating little phrases, helping to spell by ear **fat cat** and **fat cats**, i.e. 'Ffffaat caaa...t' (avoid 'cuh...at'). Let them also try **on** and **off** and this silly sentence: **I sat on his gift**. After each try, write the words on the board for the children to check.

Action sentences

Can you nod
if I smile?

Hand out *Flashcard* 50 to various pairs or groups of children, and any other *Flashcards* you wish to revise, and ask them to read the sentence side of the card in silence and then to respond to it silently.

Consolidation

Workbooks

Guide the children through the exercises on pages 18 and 19 of *Programme One Workbook 2* to consolidate learning of Fireman Fred's letter shape and sound. Draw special attention to his name and to the words **Finish/finish**, **four**, **finger** and **Fill** in the instruction text.

Storybooks

For further listening practice, read the *Letterland Storybook: Eddy Elephant and the Forest Fire* aloud and draw the children's attention to the recurring 'fff...' sound.

STEP 14
Poor Peter

Objectives

To teach the letter shapes and sound for **p** and **P**, and word building.

What you need

☆ *Programme One Picture Code Cards*: Poor Peter (**p**), Poor Patsy (**p**) and all the cards covered so far

☆ *Programme One Flashcards*: 52-55 and all the character name cards covered so far

☆ *Class Wall Frieze*

☆ *Handwriting Songs Cassette*

☆ *Alphabet Songs Cassette*

☆ *Programme One Workbook 3*: pages 2 and 3

☆ *Storybook: Poor Peter's Penguin Pals*

Preparation

☆ **Letters for picture coding**
Prepare thick black **p**-shapes on pieces of card or paper for each child to picture code.

Quick revision

Start with a quick revision of all the letters learnt so far, using the relevant *Picture Code Cards* as well as any character name *Flashcards*. You have 27 cards to practise now in random order: **a** (2), **c**, **d** (2), **f** (2), **ff**, **g** (2), **h**, **i** (3), **m** (2), **n** (2), **o** (3), **s** (2), **ss** and **t** (2) and **y**. Can the children reel off the sounds only? From the plain sides only? Can they respond swiftly to the character name *Flashcards* too? And to any spelling pictures on the walls? (For more information, see **Revising letters** on page 24.)

Introducing Poor Peter

Poor Peter is a puppy with a problem. Most children's response to this character is one of fond sympathy, perhaps because nearly everyone (children and adults alike) is sensitive in some way about themselves. Poor Peter's problem is his ears which are long and floppy. Everybody else likes his long, floppy ears, but not Poor Peter. He hates the way they droop.

Distribute your prepared **p**-shapes for the children to picture code with crayons.

Poor Peter's letter shape

The emphasis on droopy ears is, of course, a strategy for emphasising the down stroke of **p** in contrast to the **b** and **d** shapes. Entrust the children with the job of cheering Peter up by always stroking him properly.

Introduce Poor Peter's handwriting verse (set to music on the *Handwriting Songs Cassette*) to teach the correct stroke for **p**:

> Pat Poor Peter properly.
> First stroke down his ear,
> then up and round his face
> so he won't shed a tear.

Choose children to demonstrate the stroke on the *Class Wall Frieze* or *Picture Code Card*. Write a huge **p** on the board for them to air trace while they sing or chant the verse again.

Poor Peter's words

paint*	pink*
paper*	play*
parcel*	please*
park*	pond
party*	pony*
pass*	present*
paw*	pretty*
pen*	puddle
pencil*	pull*
pet*	puppy*
picture*	purple
pig*	put*

* High usage words

Poor Peter's sound

Poor Peter not only has a problem with his ears, but to make matters worse, this poor puppy has a second problem: he can't bark! The only sound he can make is a funny little, very quiet 'p...' sound. He makes this sound by shutting his mouth and blowing through his lips. (Get the children to do the same. Make sure they don't add voice.)

The reason that Poor Peter can't bark is that he is a Letterland puppy. So naturally he makes a special sound instead of barking the way ordinary dogs in our land do. He should really be pleased, and proud of his special sound, but he's not.

Encourage the children to feel protective towards him.

It is important to remember that **p** is a voiceless consonant, so any voice between it and the next letter will distort its sound into 'puh'. Make sure that the children whisper the 'p...' sound as they sing Poor Peter's song on the *Alphabet Songs Cassette.*

Introducing Poor Patsy

Poor Peter has a best friend called Poor Patsy. (She has eyelashes, no tear and a pink collar.) Introduce her, using the appropriate *Picture Code Card,* when children want to spell words like **paper** and words containing **pp**. Poor Patsy can be used for the *second* **p** of the pair.

Explaining the capital P shape

In most words Poor Peter rests his chin on the line, but for capital P he takes a deep breath and then does his own special trick. He pops up! He hopes, with this trick, to make his ears pop up, too and stay up. Sadly, he is always disappointed. They still droop even after he has popped up. Poor, poor Peter! But he keeps on trying all the same, every time he begins an important word.

Compare the position of **P** and **p** on *Flashcards* 52-55 with the children.

Practising Poor Peter's shape and sound

Poor Peter puzzle

The children can help you to paint a picture of Poor Peter. Turn it into a Poor Peter jigsaw puzzle by cutting it up and getting the children to put it back together again.

Poor Peter in blends

Some of your children may be ready to practise the blends with **p**. In Section 3, you will find information on **pl** (page 150) and **pr** (page 152).

Word building with Poor Peter

Live spelling: pat, pot, pots, stop, spot, spots, dots

Ask children to build the words **pat**, **pot** and **pots**. Next see who can discover two more words which they can make just by children changing places? (**stop** and **spot**) Where could they then add another 'hiss'? (**spots**) Which two letters would have to go to change **spots** into **dots**?

Action sentences

Hand out *Flashcard* 55 to various pairs or groups of children, and any other *Flashcards* you wish to revise, and ask them to read the sentence side of the card in silence and then to respond to it silently.

Consolidation

Workbooks

Guide the children through the exercises on pages 2 and 3 of *Programme One Workbook 3* to consolidate learning of Poor Peter's letter shape and sound. Draw special attention to his name and to the words **pictures**, **picture** and **Picture code** in the instruction text.

Storybooks

For further listening practice, read the *Letterland Storybook: Poor Peter's Penguin Pals* aloud and draw the children's attention to the recurring 'p...' sound.

STEP 15
Kicking King

Objectives

To teach the letter shapes and sound for **k** and **K**, and word building.

What you need

☆ *Programme One Picture Code Cards*: Kicking King (**k**) and all the cards covered so far

☆ *Programme One Flashcards*: 56-58 and all the character name cards covered so far

☆ *Class Wall Frieze*

☆ *Handwriting Songs Cassette*

☆ *Alphabet Songs Cassette*

☆ *Programme One Workbook 3*: pages 4 and 5

☆ *Storybook: Kicking King Lost in Letterland*

Preparation

☆ **Letters for picture coding** Prepare thick black **k**-shapes on pieces of card or paper for each child to picture code.

Quick revision

Quickly revise all the letters learnt so far, including the blends **pa**, **pi** and **po**, as well as any character names.

Introducing Kicking King

The Letterland explanation for why the **k** sound occurs relatively infrequently at the beginning of words is a practical one. There is not much room for a good kick at the start of a word, or in the middle for that matter. That is why you see Kicking King so often at the end of words instead, where he has plenty of room to kick!

Hold up the pictogram side of the Kicking King *Picture Code Card*.

*Not every country has a **k**ing, but Letterland has one, and he is a good, **k**ind **k**ing, so everyone likes him. He is also very good at sports. He can **k**ick a ball farther than anyone else in all his **k**ingdom. You will often see him practising his **k**ick in words.*

Turn the card to the plain side, so the children can indicate and discuss where the king's body fits in. Distribute your prepared **k**-shapes for picture coding.

Kicking King's letter shape

Introduce Kicking King's handwriting verse (set to music on the *Handwriting Songs Cassette*) to teach the correct stroke for **k**:

> Kicking King's body is a straight stick.
> Add his arm, then his leg, so he can kick!

Choose children to demonstrate the stroke on the *Class Wall Frieze* or *Picture Code Card*. Write a huge **k** on the board for them to air trace while they sing or chant the verse again.

Kicking King's sound

Let's discover Kicking King's sound. Just start to say 'Kicking King'. Whisper it slowly and carefully and you should hear his sound in the back of your throat three times: 'k..., k..., k...'.

Let the children examine the **Kicking King** *Flashcard* (56), so they can see him appearing three times as well as hearing him.

Make sure the children whisper the recurring 'k...' sound when they sing Kicking King's song on the *Alphabet Songs Cassette*.

Explaining the capital K shape

Sometimes Kicking King looks bigger at the beginning of words. That's because he takes a deep breath. Who else have we met who does that getting-bigger trick to start important words?

Show how it is mainly the King's arm and leg that become bigger. Compare the **K** and **k** shapes on both sides of *Flashcards* 57 and 58.

Comparing the sounds for c and k

Can you think of someone else in Letterland who makes a 'k...' sound just like the King?

Get everyone to whisper 'Clever Cat' and then 'Kicking King', so that they can hear and *feel* the identical sounds in their throats.

Clever Cat is very proud to share the same sound as Kicking King.

Ways of predicting when to use **c**, **k** or **-ck** are explained in Programme Two. (See page 130 for information on **-ck**.)

Word building with Kicking King

Live spelling: king, sing and song

The children should hear the **-ng** story on page 135 of Section 3 before they start building the words **king**, **sing** and **song**. Knowing the **-ng** story will also help them to read a vast number of words ending in **-ing**, so now is an excellent time to introduce it.

Consolidation

Workbooks

Guide the children through the exercises on pages 4 and 5 of *Programme One Workbook 3* to consolidate learning of Kicking King's letter shape and sound. Draw special attention to his name and to the word **kite** in the instruction text.

Storybooks

For further listening practice, read the *Letterland Storybook: Kicking King Lost in Letterland* aloud and draw the children's attention to the recurring 'k...' sound.

Kicking King's words

kaleidoscope	kid
kangaroo	kilo*
keep*	kind*
kennel*	king*
ketchup	kiss
kettle	kitchen*
key	kite*
kick	kitten*

* High usage words

STEP 16a
Eddy Elephant

Objectives

To teach the letter shapes for **e** and **E**, the short vowel sound 'ĕ...', the silent **e**, the irregular **e** as in **they**, and word building.

What you need

- ☆ *Programme One Picture Code Cards*: Eddy Elephant (ĕ), Silent (grey) **e**, Mr Mean-E (**e**) and all the cards covered so far

- ☆ *Programme One Flashcards*: 59-61 and all the character name cards covered so far

- ☆ *Class Wall Frieze*

- ☆ *Handwriting Songs Cassette*

- ☆ *Alphabet Songs Cassette*

- ☆ *Programme One Songs Cassette*

- ☆ *Programme One Workbook 3*: pages 6, 7 and 9

- ☆ *Storybook: Eddy Elephant and the Forest Fire*

- ☆ *Links Group 1: Eddy Elephant*

Preparation

☆ **Letters for picture coding**
Prepare thick black **e**-shapes on pieces of card or paper for each child to picture code.

☆ **'Entrance' and 'exit' signs**
Write out the words **Entrance** and **Exit** on separate sheets of paper, using a thick black felt-tip pen, allowing enough space for the children to picture code the words. Make enough copies for each child.

Quick revision

Start with a quick revision of all the letters learnt so far.

Introducing Eddy Elephant

Begin with a discussion about different kinds of pets. Lead up to this question:

> *Do you know anyone who has an **e**lephant for a pet? Well in Letterland there is a man who really does have an **e**lephant. This **e**lephant is called **E**ddy **E**lephant.*

Show the pictogram side of the *Picture Code Card*.

> *You can tell that he's a Letterland **e**lephant, because he always points his trunk in the Reading Direction, like this.*

Turn the card to the plain side.

> *Even when you can't see **E**ddy **E**lephant's face in his letter, you can still see his trunk pointing in the Reading Direction. You show me where his trunk is.*

Let several children come and touch the plain side of the card. Keep turning over to the pictogram side to confirm their findings.

You can now distribute your prepared **e**-shapes for the children to picture code.

Eddy Elephant's letter shape

Introduce Eddy Elephant's handwriting verse (set to music on the *Handwriting Songs Cassette*) to teach the correct stroke for **e**:

> Ed has a headband. Draw it and then stroke round his head and his trunk to the end.

Choose children to demonstrate the stroke on the *Class Wall Frieze* or *Picture Code Card*. Write a huge **e** on the board for them to air trace while they sing or chant the verse again.

Eddy Elephant's sound

Eddy Elephant expects that some of you children might be able to guess what sound he makes in words.

Have you noticed that all you have to do is start to say Sammy Snake's name to make his hissing sound 'Sssammy...Sss...'? Or start to say 'Munching Mike' to make his 'Mmm...' sound? So if you start to say 'Eddy Elephant', you can discover Eddy Elephant's sound.

Elicit 'ĕ...' from the children.

Yes! Eddy Elephant enjoys saying 'ĕ...' ever so much in lots of words every day!

Let the children practise this new vowel sound by singing Eddy Elephant's song on the *Alphabet Songs Cassette*.

Explaining the capital E shape

Now there is a special trick which Eddy Elephant has learned to do all by himself. He would like you to see it. He only does it at the beginning of names and very important words. This is what he does.

Point to the capital **E** on the *Class Wall Frieze*.

He sits down on end and points...not just his trunk...but everything in the Reading Direction: his back legs, his front legs...and his trunk. He calls this his 'Elephant-on-End' trick.

Read and compare the words with **E** and **e** on both sides of *Flashcards* 59, 60 and 61, and look for EXIT signs.

The silent e

Curiously, although Eddy Elephant loves making a sound to start the word end, his sound never turns up at the ends of words. Instead, if you ever see his letter at the end of a word, it will be empty! Eddy Elephant is not there. So of course his letter will make no sound at all.

Everyone in Letterland calls these empty letters 'silent e's'. Here is a silent e, just a plain grey letter.

Show the grey **e** *Picture Code Card*.

Take time, either now or later, to help the children to deduce this fact by looking at and listening to any words encountered so far with silent **e**'s at the end, e.g. **gone**, **house** and **horse**. (For words ending in -**ve** (the Vase-Prop **e**), see page 103.)

When picture coding names, use grey paint or crayons, or write the silent **e** in dots (as though it is fading away like its sound). The more advanced concept of the Silent Magic **e** will be covered later on (see page 161).

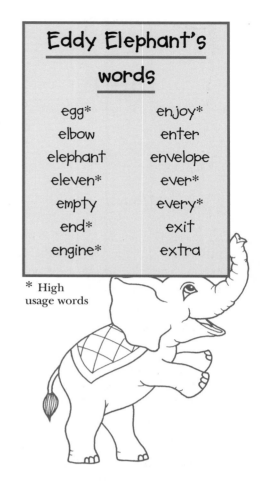

Eddy Elephant's words

egg*	enjoy*
elbow	enter
elephant	envelope
eleven*	ever*
empty	every*
end*	exit
engine*	extra

* High usage words

End

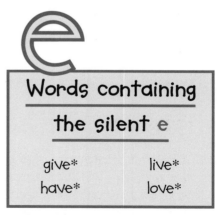

Words containing the silent e

give*	live*
have*	love*

* High usage words

Anne

they

Mr Mean-E (the e as in they)

The word **they** has been misspelt as **thay** millions of times by millions of children in every country where English is taught, and patiently (or impatiently) corrected by millions of teachers.

Introduce Mr Mean-E early on to make sure that none of your children join these millions.

Here is a useful rhyme for remembering Mr Mean-E's sound:

> Mr Mean-E, he looks like an **e**,
> but he tricks us all by saying 'a̅...'
> He's too mean to be seen very often in words,
> but you **can** see him in the word **they**!

The music for this rhyme is on the *Programme One Songs Cassette*.

Let everyone picture code the word **they** with this very different **e**, an old scrooge and a real 'meany' (Mean-E). Challenge the children to make sure that old Mr Mean-E cannot gloat over their mistake. Don't let him fool them just because he sounds exactly like Mr A in this particular word. See also *Programme One Copymaster* 69.

The box on the left contains some of the very few words that Mr Mean-E appears in. You may like to talk about these examples now or later on.

Mr Mean-E's words

eight*	obey
grey*	they*

* High usage words

Practising Eddy's shape and sound

Eddy Elephant and other e's in names

Let any children with the short Ĕ or ĕ in their names (e.g. **E**lliot, **E**mily, **J**essica, etc.) picture code them with Eddy Elephant. For names containing the long ē, such as **E**ve, see page 97. Remember to use a wiggly line under any irregular **e**'s (e.g. in Rach**e**l). Try to avoid children picture coding any silent **e**'s in their names with Eddy Elephant. If the deed is already done, do not worry: just draw a wiggly line beneath their elephant. Their coding will still have helped to remind them of the correct letter sequence for their name. The more accurate coding with a grey or dotted silent **e**, however, should be used next time.

Entrance and exit signs

Hand out your prepared 'Entrance' and 'Exit' signs for each child to picture code and take home to put on either sides of their bedroom doors.

Word building with Eddy Elephant

Live spelling: ten ➤ tent, tents, man, men ➤ mess

Ask five children to hold or wear the *Picture Code Cards* for Ticking Tess, Ticking Tom, Eddy Elephant, Naughty Nick and Sammy Snake. Use these letters to explore the effects on word meaning as you slowly say and they build each of the following:

ten ➤ **net** ➤ **nets** ➤ **nest** ➤ **sent** ➤ **tent** ➤ **tents**

Bring in five more children with the cards for Munching Mike, Annie Apple, Impy Ink and Sammy and Sally Snake together to discover what just changing the vowel does to word meaning.

man ➤ **men**
miss ➤ **mess**

Slow speak dictation

The following are possible suggestions for slow speak words: **dot**, **pot**, **pet**, **get**, **got**, **yes**, **end**, **send**, **spend** and **spent**. These words focus on the short 'ŏ...' sound (for revision purposes) and the new short 'ĕ...' sound. Where you cannot prolong an initial consonant without adding an unwanted 'uh' sound, e.g. 'duh...o...t', combine the first two letters instead: 'do...t', telling the children first to listen for *two* sounds at the beginning of the next word you speak.

Consolidation

Workbooks

Guide the children through the exercises on pages 6, 7 and 9 of *Programme One Workbook 3* to consolidate learning of Eddy Elephant's letter shape and his short 'ĕ...' sound. Draw special attention to his name in the instruction text.

Storybooks

For further listening practice, read the *Letterland Storybook: Eddy Elephant and the Forest Fire* or *Letterland Links Group 1: Eddy Elephant* aloud again and draw the children's attention to the recurring short 'ĕ...' sound.

Cassette

Sing or listen to **Eddy Elephant** and Eddy Elephant's verse (in particular) of the **Vowel Sounds Song** on the *Programme One Songs Cassette.*

STEP 16b
Mr E, the Easy Magic Man

Objectives

To teach the long vowel ē and word building.

What you need

☆ *Programme One Picture Code Cards*: Mr E (ē) and Eddy Elephant (ĕ)

☆ *Programme One Flashcards*: 8, 29, 47 and 62

☆ *Class Wall Frieze*

☆ *Programme One Songs Cassette*

☆ *Programme One Workbook 3*: pages 8 and 9

☆ *Storybook: The Vowel Street Party*

☆ *Links Group 1: Five Vowel Men*

Introducing Mr E, the Easy Magic Man

Show the pictogram side of the Mr E *Picture Code Card*.

> *Here is the lucky man who has Eddy Elephant for a pet. His name is Mr **E**. Eddy Elephant feels lucky too, belonging to Mr **E**, because Mr **E** is the **E**asy Magic Man. He knows lots of magic tricks. All these tricks would be difficult for you or me to do, but not for Mr **E**. For him they are all **eee**asy! That is why everyone calls him 'Mr **E**, the **E**asy Magic Man'.*

Hold up the card for Eddy Elephant along with Mr E's card and allow discussion.

It is useful to start picture coding a few key words with stick men now, but first link Mr E in the children's minds with the other Vowel Men.

> *Eddy Elephant's master, Mr **E**, is another Vowel Man. Who are the Vowel Men we have met so far?*

Bring out *Flashcards* 8, 29 and 47 (**Mr A**, **Mr I** and **Mr O**). Revise them briefly and introduce *Flashcard* 62 (**Mr E**). Then summarise as follows:

> *Right! Mr A collects apples in his apron. Mr I sells ink and ice cream. Mr O brings oranges from over the ocean. And these three Vowel Men are all good friends of the **E**asy Magic Man called Mr…? Right! Mr **E**! All the other Vowel Men think Mr **E** is very clever because he makes all his magic tricks look so **eee**asy. Do you think magic tricks are **e**asy?*

Explain that Mr E has worked so hard practising his magic tricks that they have become very easy for him. Explain also that when he is not busy working on a new magic trick, he loves to pop into a word and say his name, just as the other Vowel Men do.

> *Here are two little words to look out for where you can hear Mr **E** saying his name, loud and clear: **he** and **me**.*

Put these words on a chart and leave room to add four other words later (**we**, **be**, **she** and **the**). Apart from a few names (e.g. Daphne and Phoebe), these six are the *only* common words where a final **e** is not empty (silent). It is not silent, because 'Mr E himself is appearing in it'. (Strictly speaking, since we often say 'thuh' for **the**, it does not qualify, but for spelling purposes it is worth grouping it with the other five.)

Practising Mr E saying his name

Mr E in names

Show any children who have a long ē in their names, e.g. **E**ve, **P**eter, etc. how to draw a stick man right through their letters to signal Mr E's presence. Any short 'ĕ...' sounds can be picture-coded with Eddy Elephant. Don't forget to add a wiggly line under any irregular e's. Treat these names as special 'because Mr E always manages to find time to appear in them, even though he is such a busy man!'

Word building with Mr E

The word see

The word **see** is in the high usage bracket. Since **see** is also an important spelling pattern, it helps to show the children that these are not short, but long ē's. Explain that this is Mr E with his twin brother, a second Mr E. To picture code them, they can simply draw two stick men side by side. They will soon find **ee** turning up again in Step 23 inside the word **queen**.

Consolidation

Workbooks

Guide the children through the exercises on pages 8 and 9 of *Programme One Workbook 3* to consolidate learning of the long ē in words. Draw special attention to Mr E's name and the word **each** in the instruction text.

Storybooks

For further listening practice, read the *Letterland Storybook: The Vowel Street Party* or *Letterland Links Group 1: Five Vowel Men* aloud and draw the children's attention to Mr E's name in words.

Cassette

Sing or listen to Mr E's verse (in particular) of the **Vowel Men Song** on the *Programme One Songs Cassette*.

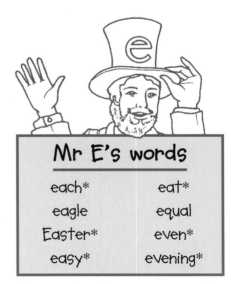

Mr E's words	
each*	eat*
eagle	equal
Easter*	even*
easy*	evening*

* High usage words

Story-telling

You have told the children 'stories' about 16 characters. Now turn the tables. Let them tell them back to you. Retelling stories encourages self-expression and consolidates learning. Encourage the children to give you a character sketch of each person or animal met in Letterland so far. Help them to include as many descriptive words as possible (both alliterative and others).

The handwriting verses

This is a good stage to revise all the handwriting verses learnt so far. If you haven't done so already, you may like to photocopy the relevant verses from the back of this guide (on pages 168-69) and send them home with the children. This way parents can be encouraged to help with handwriting practice at home.

The sixteen handwriting verses covered so far will now be 'readable', chiefly because the children can anticipate the words. This is all to the good, as they are both thinking of the message and moving their eyes along at a gentle sight-reading pace. Both are very desirable forms of reading behaviour. Listening to the *Handwriting Songs Cassette* will also play an important part in helping the children to remember the words more easily.

In **and on**

Play a version of 'Hide the thimble' to revise the words **in** and **on**.

Choose four or five children to come and write the word **in** on the board with white chalk and then to picture code the **i**'s using blue chalk. Choose four or five more children to do the same with **on**, picture coding the **o**'s in orange chalk.

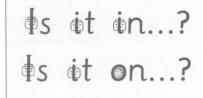

Then write the phrases **Is it in...?** and **Is it on...?** on the right on the board, picture coding all the vowels.

Let the children come and point to the relevant phrase on the board as they ask out loud what the thimble might be *in* or *on*.

Actions to accompany the letter sounds

The rhythmic repetition of any letter's sound, accompanied by either a simple mime gesture or dance movement and background music, provides a unique kinaesthetic and acoustic experience for each child. The *Alphabet Songs Cassette* is a useful tool here. The paragraph entitled **Actions to accompany the Letterlanders** on page 28 will provide you with various ideas.

The miming of various Letterland characters (while singing the *Alphabet Songs*) can even be made worthy of a little assembly performance. For example, children can tick and turn slowly on tip-toe with arms outstretched during the Ticking Tess song.

Match the sound game

Play this game as described on page 62. For these lists of words, the children will need to make cards for **yY**, **tT**, **fF**, **sS**, **nN** and **gG**, plain on one side and picture-coded on the other, as before. Use different lists of words on different days. For a more difficult game, mix the **nN** words given here with the **mM** words listed on page 62.

yY/tT	fF/sS	nN/gG
1 yeast	1 flying fish	1 new nest
2 tractor	2 slippery slope	2 nice neighbour
3 yellow yolk	3 swimming swans	3 golden grain
4 tall trees	4 funny fork	4 growing grass
5 table top	5 silver spoon	5 never, never
6 yoghurt	6 sausage	6 gooey glue
7 teacher	7 forest of fir trees	7 nine needles
8 youngster	8 freezing fog	8 gobbling goats
9 yacht	9 fresh flowers	9 group of girls
10 triangle	10 seven seas	10 no nonsense

Slow speak dictation

Live spelling should convert easily to 'slow speak' spelling practice by now. (For more information on 'slow speaking', see **Blending** on page 19.) If some children still find putting slow speech to paper difficult, you could conduct these sessions at three levels: the children can write just the first letter of each word, or the first two only, or the whole word. Then even the less quick children will have a sense of completion and can expect credit for their efforts. See page 176-80 for a full list of words to draw from for regular practice in writing down clearly spoken words.

Display ideas

Here are a few ideas for wall displays:
- Make a tower for Ticking Tess with **t** words.
- Build a fire station out of **f** words for Fireman Fred: one word on every other brick.
- Collect **m** words to place in the jaws and around a huge picture of Munching Mike.
- Paint a seaside scene with Sammy Snake and **s** words on the sand and in the sea.
- Make a snow scene with Christmas theme words and the word **Christmas** spelt with letters the children have picture coded themselves. (See page 146 and Copymaster 72 for help with **Christmas**.)

STEP 17
Lucy Lamp Lady

Objectives

To teach the letter shapes and sound for **l** and **L**, and word building.

What you need

☆ *Programme One Picture Code Cards*: Lucy Lamp Lady (**l**), Linda Lamp Lady (**l**), Lucy and Linda together (**ll**), and all the cards covered so far

☆ *Programme One Flashcards*: 63-65 and all the character name cards covered so far

☆ *Class Wall Frieze*

☆ *Handwriting Songs Cassette*

☆ *Alphabet Songs Cassette*

☆ *Programme One Workbook 3*: pages 10 and 11

☆ *Storybook: Kicking King Lost in Letterland*

Preparation

☆ **Letters for picture coding**
Prepare thick black **l**-shapes on pieces of card or paper for each child to picture code.

Quick revision

Include the silent **e** *Picture Code Card* from now on in your daily quick revision session. Let the children respond by covering their mouths to emphasise the silent **e**. You can also show the plain sides of the Eddy Elephant, Mr E and silent **e** cards and play at guessing what or who is on the reverse.

Introducing Lucy Lamp Lady

You are now ready to introduce Lucy Lamp Lady. Describe her as helpful and protective. She lives in a lighthouse on Land's End in Letterland. She lights up Letterland with her lovely lemon-coloured light and she makes sure that no-one gets lost. Like Mr A from Asia, the Lamp Lady has come from a faraway place to live in Letterland. The children can decide where (anywhere beginning with **L**).

> *There is one striking thing about Lamp Lady's looks. She looks just like the number one! She is tall, long and thin, like number one, and her body is as straight as straight can be.*
>
> *If you are wondering why she looks just like number one, the people of Letterland sometimes wonder, too. They have thought of only one possible reason. Maybe, it is because she is a neat and tidy lady who always likes doing things carefully, one by one. Can anyone here think of any other reason why Lamp Lady looks like the number one?*

Allow discussion. There is no need to find a specific reason. It is good to keep some questions open.

Finally, distribute your prepared **l**-shapes for picture coding.

Lucy Lamp Lady's letter shape

Introduce Lamp Lady's handwriting verse (set to music on the *Handwriting Songs Cassette*) to teach the correct stroke for **l**:

> Lamp Lady looks like one long line.
> Go straight from head to foot
> and she's ready to shine!

Choose children to demonstrate the stroke on the *Class Wall Frieze* or *Picture Code Card*. Write a huge **l** on the board for them to air trace while they sing or chant the verse again.

Lucy Lamp Lady's sound

*Lucy Lamp Lady's favourite songs must be **l**ullabies, because whenever she goes into a word, it sounds as though she is starting to sing one. '**Lll**..., **lll**..., **lll**..., **lll**...', she sings.*

*So now that you have met Lucy Lamp Lady, **l**ook out for her in words and **l**isten for her sound. Can you hear her at the beginning of her name, Lucy Lamp Lady?*

Everyone should keep their mouths almost shut to avoid 'lllluh' when singing Lucy Lamp Lady's song on the *Alphabet Songs Cassette*.

Introducing Lamp Lady Linda

Lucy Lamp Lady has a best friend called Linda (with blonde hair). Introduce her, using the appropriate *Picture Code Card*, when children want to spell words like **little** and words containing **ll**. Lamp Lady Linda can be used for the *second* **l** of the pair. The story explanation for **ll** is on page 132.

Explaining the capital L shape

*For capital **L**, **L**amp **L**ady takes a deep breath and gets bigger. In her case, however, her **l**egs also grow **l**onger, so **l**ong in fact, that she has to sit down with her **l**egs on the **l**ine.*

Introduce *Flashcards* 63-65 and compare the **L**'s and **l**'s.

Practising Lucy's shape and sound

Lucy Lamp Lady in blends

Some of your children may be ready to practise the blends with **l**. In Section 3, you will find information on **-ll** (page 131), **-lk** and **-lt** (page 134), **bl**, **cl**, **fl**, **gl**, **pl** and **sl** (page 150) and **-old** (page 158).

Consolidation

Workbooks

Guide the children through the exercises on pages 10 and 11 of *Programme One Workbook 3* to consolidate learning of Lucy Lamp Lady's letter shape and sound. Draw special attention to her name and to the words **long lorry**, **letter**, **letters**, **line** and **Fill** in the instruction text.

Storybooks

For further listening practice, read the *Letterland Storybook: Kicking King Lost in Letterland* aloud and draw the children's attention to the recurring 'lll...' sound.

Lucy Lamp Lady's words	
ladder	lighthouse
lamb	like*
lamp	little*
large*	live*
laugh	long*
leaf*	look*
left*	lost*
leg*	lots*
lemon	lovely*
letter*	lunch

* High usage words

STEP 18
Vase of Violets

Objectives

To teach the letter shapes and sound for **v** and **V**, -**ve**, and word building.

What you need

- ✩ *Programme One Picture Code Cards*: Vase of Violets (**v**), the Vase-Prop **e** (-**ve**) and all the cards covered so far
- ✩ *Programme One Flashcards*: 66-68 and all the character name cards covered so far
- ✩ *Class Wall Frieze*
- ✩ *Handwriting Songs Cassette*
- ✩ *Alphabet Songs Cassette*
- ✩ *Programme One Workbook 3*: pages 12 and 13
- ✩ *Storybook: Uppy Umbrella in Volcano Valley*

Preparation

- ✩ **Letters for picture coding** Prepare thick black **v**-shapes on pieces of card or paper for each child to picture code.

Quick revision

Introduce blends with **e** (**de**, **ke**, **se**, **te**, **ye**, etc., but not **ce** or **ge**) in your quick revision, as well as the newest character name *Flashcards*.

Introducing Vase of Violets

The letter **v** has a simple shape and is one of the very few letters that never changes its sound.

Distribute your prepared **v**-shapes for picture coding while you explain that this letter is a lovely vase of violets with velvet petals and velvet leaves. These violets grow in the valleys of Letterland where children make special vases for them. They use these vases of violets to decorate words like **have** and **live**.

Vase of Violets' letter shape

Introduce Vase of Violets' handwriting verse (set to music on the *Handwriting Songs Cassette*) to teach the correct stroke for **v**:

> Very neatly, start at the top.
> Draw down your vase, then up and stop.

Choose children to demonstrate the stroke on the *Class Wall Frieze* or *Picture Code Card*. Write a huge **v** on the board for them to air trace while they sing or chant the verse again.

Vase of Violets' letter sound

Help the children to discover the sound of the letter from the beginning of its name: '**Vv**vase of **Vv**violets'. Let them count the five leaves and petals on each violet and listen to the 'vvv...' sound each time they say the number **five**. Then use the Vase of Violets' song on the *Alphabet Songs Cassette* for practice in making the correct sound.

Explaining the capital V shape

Why do some vases look bigger? Because Letterland children bring them nearer to us to show us when a word is important.

Introduce *Flashcards* 66-68 and compare the sizes of **V** and **v**.

The silent e in words like have and give

The e in the -ve ending is neither Eddy Elephant nor Mr E. So what is the reason for the silent e at the ends of words like have and live and give?

Well, in Letterland, there is a reason for most things. This e is a silent Vase-Prop e. It makes no sound at all. But it does have a special job: to stop Vase of Violets from blowing over at the end of a word. Inside words these vases are protected from the Letterland winds. Because these winds can be very strong — and of course they always blow in the Reading Direction — these very valuable vases of violets at the ends of words all need propping up.

To write the Vase-Prop e, the children can simply join up v and e as for cursive writing. They can show e as silent by writing it in dots.

Word building with Vase of Violets

Live spelling: love, have and give

To build the words **love**, **have** and **give** you will need the following *Picture Code Cards*: **l**, **o** (Oscar's Little Brother), **v**, the silent **e**, **-ve** (the Vase-Prop **e**), **h**, **ă**, **g** and **ĭ**. Let three children form **lov**. Call a group to stand to their left blowing hard, so the **v** child can mime being almost blown over. Then a silent **e** child can rush in and prop the **v** up. Repeat this sequence for **have**. For **give**, you could skip the miming and use the Vase-Prop **e** (**-ve**) card instead.

Action sentences

Hand out *Flashcard* 68 to various pairs or groups of children, and any other *Flashcards* you wish to revise, and ask them to read the sentence side of the card in silence and then to respond to it silently.

Consolidation

Workbooks

Guide the children through the exercises on pages 12 and 13 of *Programme One Workbook 3* to consolidate learning of Vase of Violets' letter shape and sound. Draw special attention to its name and to the word **over** in the instruction text.

Storybooks

For further listening practice, read the *Letterland Storybook: Uppy Umbrella in Volcano Valley* aloud and draw the children's attention to the recurring 'vvv...' sound.

Vase-Prop e words	
above*	live*
forgive	love*
give*	move*
glove*	olive
have*	prove

* High usage words

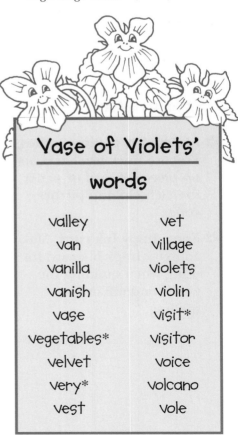

Vase of Violets' words	
valley	vet
van	village
vanilla	violets
vanish	violin
vase	visit*
vegetables*	visitor
velvet	voice
very*	volcano
vest	vole

* High usage words

STEP 19
Wicked Water Witch

Objectives

To teach the letter shapes and sound for **w** and **W**, and word building.

What you need

☆ *Programme One Picture Code Cards*: Wicked Water Witch (**w**) and all the cards covered so far

☆ *Programme One Flashcards*: 69-71 and all the character name cards covered so far

☆ *Class Wall Frieze*

☆ *Handwriting Songs Cassette*

☆ *Alphabet Songs Cassette*

☆ *Programme One Workbook 3*: pages 14 and 15

☆ *Storybook: The Wicked Witch's Wish*

Preparation

☆ **Letters for picture coding** Prepare thick black **w**-shapes on pieces of card or paper for each child to picture code.

☆ **Extra Impy Ink card** Make an extra Impy Ink card for using when building the word **windmill** in live spelling.

Quick revision

Limit your quick revision to recently learnt letters and character name *Flashcards*, and to consonant/short vowel blends, e.g. **da**, **de**, **di**, **do**; **fa**, **fe**, **fi**, **fo**; **va**, **ve**, **vi**, **vo**, etc.

Introducing Wicked Water Witch

This letter is a real trouble-maker for any child who wants to learn how to read and spell well and this is not mere fiction! The presence of **w** in words accounts for many shifts in vowel sounds, both predictable (e.g. **aw**, **ow** and **ew**) and less predictable (e.g. one-off words such as **was**, **want**, **woman** and **world**). Use this witch as a catalyst by presenting her as a character for the children to outwit. To do this they will have to learn all her wicked ways in words!

On the Wicked Water Witch *Picture Code Card*, liken the middle of her letter to a very small island with two wells on either side. These wells hold all the water she needs for her wicked spelling spells.

Next write six capital **M**'s and six capital **W**'s on the board, making the letters nice and thick. Ask six children to come and add water to the **W**'s on the board, in blue, if possible. Then let them draw the Witch perched on her island in the middle. Discuss the similarities and differences between Munching Mike's Mum's shape and the Witch's letter which holds water. Let them picture code Munching Mike's Mum as well to reinforce the differences. In addition, distribute your prepared **w**-shapes so that everyone can picture code the **w**'s.

Find a moment too to discuss what **windmills** are, as the children will be building this word later on with live spelling.

Wicked Water Witch's letter shape

Introduce Wicked Water Witch's handwriting verse (set to music on the *Handwriting Songs Cassette*) to teach the correct stroke for **w**:

> When you draw the Witch's wells,
> where she works her wicked spells,
> whizz down and up and then,
> whizz down and up again.

Choose children to demonstrate the stroke on the *Class Wall Frieze* or *Picture Code Card*. Write a huge **w** on the board for them to air trace while they sing or chant the verse again.

Wicked Water Witch's sound

Discuss where in Letterland Wicked Water Witch might live (north, south, east or west) and elicit 'West'.

Why yes! And what do you think the weather might be like where she lives in the West? Dry and sunny? Or wet and windy?

By now the children should be sensitive to alliteration. Hopefully, they will be able to answer this question correctly even before you formally teach the 'www...' sound. If not, help them to match up the initial 'www...' sound in her name with the initial 'www...' sounds in **wet** and **windy**.

Yes, the weather where the Wicked Water Witch lives is wild and wet and windy. It rains and rains, and the west wind whines through the trees day and night. The wind makes a sound like this: 'www...www...www...' Perhaps that is why the Wicked Witch makes a sound just like the wind whenever she turns up in a word!

Wicked Water Witch's song on the *Alphabet Songs Cassette* is a fun way to practise making her sound correctly.

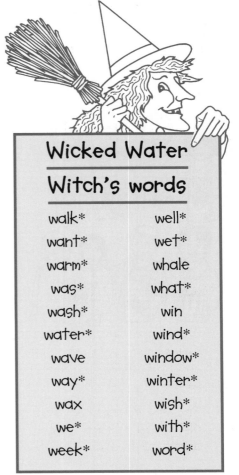

Wicked Water Witch's words	
walk*	well*
want*	wet*
warm*	whale
was*	what*
wash*	win
water*	wind*
wave	window*
way*	winter*
wax	wish*
we*	with*
week*	word*

* High usage words

Explaining the capital **W** shape

The children will have already met the capital **W** shape when you were introducing Wicked Water Witch. Like many other Letterland characters, Wicked Water Witch takes a deep breath and gets bigger when she has a chance to start an important word. Her wells even hold more water!

Introduce *Flashcards* 69 and 71 and compare **W** and **w** on both sides.

Practising the Witch's shape and sound

Wicked Water Witch in blends and digraphs

Some of your children may be ready to practise the blends and digraphs with **w**. In Section 3, you will find information on **wh** (page 142), **sw** (page 155) and **tw** (page 157).

Spelling was and saw

The word **was** ranks among the 12 most used words in the English language. See *Copymaster* 70 for help in spelling **was** and its reverse image **saw**.

Word building with Wicked Water Witch

Live spelling: wind, mill and windmill

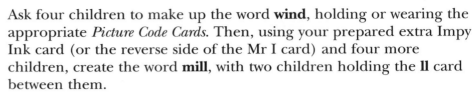

Ask four children to make up the word **wind**, holding or wearing the appropriate *Picture Code Cards*. Then, using your prepared extra Impy Ink card (or the reverse side of the Mr I card) and four more children, create the word **mill**, with two children holding the **ll** card between them.

Ask the eight children to move together to form the word **windmill**, and help them to discover what bigger word the two smaller words have made.

Finally, appoint eight new children to form the word **windmill** again. This time the rest of the class should guide them into the right sequence, by saying the word **windmill** in 'slow speak'.

Slow speak dictation

Use either the phrases or sentences below for slow speak dictation:

get well	can swim	will wish
west wind	went back	wet windmill

We will get wet.	The wind is from the west.
We will miss him.	She can swim in the wells.

Give the children a chance to check their work after each phrase or sentence, by writing it on the board. You may need to write **The** or **the** on the board first for them.

Action sentences

Hand out *Flashcard* 70 to various pairs or groups of children, and any other *Flashcards* you wish to revise, and ask them to read the sentence side of the card in silence and then to respond to it silently.

Consolidation

Workbooks

Guide the children through the exercises on pages 14 and 15 of *Programme One Workbook 3* to consolidate learning of Wicked Water Witch's letter shape and sound. Draw special attention to her name and to the words **wavy**, **with** and **words** in the instruction text. Also point out the tricky word **Write**, where the Witch makes no sound at all. (For the story explanation, see Programme Two.)

Storybooks

For further listening practice, read the *Letterland Storybook: The Wicked Witch's Wish* aloud and draw the children's attention to the recurring 'www...' sound.

STEP 20
Jumping Jim

Objectives

To teach the letter shapes and sound for **j** and **J**, and word building.

What you need

☆ *Programme One Picture Code Cards*: Jumping Jim (**j**) and all the cards covered so far

☆ *Programme One Flashcards*: 72-74 and all the character name cards covered so far

☆ *Class Wall Frieze*

☆ *Handwriting Songs Cassette*

☆ *Alphabet Songs Cassette*

☆ *Programme One Workbook 3*: pages 16 and 17

☆ *Storybook: Impy Ink's Invisible Ink (Jumping Jim in the Jungle)*

Preparation

☆ **Letters for picture coding**
Prepare thick black **j**-shapes on pieces of card or paper for each child to picture code.

Quick revision

Focus your quick revision on consonant/short vowel blends, as on page 104. Also include **sp**, **st** (whispered); **spa**, **spe**, **spi**, **spo**; and **sta**, **ste**, **sti**, **sto**, using the relevant *Picture Code Cards*.

Introducing Jumping Jim

The letter **j** is almost unique in the English alphabet, because it never changes its sound or becomes a silent letter. This means that you can introduce Jumping Jim as a good, reliable fellow who can always be counted upon.

Like many athletes in the modern Olympics, Jumping Jim is also a champion. Thus you can present him as a hero: the all-time high-jumping champion of Letterland! Not only can he jump sky high (witness the capital letter shape), but he can even juggle while he jumps!

Jumping Jim always jumps in the Reading Direction in words, so of course, the curve of his letter shape must show his knees bending round to his jogging shoes behind him.

*Jumping Jim juggles with balls, so fast, that you can never see more than one ball at a time [the **j**-dot]. Just think how difficult it must be to juggle while you jump. It is almost impossible! No wonder Jumping Jim wins all the jumping competitions held in Letterland every January, June and July.*

Distribute your prepared **j**-shapes for picture coding.

Let the children try jumping and juggling around the playground (in the Reading Direction ideally) during playtime. They will soon see for themselves how impossible it is to do *both* at once, and really admire Jumping Jim for knowing how.

Jumping Jim's letter shape

Introduce Jumping Jim's handwriting verse (set to music on the *Handwriting Songs Cassette*) to teach the correct stroke for **j**:

> Just draw down Jim, bending his knees.
> Then add the one ball which everyone sees.

Choose children to demonstrate the stroke on the *Class Wall Frieze* or *Picture Code Card*. Write a huge **j** on the board for them to air trace while they sing or chant the verse again.

Jumping Jim's sound

Let the children discover Jumping Jim's sound by *beginning* to say his name: 'j..., j..., j...'. Discourage 'juh' by keeping the jaw closed. Practise Jumping Jim's sound on the *Alphabet Songs Cassette*.

J is a low frequency letter, as so many words are spelt with a soft **g** instead. If you present Jumping Jim as a somewhat modest champion, this will help children when choosing whether to spell a word with **j** or **g**. The odds are very much in favour of **g**.

Explaining the capital J shape

Capital **J** will not be needed very often, because words beginning with it are also few and far between. Names, however, are a different matter. Because these are all-important words, Jumping Jim likes nothing better than to start a child's name with a sky-high jump (e.g. in Jessica, Jack, James, etc.)! Introduce *Flashcards* 72, 73 and 74 and compare the **J** and **j** shapes on both sides.

Practising Jumping Jim's shape and sound

Jumping Jim in names

If you have any children with foreign names, where **J** sounds like **Y**, help them to decide on a reason themselves, e.g. 'Jim must be juggling yellow yo-yos up there in the clouds – just for a change!'

Word building with Jumping Jim

Live spelling: jog, jig, jam, jet and jacket

Practise all the short vowels learnt so far by asking the children to make up the words **jog**, **jig**, **jam**, **jet** and **jacket**, and then to write them down, too.

Consolidation

Workbooks

Guide the children through the exercises on pages 16 and 17 of *Programme One Workbook 3* to consolidate learning of Jumping Jim's letter shape and sound. Draw special attention to his name and to the word **jigsaw** in the instruction text.

Storybooks

For further listening practice, read the *Letterland Storybook: Impy Ink's Invisible Ink* (*Jumping Jim in the Jungle*) aloud and draw the children's attention to the recurring 'j...' sound.

Jumping Jim's words

jacket	journey
jam*	joy
January*	jug
jar	juggle
jaw	juice
jelly*	July*
jigsaw	jump*
job*	jumper
jog	June*
joke	jungle
jolly	just*

* High usage words

STEP 21
Bouncy Ben

Objectives

To teach the letter shapes and sound for **b** and **B**, and word building.

What you need

☆ *Programme One Picture Code Cards*: Bouncy Ben (**b**), Bouncy Barbara (**b**) and all the cards covered so far

☆ *Programme One Flashcards*: 75-77 and all the character name cards covered so far

☆ *Class Wall Frieze*

☆ *Handwriting Songs Cassette*

☆ *Alphabet Songs Cassette*

☆ *Programme One Workbook 4*: pages 2 and 3

☆ *Storybook: Bouncy Ben's Birthday*

Preparation

☆ **Letters for picture coding**
Prepare thick black **b**-shapes on pieces of card or paper for each child to picture code.

Quick revision

Revise three letters at a time by focusing on **cla**, **fla**, **pla**, **sla**; **cle**, **fle**, **ple**, **sle**; **cli**, **fli**, **pli**, **sli** and **clo**, **flo**, **plo** and **slo**. Remember to whisper **c**, **f**, **p** and **l**.

Introducing Bouncy Ben

Another very lively letter comes next: Bouncy Ben. Bouncy Ben is a bright-eyed, brown bunny, who bounces along in words saying 'b..., b..., b...' as he bounces.

No doubt you will have had to tell curious children who this character is on the *Class Wall Frieze* long before now. The delay in focusing on him, however, is deliberate. It is one more precaution against **b**/**d** confusions. Your use of the pronouns **she**/**her**/**hers** for Dippy Duck and **he**/**him**/**his** for Bouncy Ben will help, too, whereas the traditional use of **it** for both **b** and **d** does not.

> *Bouncy **B**en has **b**ig **b**rown ears which stick up straight as he **b**ounces along in the Reading Direction. Far from being unhappy about his ears like Poor Peter, **B**ouncy **B**en often **b**oasts about his ears, **b**ecause they are so **b**ig and **b**rown and **b**eautiful!*
>
> *Bouncy **B**en has six **b**rothers and he lives in a **b**urrow! His **b**urrow is...*

Let the children decide. It could be by a bridge, along a river bank, beside some bluebells and buttercups, or even all three!

Finally, distribute your prepared **b**-shapes for picture coding.

Bouncy Ben's letter shape

Introduce Bouncy Ben's handwriting verse (set to music on the *Handwriting Songs Cassette*) to teach the correct stroke for **b**:

> Brush down Ben's big, long ears.
> Go up and round his head so his face appears!

Choose children to demonstrate the stroke on the *Class Wall Frieze* or *Picture Code Card*. Write a huge **b** on the board for them to air trace while they sing or chant the verse again.

Bouncy Ben's sound

Bouncy Ben's sound (as with all the other Letterland characters) is reliably at the beginning of his name. Make sure the children avoid saying 'buh' by keeping their mouths almost shut. They can practise it using Bouncy Ben's song on the *Alphabet Songs Cassette*.

Introducing Bouncy Barbara

Bouncy Ben has a best friend called Bouncy Barbara (with eyelashes). Introduce her, using the appropriate *Picture Code Card*, when children want to spell words like **baby** and words containing **bb**. They particularly like being in the word **rabbit** together! Bouncy Barbara can be used for the *second* **b** of the pair.

Explaining the capital B shape

Point to the capital **B** pictogram on the *Class Wall Frieze* showing Bouncy Ben doing his balancing trick:

To begin important words, Bouncy Ben always balances his bright blue ball between his beautiful, big brown ears. He bets you can't do that!

The children will enjoy play-acting Bouncy Ben balancing a ball or balloon between their 'ears ' (arms) just like the capital **B**.

Introduce *Flashcards* 75, 76 and 77. Compare the **B** and **b** shapes and encourage the children to read both sides of the card.

Word building with Bouncy Ben

Live spelling: big, beg, bag, bags and blob

Revise the short vowel sounds together with **b**. Let the children build **big**, then change **i** to **e**, and then **e** to **a** to discover they have made **beg** and **bag**. Slow speak **bags** so they know to add the Sleepy Sammy *Picture Code Card*, and then 'blllo...b' (**blob**), ending with the Bouncy Barbara card.

Consolidation

Workbooks

Guide the children through the exercises on pages 2 and 3 of *Programme One Workbook 4* to consolidate learning of Bouncy Ben's letter shape and sound. Draw special attention to his name and to the words **begin** and **blue** in the instruction text.

Storybooks

For further listening practice, read the *Letterland Storybook: Bouncy Ben's Birthday* aloud and draw the children's attention to the recurring 'b...' sound.

Bouncy Ben's words

baby*	blue*
bad*	boat*
balance	bounce
ball*	bread*
bat*	breakfast*
beautiful*	bridge*
bed*	brown*
bee*	bubble
big*	bun
bird*	bus*
birthday*	butter*
biscuit	butterfly

* High usage words

Objectives

To teach the letter shapes for **u** and **U** and the short vowel sound 'ǔ...', and word building.

What you need

☆ *Programme One Picture Code Cards*: Uppy Umbrella (ǔ) and all the cards covered so far

☆ *Programme One Flashcards*: 78-81 and all the cards covered so far

☆ *Class Wall Frieze*

☆ *Handwriting Songs Cassette*

☆ *Alphabet Songs Cassette*

☆ *Programme One Songs Cassette*

☆ *Programme One Workbook 4*: pages 4, 5 and 7

☆ *Storybook: Uppy Umbrella in Volcano Valley*

☆ *Links Group 1: Uppy Umbrella*

Preparation

☆ **Letters for picture coding** Prepare thick black **u**-shapes on pieces of card or paper for each child to picture code.

☆ **Spelling pictures** Write out the words **bus**, **sun** and **cup** on separate sheets of paper, using a thick black felt-tip pen, allowing enough space for the children both to picture code and illustrate the words' meanings. Make enough copies for each child.

Quick revision

Let this revision time be a more thorough one before arriving at a new milestone: introducing the fifth and final vowel. Run rapidly through the 'Quick dash' routine, asking for the single letter *sounds* only. Whenever the response is not instant, revise just those *Picure Code Cards* again until they are. Alternatively, pair up the children to do 'Quick dashes' with each other. Some children may also benefit from more practice in blending into a vowel.

Children can also test each other on reading the *Flashcard* names, words and sentences. Since they have now had 77 *Flashcards*, you may like to divide them into seven groups of ten cards each to circulate around the class.

Introducing Uppy Umbrella

Bring in a real umbrella to help you to introduce Uppy Umbrella. Open and close your umbrella and discuss the weather in general.

*Sometimes in Letterland it can be very rainy indeed. People find that one minute it is sunny; the next minute, the rain is pouring down! That's why you are lucky if you have an **umbrella** to stand **under**. Put **up** your **umbrella** and you will stay just as dry as if the sun were still shining.*

*All the **umbrellas** are very **understanding**. They are very glad to let anyone stand **under** them who doesn't want to get wet.*

Hold up the plain side of the Uppy Umbrella *Picture Code Card*.

*The sudden rainstorms in Letterland mean that this letter has to be looked after very carefully, because it is shaped rather like a tub. People call it the 'umbrella-letter' because it always needs an **umbrella** above it to keep it from filling **up** with water when it rains. The important job of keeping this letter dry goes to **U**ppy **U**mbrella. Would you like to see what **U**ppy **U**mbrella looks like?*

You can now show the pictogram side of the card.

*Here she is! She is a happy-go-lucky little **umbrella** who loves getting wet! But she never lets her **umbrella**-letter get wet. Oh no! She keeps it covered **up**, not only on rainy days, but on sunny days, too. Think how dreadful it would be if the Wicked Water Witch were to fill it **up** with water to use for some of her wicked spelling spells!*

Distribute your prepared **u**-shapes for picture coding.

111

Uppy Umbrella's letter shape

Introduce Uppy Umbrella's handwriting verse (set to music on the *Handwriting Songs Cassette*) to teach the correct stroke for **u**:

> Under the umbrella draw a shape like a cup.
> Then draw a straight line so it won't tip up.

Choose children to demonstrate the stroke on the *Class Wall Frieze* or *Picture Code Card*. Write a huge **u** on the board for them to air trace while they sing or chant the verse again.

Uppy Umbrella's sound

*When you see **U**ppy **U**mbrella's letter, you will usually hear her saying 'ŭ...' as she carefully covers **u**p her letter.*

Let the children stand up and form protective umbrella shapes with their arms and mime Uppy Umbrella while singing her song on the *Alphabet Songs Cassette*.

Explaining the capital U shape

For starting important words, Uppy Umbrella just has to take a deep breath to get bigger, like many of her Letterland friends.

Introduce *Flashcards* 78-81. Compare the **U** and **u** shapes and encourage the children to read the words on both sides of the cards.

Practising Uppy's shape and sound

Uppy Umbrella in names

To picture code children's names, the usual considerations apply. Short vowels will need the umbrella coding, long vowels will need a stick man coding (see page 42 for more information) and any irregularly pronounced u's (as in Laura) should have a wiggly line beneath them.

* High usage words

Uppy Umbrella's words	
ugly	unhappy
umbrella	unless
unbutton	until*
uncle*	unusual
under*	up*
underneath	upside down
understand	upstairs
undone*	us*

Word building with Uppy Umbrella

Live spelling: up, us, fun, sun, luck and stuck

Let the children build the first four words (**up**, **us**, **fun** and **sun**) by taking away and adding letters beside Uppy Umbrella. Then slow speak 'lllu...ck' and discuss who might make the 'k...' sound: Clever Cat, Kicking King or both? (For more information about **-ck**, see page 130.) Likewise, a similar discussion can take place for **stuck**.

Spelling pictures

Hand out your prepared spelling pictures for the words **bus**, **sun** and **cup** and ask the children to picture code them. When they have done this, they can then illustrate the words' meanings on the same sheets, as many times as space allows.

Action sentences

Hand out *Flashcards* 79, 80 and 81 to various pairs or groups of children, and any other *Flashcards* you wish to revise, and ask them to read the sentence sides of the cards in silence and then to respond to them silently.

Consolidation

Workbooks

Guide the children through the exercises on pages 4, 5 and 7 of *Programme One Workbook 4* to consolidate learning of Uppy Umbrella's letter shape and her short 'ŭ...' sound. Draw special attention to her name in the instruction text.

Storybooks

For further listening practice, read the *Letterland Storybook: Uppy Umbrella in Volcano Valley* or *Letterland Links Group 1: Uppy Umbrella* aloud and draw the children's attention to the recurring short 'ŭ...' sound.

Cassette

Sing or listen to **Uppy Umbrella** and Uppy Umbrella's verse (in particular) of the **Vowel Sounds Song** on the *Programme One Songs Cassette*.

STEP 22b
Mr U, the Uniform Man

Objectives

To teach the long vowel **ū** and word building.

What you need

☆ *Programme One Picture Code Cards*: Mr U (**ū**)

☆ *Programme One Flashcards*: 82 and 83

☆ *Class Wall Frieze*

☆ *Programme One Songs Cassette*

☆ *Programme One Workbook 4*: pages 6 and 7

☆ *Storybook: The Vowel Street Party*

☆ *Links Group 1: Five Vowel Men*

Preparation

☆ **Spelling pictures** Write out the word **you** using a thick black felt-tip pen, allowing enough space for the children both to picture code and illustrate the word's meaning, if possible. Make enough copies for each child.

Introducing Mr U, the Uniform Man

Hold up the Mr U *Picture Code Card*, with the pictogram side showing.

*You can tell that umbrellas must be important in Letterland, because an important looking man called Mr U, the **U**niform Man, has the job of looking after them all. We know he must be important. Otherwise, he wouldn't be wearing a **u**niform!*

Introduce both sides of *Flashcards* 82 and 83.

Practising Mr U saying his name

Mr U in names

Show any children with the long **ū** in their names how to draw a stick man right through the **U** or **u** to signal Mr U's presence. As you have done with the other long vowels, treat these names as special for having a Vowel Man in them.

Word building with Mr U

Spelling pictures

Hand out your prepared spelling pictures for the word **you** and ask the children to picture code just the letters **y** and **u**. Help them to notice that in this word, Yellow Yo-yo Man is making his usual sound, **o** is silent, and Mr U is saying his name. (The letter **o** can be written in grey or dotted lines.) To illustrate the meaning of the word **you**, the children can draw a hand pointing to a face or whole person.

Consolidation

Workbooks

Guide the children through the exercises on pages 6 and 7 of *Programme One Workbook 4* to consolidate learning of the long $\bar{u}$ in words. Draw special attention to Mr U's name in the instruction text.

Storybooks

For further listening practice, read the *Letterland Storybook: The Vowel Street Party* or *Letterland Links Group 1: Five Vowel Men* aloud and draw the children's attention to Mr U's name in words.

Cassette

Sing or listen to Mr U's verse (in particular) of the **Vowel Men Song** on the *Programme One Songs Cassette*.

Mr U's words	
unicorn	use*
uniform	useful
united	

* High usage words

STEP 23
Quarrelsome Queen

Objectives

To teach the letter shapes and sound for **q** and **Q**, and word building.

What you need

- ☆ *Programme One Picture Code Cards*: Quarrelsome Queen (**q**), Quarrelsome Queen and the Royal Umbrella together (**qu**), and all the cards covered so far

- ☆ *Programme One Flashcards*: 84-86 and all the character name cards covered so far

- ☆ *Class Wall Frieze*

- ☆ *Handwriting Songs Cassette*

- ☆ *Alphabet Songs Cassette*

- ☆ *Programme One Workbook 4*: pages 8 and 9

- ☆ *Storybook: Quarrelsome Queen's Quiz*

Preparation

- ☆ **Letters for picture coding** Prepare thick black **qu**-shapes on pieces of card or paper for each child to picture code.

- ☆ **Spelling pictures** Write out the words **queen** and **queen bee** on separate sheets of paper, using a thick black felt-tip pen, allowing enough space for the children both to picture code and illustrate the words' meanings. Make enough copies for each child.

Quick revision

Revise all the letters learnt so far, using the relevant *Picture Code Cards*, as well as any character name *Flashcards*.

Introducing Quarrelsome Queen

The words beginning with **qu** determine the temperament of Letterland's queen. She is beautiful, of course, as all queens traditionally seem to be, but she is also quick to quarrel. That is why everyone calls her 'Quarrelsome Queen'.

The characterisation of the queen can provide fruitful discussion material. Children know at first hand about cross adults. A chance to discuss with you anyone they know who gets cross as quickly as Quarrelsome Queen can give them an opening to talk.

*The **q**ueen **q**uarrels with the king and everyone else in Letterland. Normally, she has no less than nine **q**uarrels a day, which may explain why her letter looks like the number 9.*

*She is also proud of her splendid long hair. That is why she insists on taking her royal umbrella with her wherever she goes. Just think! Supposing it suddenly rained on her beautiful hair! She is certain to **q**uarrel with anyone who tries to stop her from keeping her umbrella right beside her in words!*

In fact, there is not one word in the whole English language where the letter **q** appears without a **u**.

Further proof as to how quarrelsome this queen can be lies in the fact that she refuses to face in the Reading Direction in words. She will certainly quarrel with anyone who tries to turn her round!

Before distributing your prepared **qu**-shapes for the children to picture code, hold up the pictogram side of the **qu** *Picture Code Card*. Explain that the umbrella is not Uppy, but the Queen's very own royal umbrella, which only ever appears beside her in words.

Quarrelsome Queen's letter shape

Introduce Quarrelsome Queen's handwriting verse (set to music on the *Handwriting Songs Cassette*) to teach the correct stroke for **q**:

> Quickly go round the Queen's cross face.
> Then comb her beautiful hair into place.

Choose children to demonstrate the stroke on the *Class Wall Frieze* or *Picture Code Card*. Write a huge **q** on the board for them to air trace while they sing or chant the verse again.

Quarrelsome Queen's sound

The queen's sound is a '**qu**iet' sound. As with all of the letters, it will be on the children's lips the moment they *start* to say her name. The **qu** sound is difficult, however, because it is really *two* letters' sounds said rapidly together: **cw**. To any child who spells, for example, **quick** starting with **cw** or **kw**, explain that one good thing about the queen is that she saves Clever Cat and Kicking King from ever having to be next to the Wicked Water Witch in a word!

Practise her sound with the help of Quarrelsome Queen's song on the *Alphabet Songs Cassette*.

Quarrelsome Queen's words

quack	quick*
quarrelsome	quiet
quarter*	quill
queen*	quilt
question	quite*
queue	quiz

* High usage words

Explaining the capital Q shape

The capital Q shape is Quarrelsome Queen's Quiet Room, where she goes to recover from all her quarrelling. Help the children to notice how she won't even go into her Quiet Room without keeping her precious umbrella within reach, i.e. they must *never* write either small **q** or capital **Q** without adding a **u**. (Exceptions are always foreign words.)

Introduce *Flashcards* 84, 85 and 86. Encourage the children to compare the **Qu** and **qu** spelling pattern and to read both sides of the cards.

Practising the Queen's shape and sound

Quarrelsome Queen's collection

Ask the children to collect words with **qu** in them, checking to see for themselves, in every case, whether it is really true that the queen never appears in a word without her umbrella.

Word building with Quarrelsome Queen

Live spelling: queen, see, seen, keep and sleep

To start with, write the word **queen** on the board. Then appoint a queen and an umbrella child (the 'Royal Umbrella') to hold the **qu** *Picture Code Card* together, two Mr E's and a Naughty Nick to build the word. For the *second* Mr E, use the plain side of the Eddy Elephant card. Explain that Eddy Elephant never turns up in a word with another elephant right beside him: elephants are too big to do that. Instead, two **e**'s side by side will always be Mr E and his twin brother, both saying their name '**E**' loud and clear.

Place the two Mr E's and Naughty Nick on the left of the class. Put the queen and umbrella child on the class' right. The queen should then pull the umbrella child to the centre of the room, crossly muttering 'qu..., qu..., qu...' as they both move *against* the Reading Direction. The others then join her from the left to form **queen**. Finally, they pronounce the three sounds in sequence: 'qu...ee...nnn', '**queen**'! Go on to make **see**, **seen**, **keep** and **sleep**.

Spelling pictures

Hand out your prepared spelling pictures for the words **queen** and **queen bee** and ask the children to picture code them. When they have done this, they can then illustrate the words' meanings on the same sheets, as many times as space allows.

Action sentences

Hand out *Flashcards* 85 and 86 to various pairs or groups of children, and any other *Flashcards* you wish to revise, and ask them to read the sentence sides of the cards in silence and then to respond to them silently.

Consolidation

Workbooks

Guide the children through the exercises on pages 8 and 9 of *Programme One Workbook 4* to consolidate learning of the **qu** letter shapes and sound. Draw special attention to the queen's name in the instruction text.

Storybooks

For further listening practice, read the *Letterland Storybook: Quarrelsome Queen's Quiz* aloud and draw the children's attention to the recurring 'qu...' sound.

STEP 24
Robber Red

Objectives

To teach the letter shapes and sound for **r** and **R**, and word building.

What you need

✫ *Programme One Picture Code Cards*: Robber Red (**r**) and all the cards covered so far

✫ *Programme One Flashcards*: 87-89 and all the character name cards covered so far

✫ *Class Wall Frieze*

✫ *Handwriting Songs Cassette*

✫ *Alphabet Songs Cassette*

✫ *Programme One Workbook 4*: pages 10 and 11

✫ *Storybook: Robber Red and the Robot*

Preparation

✫ **Letters for picture coding** Prepare thick black **r**-shapes on pieces of card or paper for each child to picture code.

✫ **Spelling pictures** Write out the words **red** and **ring** on separate sheets of paper, using a thick black felt-tip pen, allowing enough space for the children both to picture code and illustrate the words' meanings. Make enough copies for each child.

Quick revision

The **q** and **qu** *Picture Code Cards* will now be included in your quick revision sessions. From now on, no-one should make a sound when you hold up the single **q** card: only when you hold up the **qu** card. This way you emphasise that the queen won't even *speak* unless you give her her umbrella.

Introducing Robber Red

The vitality of Letterland stems in part from the many parallels to real life. The figure of Robber Red produces yet another of these parallels. In real life there *are* people who break rules and laws. All children will know at least a little about what it means to take something which does not belong to them or to have something taken from them, which may explain why they are invariably intrigued by Letterland's chief law-breaker, Robber Red. Robber Red is the ringleader of a gang of trouble-makers. He draws upon the excitement inherent in the reality of right and wrong. As a result, once you have alerted them to his shape and sound, they love to 'catch' him in words.

Hold up the plain side of the Robber Red *Picture Code Card*.

The Wicked Water Witch is not the only trouble-maker in Letterland. This card shows you the letter shape of a man called Robber Red. Robber Red always runs in the Reading Direction growling 'rrr...' as he runs.

Encourage the children to imagine the upright line as the robber's body and the rightward line as Robber Red's outstretched arm. Discuss where his head and legs must be. Before turning to the pictogram side, discuss colour.

What colour do you think Robber Red's clothes will be?

They will know that the answer is 'red' from the *Class Wall Frieze*. Show the pictogram side of the *Picture Code Card*.

Yes, rrred. All his clothes are red. His cap is red. His trousers are red. His socks are red. His boots are red. Even his hair is red, really red, just as red as his red clothes! So now you know why everyone in Letterland calls this bad man Robber Red!

While the children are picture coding your prepared **r**-shapes, let them think of things that Robber Red might run off with, i.e. things beginning with his sound, such as **r**ulers and **r**adios.

Robber Red's words

rabbit*	robber
race*	robot
radio*	rock*
rain*	roll
rascal	roller
rat*	skates
read*	roof
ready*	rope*
really*	roses
red*	round*
ride*	rubber*
right*	rules
ring*	run*
road*	

* High usage words

children	read	run
every	red	street
from	right	three
green	road	train
rabbit	room	tree
ran	round	very

Robber Red's letter shape

Introduce Robber Red's handwriting verse (set to music on the *Handwriting Songs Cassette*) to teach the correct stroke for **r**:

> Run down Robber Red's body.
> Go up to his arm and his hand.
> Then watch out for this robber
> roaming round Letterland.

Choose children to demonstrate the stroke on the *Class Wall Frieze* or *Picture Code Card*. Write a huge **r** on the board for them to air trace while they sing or chant the verse again.

Robber Red's sound

The sound of **r** is difficult to pronounce in isolation, because it distorts so easily to 'ruh' or 'er', so take every opportunity to emphasise his sound accurately in running speech. The word **red** gives you repeated opportunities. Everyone should keep their mouths almost shut as they practise the 'rrr..' sound in Robber Red's song on the *Alphabet Songs Cassette*.

Explaining the capital R shape

*When **R**obber **R**ed takes a big breath to start an important word, he certainly gets bigger! He also looks fatter! Why the big bulge in front? Because he has just stuffed some stolen goods inside his sweater to hide them from us! He also hopes that by changing his shape he will make it more difficult for you to **r**ecognise him!*

Now is the time to picture code the initial **R** on your Reading Direction sign. Look, too, at *Flashcards* 87, 88 and 89, comparing the use of **R** and **r** and encouraging the children to read the sentences.

Practising Robber Red's shape and sound

Robber Red's gang

Of the 250 most used words in the English language, 58 of them contain an **r**. Yet the children will only be able to hear Robber Red 'growling' in 18 of them, listed left.

You will not, however, have to apologise for the exceptions. Simply blame them on Robber Red's gang instead. Like the Wicked Water Witch, Robber Red likes to make learning to read as hard as he can! This is why he has a robber gang.

At this stage, encourage the children to learn irregular words like **are**, **her**, **or**, **our**, **your**, **bird** and **year**, etc. as whole-word shapes. Use wiggly lines beneath these words to ensure that they do not waste time trying to sound out these words.

The children will be meeting the Robber gang soon in Programme Two.

Robber Red in blends

Some of your children may be ready to practise the blends with **r**. In Section 3, you will find information on **br**, **cr**, **dr**, **fr**, **gr**, **pr** and **tr** (page 152).

Word building with Robber Red

Live spelling: red, read, tree, three and green

The word **red** will be easy for the children to build, but you will need to explain that the next same sounding word, **read**, has a silent letter in it. Ask the children to replace Eddy Elephant with Mr E, and then give them the hint that another Vowel Man will come next, just to keep Mr E company. Let them see which one looks right. They can then go on to building **tree** (using the reverse side of the Eddy Elephant *Picture Code Card* for the second Mr E). You will need to have told them the **th** story to build **three** (see page 140), or alternatively, go on to build **green**.

Spelling pictures

Hand out your prepared spelling pictures for the words **red** and **ring** and ask the children to picture code them. When they have done this, they can then illustrate the words' meanings on the same sheets, as many times as space allows.

Consolidation

Workbooks

Guide the children through the exercises on pages 10 and 11 of *Programme One Workbook 4* to consolidate learning of Robber Red's letter shape and sound. Draw special attention to his name in the instruction text.

Storybooks

For further listening practice, read the *Letterland Storybook: Robber Red and the Robot* aloud and draw the children's attention to the recurring 'rrr...' sound.

your bird

STEP 25
Max and Maxine

Objectives

To teach the letter shapes and sound for **x** and **X**, and word building.

What you need

- ✿ *Programme One Picture Code Cards*: Max and Maxine (**x**) and all the cards covered so far

- ✿ *Programme One Flashcards*: 90-92 and all the character name cards covered so far

- ✿ *Class Wall Frieze*

- ✿ *Handwriting Songs Cassette*

- ✿ *Alphabet Songs Cassette*

- ✿ *Programme One Workbook 4*: pages 12 and 13

- ✿ *Storybook: Zig Zag Zebra Saves the Day*

Preparation

- ✿ **Letters for picture coding**
  Prepare thick black **x**-shapes on pieces of card or paper for each child to picture code.

Quick revision

Take a 'Quick dash' through all the letters and character names learnt so far.

Introducing Max and Maxine

You can describe the letter **x** as being a very 'loving letter', because when it stands on its own it means a kiss. Show the **x** *Picture Code Card* on the plain side first, and discuss the shape as being like two crossed sticks.

On the pictogram side, you can introduce Letterland's young cousins, Max and Maxine. Max has just given Maxine a kiss because today she is six.

Explain that they won't spot Max and Maxine kissing very often in words (there are only two in the 250 most used English words: **next** and **box**), but they must keep a sharp look-out for them all the same.

Finally, distribute your prepared **x**-shapes for picture coding.

Max and Maxine's letter shape

Introduce Max and Maxine's handwriting verse (set to music on the *Handwriting Songs Cassette*) to teach the correct stroke for **x**:

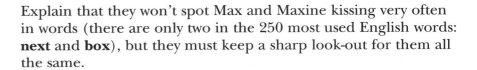

> Fix two sticks, to look like this.
> That's how to draw a little kiss.

Choose children to demonstrate the stroke on the *Class Wall Frieze* or *Picture Code Card*. Write a huge **x** on the board for them to air trace while they sing or chant the verse again.

Max and Maxine's sound

Explain that whenever Max and Maxine give each other a kiss above their letter, they do it to remind us of their letter's sound in words. It is 'k-ss': the word 'kiss' said in a whisper so that we do not hear the vowel. Get everyone to whisper 'k-ss', listening to themselves carefully, paying special attention to their own throat and tongue movements. Make sure the children also whisper 'k-ss' as they practise it in Max and Maxine's song on the *Alphabet Songs Cassette*.

Let the children listen together for the **x** sound in sentences such as: 'Can Ma**x** fi**x** the bo**x**?' and *Flashcards* 90-92. It is helpful if they whisper the whole sentence to make the 'k-ss' sound easier to notice.

Explaining the capital X shape

Like many other Letterlanders, Max and Maxine just take a deep breath and get bigger when they need to start important words. However, when they do start words they do *not* make their usual sound of 'k-ss', e.g. in words like **x-ray**, **xylophone**, etc. (see **X-rays and xylophones** below).

X-rays and xylophones

Pictures of x-rays or xylophones on alphabet friezes are not pedagogically sound for the introductory stages of alphabet teaching. They are entirely misleading, since in each case, they only really apply to two words that children are likely to meet: 'eks' as in **x-ray** and **Xmas** and 'zzz...' as in **xylophone** and **xerox**. Both ignore the 'k-ss' sound within many more useful words, e.g. **fix**, **mix**, **six**, **ox**, **box**, **fox**, **wax**, **next**, **expect**, **extra**, etc.

If children ask about the 'zzz...' sound at the start of **xylophone** or **xerox**, explain it as follows:

At the start of just two or three words, Max has a quick snooze, instead of giving Maxine a kiss. That is why he makes a 'zzz...' sound instead of his usual 'k-ss' sound.

Practising Max and Maxine's shape and sound

Exit signs

Let the children design their own **EXIT** signs, picture code all four letters and take them home to display on the inside of a back door.

Spelling: -x or -cks?

When it comes to spelling the 'k-ss' sound, one reason that Max and Maxine are seldom seen is because the job is often done by three other letters instead. Leave the children to guess 'who' these three might be (Clever Cat, Kicking King and Sammy Snake).

Max and Maxine's words

box*	mixture
exit	next*
expect*	six*
extra	sixteen*
fix*	sixty*
fox*	taxi
mix	wax

* High usage words

_ x	- cks
fox fix	socks ticks
box	blocks picks
wax	bricks packs
	kicks pecks
	rocks
	tricks
	necks
	backs

You may like to start two lists for -**x** and -**cks**, to discover gradually exactly how few words appear in the -**x** list compared with -**cks** list.

Some children may also discover words ending in -**ks** (**looks** and **weeks**) and -**kes** (**makes** and **likes**). Help them to start a third and a fourth list.

Word building with Max and Maxine

Live spelling: six, fix, fox, box and next

Help the children to build the words **six**, **fix**, **fox**, **box** and **next**. Either one or two children can hold the **x** *Picture Code Card*.

Action sentences

Hand out *Flashcards* 91 and 92 to various pairs or groups of children, and any other *Flashcards* you wish to revise, and ask them to read the sentence sides of the cards in silence and then to respond to them silently.

Consolidation

Workbooks

Guide the children through the exercises on pages 12 and 13 of *Programme One Workbook 4* to consolidate learning of Max and Maxine's letter shape and sound. Draw special attention to their names in the instruction text and to the 'k-ss' sound in each of their names.

Storybooks

For further listening practice, read the *Letterland Storybook: Zig Zag Zebra Saves the Day* aloud and draw the children's attention to the recurring 'k-ss' sound.

STEP 26
Zig Zag Zebra

Objectives

To teach the letter shapes and sound for **z** and **Z**, and word building.

What you need

☆ *Programme One Picture Code Cards*: Zig Zag Zebra (**z**), Zoe Zebra (**z**) and all the cards covered so far

☆ *Programme One Flashcards*: 93-95 and all the character name cards covered so far

☆ *Class Wall Frieze*

☆ *Handwriting Songs Cassette*

☆ *Alphabet Songs Cassette*

☆ *Programme One Workbook 4*: pages 14 and 15

☆ *Storybook: Zig Zag Zebra Saves the Day*

Preparation

☆ **Letters for picture coding**
Prepare thick black **z**-shapes on pieces of card or paper for each child to picture code.

Quick revision

Quickly revise all the letters learnt so far, using the relevant *Picture Code Cards,* as well as any character name *Flashcards.*

Introducing Zig Zag Zebra

Zig Zag Zebra tends to be a favourite among quiet and withdrawn children, because she is a very shy zebra, rarely showing herself in words. (As already explained, the **z** sound is created more often by **s** than **z**.)

Introduce either side of the Zig Zag Zebra *Picture Code Card* first, but make sure that the children study both sides carefully to notice orientation. Elicit their observation that Zig Zag Zebra is *not* facing in the Reading Direction. See if they can remember who else is *not* facing in the Reading Direction (Golden Girl and Quarrelsome Queen). Thus three letters 'look left' instead of to the right: Golden Girl because she gets giddy, the Queen because she is quarrelsome and Zig Zag Zebra because she is so shy (shy people and animals often turn around and face the other way).

> *Zig **Z**ag **Z**ebra moves very, very fast. She will **z**ip into a word and **z**ip out again so fast, that you hardly have time to hear her making a tiny little '**zzz**...' sound.*

You can now distribute your prepared **z**-shapes for the children to picture code.

Zig Zag Zebra's letter shape

Introduce Zig Zag Zebra's handwriting verse (set to music on the *Handwriting Songs Cassette*) to teach the correct stroke for **z**:

> Zip along Zig Zag's nose.
> Stroke her neck...,
> stroke her back... Zzzoom!
> Away she goes.

Choose children to demonstrate the stroke on the *Class Wall Frieze* or *Picture Code Card*. Write a huge **z** on the board for them to air trace while they sing or chant the verse again.

Zig Zag Zebra's sound

*Who else makes a 'zzz...' sound in words? Sammy Snake, of course. **Zig Zag Zebra** makes exactly the same sound as Sammy Snake when he is sleepy, but not because she is having a quiet snooze. Far from it. She says '**zzz...**' because she is whizzing along so fast!*

Sing Zig Zag Zebra's song on the *Alphabet Songs Cassette*.

Introducing Zoe Zebra

Zig Zag Zebra has a shy best friend called Zoe Zebra. Introduce her, using the appropriate *Picture Code Card*, when children want to spell words containing **zz**. Zoe Zebra can be used for the *second* **z** of the pair.

*Every once in a blue moon, if you are lucky, you might see **Zig Zag Zebra** whizzing along with her best friend **Zoe Zebra** in a word. Then the sight of not just one, but two stripy **zebras**, both whizzing in one word is enough to make anyone quite dizzy!*

Explaining the capital Z shape

Like a number of other letters, to start an important word Zig Zag Zebra just takes a deep breath and gets bigger. Introduce *Flashcards* 93-95 and compare **z** and **Z** on both sides.

Word building with Zig Zag Zebra

Live spelling: zebra, zero and zoo

Give help in building the words **zebra**, **zero** and **zoo**.

Action sentences

Hand out *Flashcard* 95 to various pairs or groups of children, and any other *Flashcards* you wish to revise, and ask them to read the sentence side of the card in silence and then to respond to it silently.

Consolidation

Workbooks

Guide the children through the exercises on pages 14 and 15 of *Programme One Workbook 4* to consolidate learning of Zig Zag Zebra's letter shape and sound. Draw special attention to her name in the instruction text.

Storybooks

For further listening practice, read the *Letterland Storybook: Zig Zag Zebra Saves the Day* aloud.

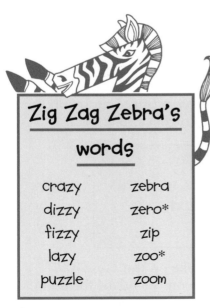

Zig Zag Zebra's
words

crazy	zebra
dizzy	zero*
fizzy	zip
lazy	zoo*
puzzle	zoom

* High usage words

126

The importance of vowels

Revise both the short vowels and the Vowel Men by singing or listening to the **Vowel Sounds Song** and the **Vowel Men Song** on the *Programme One Songs Cassette*. Appoint five children for each song to hold up the appropriate *Picture Code Card* for each verse and let them sing out their name as it is mentioned.

You can now demonstrate the importance of vowels in words by giving out all the consonant *Picture Code Cards* except for **r**, **y** and **w**. Ask the children to make a few words with these 18 cards. They will soon discover that they cannot even make one! No combination is either pronounceable or meaningful. Why not? Because Annie Apple, Eddy Elephant, Impy Ink, Oscar Orange, Uppy Umbrella and the Vowel Men are all missing. Help the children to deduce how important these five characters and their owners are. Nobody can make a single word without at least one vowel in it!

Convenient general terms from now on for talking about the vowels will be 'Vowel Men' for long vowels and 'Vowel Men's belongings' for short vowels. You will soon be able to shorten these two phrases to the single word 'vowel', since it has by now acquired meaning in the context of Letterland.

Note A few words may seem to contain no vowel because **y** is 'doing a job' for a vowel, as in **try** or **why**. (These other 'jobs' of the Yo-yo Man are fully explained in Programme Two.)

Frieze game

Develop the racing game described on page 63, matching *all* the letters of the alphabet on the *Picture Code Cards* to the letters on the *Class Wall Frieze*. Using the full **a-z**, this matching game becomes more exciting. It also provides good preparation for dictionary work. A child who has run to the middle of the frieze to match Munching Mike and nearly to the far end for the Wicked Water Witch, will soon remember where to look in a dictionary for **m** and **w**.

Sentence-building

Make up short sentences from words learnt so far, e.g.

Is Fred fat?   **I am glad.**   **We can win.**

Make a plain letter card for each of the letters in the words.

Divide the children into groups (seven, eight or nine children to match the number of letters in the sentence). Hand out a letter card to each child and ask them to picture code their letter. The group then has to work out words to create the sentence. Any capital letters, full stops and question marks will all give them clues.

When they have done it, cut out their letters more closely and mount them on the wall for other children to read.

Sentence reading

Let the children practise reading the sentence sides of all the *Flashcards*. Those who have no difficulty with them are well on their way to fluent reading.

Popularity graph

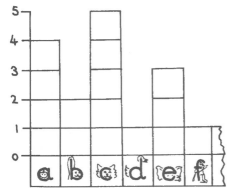

Do a survey to find which Letterland character each child likes best and then get the children to help you make a graph to show the results. Many opportunities for discussion can arise from it, involving both numbers and letters.

Match the sound game

Play this game as described on page 62. These combinations are more difficult. Again, watch out for any children who have difficulty. Their hearing may need checking, or they may just need more exercises like these to improve their auditory discrimination.

For the following lists of words, the children will need to make cards for **pP**, **bB**, **vV**, **wW**, **rR**, **lL**, **cC**, **gG**, **iI**, **eE**, **oO** and **uU**, plain on one side and picture-coded on the other, as before. Use different lists of words on different days.

pP/bB
1 potato
2 broken basket
3 pinpoint
4 bubbles
5 postman
6 big bonfire
7 price
8 brakes
9 printed papers
10 bits and bobs

vV/wW
1 varnish
2 warning
3 violin
4 waste
5 visor
6 wobble
7 visitor
8 wet washing
9 vegetables
10 warning

rR/lL
1 rhyme and rhythm
2 lullaby
3 restaurant
4 light load
5 rough ride
6 loft
7 radiator
8 life line
9 rising rocket
10 label

cC/gG
1 cold carrots
2 glass greenhouse
3 careful climber
4 garden gloves
5 clever clown
6 cosy cot
7 garage
8 crusty crumbs
9 grey gull
10 grateful granny

iI/eE
1 impossible
2 envelope
3 illness
4 elbow
5 infant
6 endless
7 interesting
8 edge
9 immediately
10 ever so

oO/uU
1 understand
2 on and on
3 upside down
4 oblong
5 uncle
6 ostrich
7 undone
8 otter
9 unfortunate
10 olives

SECTION 3

WORD ENDINGS
Clever Cat and Kicking King

Objective

To teach the ending -ck (as in the word **luck**).

What you need

☆ *Programme One Picture Code Cards*: -ck and all the cards covered so far

☆ *Programme One Copymasters*: 1 and 3

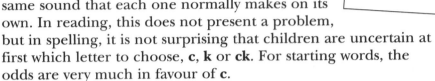

Introducing -ck

The -ck ending is special in that the two letters, **c** and **k**, represent only one sound. They 'share' the same sound that each one normally makes on its own. In reading, this does not present a problem, but in spelling, it is not surprising that children are uncertain at first which letter to choose, **c**, **k** or **ck**. For starting words, the odds are very much in favour of **c**.

*Clever Cat is proud to begin far more words than Kicking King, because the King finds ki**ck**ing too cramped at the start of words.*

For proof, let the children compare the size of the **c** and **k** sections of any dictionary. Inside words, the odds favour **c** again.

At the end of short (one-syllable) words there are three options: **-k**, **-ke** and **-ck**. A cluster of frequently used words end in **-k**: **look**, **took**, **week**, **speak**, etc. Another cluster ends in **-ke**: **make**, **take**, **like**, **bike**, etc., while over 85 useful one-syllable, short vowel words end in **-ck**.

*Clever Cat loves watching the Kicking King practise his ki**ck**s at the end of short qui**ck** words, where he does most of his really big ki**ck**s.*

The time to choose **-c** on its own at the end of a word is when the word has two or more syllables. In Letterland terms, 'Clever Cat proudly finishes *longer* words all by herself'. Examples include **comic**, **picnic** and **fantastic**.

Word building with the -ck ending

Live spelling: back/black **and** quick/trick

Hand out all ten short and long vowels, as well as the **-ck**, **b**, **l**, **t** and **r** cards. Call out the words **back**, **black**, **quick** and **trick**. After each one, ask 'Is there a Vowel Man in this word?' Simply seeing that none of the Vowel Men cards get used will highlight this short vowel plus **-ck** spelling pattern. If you like, go on to build **lock**, **stick**, **rock**, **rocket**, **thick**, **chick** or **chicken**.

Consolidation

Copymasters

Programme One Copymasters 1 and 3 provide practice in the **-ck** ending.

Words ending in and containing -ck

back*	rock
black*	rocket
block	sick
brick	socks
check	speck
chicken*	stick*
clock*	suck
duck*	thick
flock	ticket
lock	track
luck	trick
pack	truck
quick*	

* High usage words

Objective

To teach the shared sounds -**ff**, -**ll** and -**ss** at the end of words (as in the words **off**, **will** and **fuss**).

What you need

☆ *Programme One Picture Code Cards*: Fireman Fred and Frank together (**ff**), Lucy and Linda together (**ll**), Sammy and Sally Snake together (**ss**) and all the cards covered so far

☆ *Programme One Copymasters*: 2 and 3

Introducing the shared sounds

In Letterland, double consonants are described as 'shared sounds' to show that they are both of equal importance. They pair up to make exactly the same sound at the same time. Their timing is so perfect that we hear it as one sound. In fact, their behaviour is more like that of partners. Both are equally essential to the structure and pronunciation of the word. The term 'best friend' is a useful way to refer to any second letter in a pair. By using this term now, you will be paving the way for understanding a major predictive strategy: when to double the consonant, which will be explained in Programme Two.

This section just deals with three *final* shared sounds, provided on the **ff**, **ll** and **ss** *Picture Code Cards*. They are different simply because they are permanent features at the end of many one-syllable, short-vowel words. Introduce -**ff** early on if only to ensure that your children use both of these 'best friends at the end' in the important high usage little word **off**.

Best friends at the end: -ff

*One of Fireman Fred and Frank's favourite spots in words is at the end. For example, Fireman Fred never sets off to fight a fire without his best friend and fellow fireman, Fireman Frank. That is why you always see two firemen in the word **off**.*

Words ending in —ff

cliff	scoff
fluff	sniff
huff	staff
off*	stuff
puff	

* High usage words

Both firemen share their **f** sound at the end of the nine short words in the box (see above). There are not many other words which end in -**ff**.

Best friends at the end: -ll

You will usually see two Lamp Ladies at the end of short words. Why? Well, Lucy Lamp Lady feels a bit lonely at the end of little words. So she calls in her best friend Linda for company. They share their sound and light up lots of little words very well.

* High usage words. (See also *Copymaster* 2 for help with **pull**.)

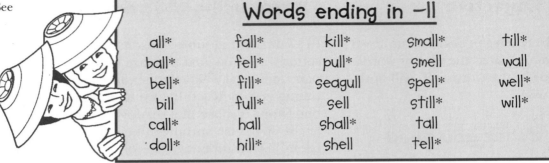

Words ending in –ll

all*	fall*	kill*	small*	till*
ball*	fell*	pull*	smell	wall
bell*	fill*	seagull	spell*	well*
bill	full*	sell	still*	will*
call*	hall	shall*	tall	
doll*	hill*	shell	tell*	

(For a special explanation of **all**, **full** and also **-al** and **-ful**, see the Giant All and Giant Full stories in Programme Two.)

Best friends at the end: -ss

Sammy Snake's best friend is his sister, Sally Snake. They both love to hiss at exactly the same time at the ends of short words, especially at the end of the word hiss!

(For the many words ending in **-less** and **-ness**, see Programme Two.)

* High usage words

Words ending in –ss

across*	dress*	hiss	mess
address	fuss	illness*	miss*
class*	glass	kiss	pass*
cress	grass*	less	press
cross*	guess*	loss	princess*

Word building with the shared sounds

Live spelling and slow speak dictation

Use any combination of the words in the boxes. For variety, try dictating short phrases, such as **will miss you**, **such a fuss**, **his address** or **shall sit still**.

Consolidation

Copymasters

Programme One Copymasters 2 and 3 provide practice in the shared sounds **-ff**, **-ll** and **-ss**.

WORD ENDINGS
Nick and a friend at the end

Objective

To teach the endings **-nd** and **-nt** (as in the words **hand** and **tent**).

What you need

☆ *Programme One Picture Code Cards*: **nd**, **nt** and all the cards covered so far

☆ *Programme One Copymasters*: 4-6

Introducing -nd and -nt

The **-nd** and **-nt** endings feature in several frequently used words (e.g. **end**, **friend**, **hand**, **went** and **want**), so it helps if the children learn early on to identify these consonant blends easily. Find a good moment to draw their attention to Naughty Nick's and Dippy Duck's '...nnnd' sound in the words **sound** and **blend**. Also see if anyone has noticed that very same sound at the end of **Letterland**! (See also **'Kind' words and 'old' words** on page 158 which features the ending **-ind**: Mr I saying his name before **-nd**.) When focusing on the **-nt** blend, a good word to use as you praise good work is, of course, **excellent**!

Word building with the -nd and -nt endings

Live spelling: and → blend and end → friend

Let the children form **and**, **band**, **bend** and **blend** as you slow speak these words. Follow on with **end**, **send**, **spend** and then **friend**. Explain first that Mr I is their silent friend just before the end part of the word **friend**.

Consolidation

Copymasters

Programme One Copymasters 4-6 provide practice in the **-nd** and **-nt** endings.

Words ending in -nd

and*	England*	land*	send*
around*	fond	lend	spend*
band*	found*	mend	stand*
bend	friend*	pond	understand
blend	hand*	pretend	wind
blond	handstand	sand	
end*	intend	second*	

Words ending in -nt

ant	present*
excellent	spent*
hunt*	tent
moment	want*
pant	went*

* High usage words

133

WORD ENDINGS
Lucy Lamp Lady and a friend at the end

Objective

To teach the endings **-lk** and **-lt** (as in the words **milk** and **salt**).

What you need

☆ *Programme One Picture Code Cards*: **lk**, **lt** and all the cards covered so far

☆ *Programme One Copymasters*: 7

Introducing -lk and -lt

It is good to be able to spell the **-lk** and **-lt** sounds easily, even though there are relatively few words in each group.

*We know that Lucy Lamp Lady loves to wa**lk** and ta**lk** with the King. What a pity there are not many words where she has a chance to shine quietly right beside her king!*

*Lucy Lamp Lady and Ticking Tess have always fe**lt** that it would be good to be side by side in lots of words, but each of them is needed so often in other words, that chances to be together are difficu**lt** to find.*

Word building with the -lk and -lt endings

Live spelling: walk/talk and left/felt

Write the words **walk** and **talk** on the board and invite speculation. Ask the children why Annie Apple is making an unusual sound. (This is an open-ended question: there are no wrong answers.) Wipe out the words and call them out to build in live spelling. Instead of sounding out 'lll...', let the **l** child simply turn and smile silently at the **k** child.

Four children can then go on to build **left**. Next, ask them to work out how they could make a new word using exactly the same letters, but in a new order (**felt**). Congratulate them on discovering one of the few words in which Lucy and Tess manage to be together.

Consolidation

Copymasters

Programme One Copymaster 7 provides practice in the **-lk** and **-lt** endings.

Words ending in −lk

chalk	silk	talk*
folk	stalk	walk*
milk*	sulk	

Words ending in −lt

adult	insult	salt*
belt	melt	spilt
difficult	quilt	wilt
felt*	result	

* High usage words

CONSONANT DIGRAPHS
Nick and Golden Girl

Objective

To teach the digraph **-ng** (as in the word **sing**).

What you need

☆ *Programme One Picture Code Cards*: **ng** and all the cards covered so far

☆ *Programme One Copymasters*: 8 and 10

☆ *Programme One Songs Cassette*

Words ending in —ng

along*	morning*
bang*	reading*
bring*	ring*
bringing*	ringing*
building*	sing*
evening*	singing*
fishing*	song*
going*	spelling*
hang	spring*
interesting*	sting
king*	string*
long*	strong*
looking*	thing*
making*	writing*

* High usage words

Introducing -ng

Letterland teaching gives high priority to the **-ng** sound for two reasons:
- The **-ng** sound usually occurs at the *end* of words, enabling you to alert the children to look not just at the start, but also at the full length of words.
- The digraph **-ng** turns up often, not just in common words like **bring**, **sing** and **thing**, but in thousands of other other words ending in **-ing**.

A good time to introduce the **-ng** story is during Step 15, as **-ng** occurs twice in **Kicking King**: an opportunity too good to miss! Alternatively, just give a brief version of the story to individual children when they need help in spelling any word ending in **-ng** or **-ing**. They will still enjoy hearing the fuller story when the others are ready for it later on.

Word building with the -ng digraph

Live spelling: king, sing, song → strong

Write the word **king** in large letters on the board. Then appoint four children to form the word. Ask two children to hold the **ng** *Picture Code Card*. Lead them to discover that when Nick and Golden Girl come face to face in a word, together they make a *new* sound.

*When we say the word **king**, how do we pronounce it? You say **king**. [King.] Yes, now let's all slow speak that word, and hold on to that end sound. [Ki...ng.] It's more like a singing sound, isn't it?*

That is exactly what Nick and Golden Girl are doing: making a funny singing sound. Why? Well, we all know that Nick can be very naughty. But Golden Girl also knows that he is really a nice boy at heart, so she is very pleased to be with him every time they meet in a word. Nick is very pleased, too. They think that liking each other is their little secret. But we can tell they like each other, can't we, by the happy little singing sound they make whenever they are together in words.

Next, choose seven children to build, in turn, the words **sing**, **song**, **sting**, **string** and **strong**. These last words will prepare the way for practising the triple consonant blends later on (see page 156).

Slow speak dictation

Dictate the **Live spelling** words (see page 135). You may like to add **sang**, **singing** and **stinging**, too, or choose other words from the **-ng** box (see page 135). The highest priority **-ing** words for children to be able to read and spell are **thing** and **bring**. For help with **th**, see page 140.

Consolidation

Copymasters

Programme One Copymasters 8 and 10 provide practice in the **-ng** digraph.

Cassette

Sing or listen to the **Letterland Bells Song** on the *Programme One Songs Cassette.*

This song ensures that not only the **-ing** pattern, but also the **-ang**, **-ong** and **-ung** patterns become familiar. Recognising these three-letter strings makes many words accessible that might otherwise still be too difficult, e.g. **tangle**, **jungle**, **fingers** and **tingling**.

It is a good idea to make a series of four bells, each one with **-ing**, **-ang**, **-ong** and **-ung** on it in a different order. Point to them as the children sing out these syllables, to help them to achieve instant recognition of these letter patterns in words.

The song could also form part of an assembly presentation, with some children playing glockenspiels and triangles in time with the music on the cassette, while others sing.

CONSONANT DIGRAPHS
Nick and Kicking King

Objective

To teach the digraph **-nk** (as in the word **pink**).

What you need

☆ *Programme One Picture Code Cards*: **nk**, **th** and all the cards covered so far

☆ *Programme One Copymasters*: 9 and 10

Words containing -nk

bank*	ink
blank	junk
blanket	monkey*
blink	pink*
bunk	sink
conker	thank*
donkey	think*
drank*	trunk
drink*	

* High usage words

Introducing -nk

The story explanation for the **-nk** sound has two functions. The first is to focus children's minds on the new '...ngk' sound which occurs whenever these two letters are side by side. The cause is Naughty Nick, who likes to make a different sound behind the King's back, even though he knows that can be a bit of a nuisance. The second is to help weak spellers to avoid (or cure themselves of) typical errors like **thinck** and **thanck**. Only tell this story if and when this mistake crops up. The following **-nk** story helps children to understand that while **ck** might normally be the best choice, Naughty Nick causes the exception.

> *Clever Cat and Kicking King finish many short words together, but not when Naughty Nick is behind the King's back. Then, the naughty fellow, instead of saying 'nnn...' as usual, makes an 'ng' sound as though he was next to Golden Girl. Clever Cat is startled by his sudden change of tune, so when Nick is around, she runs away instead of staying to watch the King kick.*

Word building with the -nk digraph

Live spelling and slow speak dictation: bank → thank

Choose children to build the words **bank**, **bunk**, **ink**, **sink**, **think** and **thank** in live spelling and/or use any of these words for slow speak dictation. You could also bring in **pink**, **drink**, **drank**, **blank** and **blanket**.

Consolidation

Copymasters

Programme One Copymasters 9 and 10 provide practice in the **-nk** digraph.

CONSONANT DIGRAPHS
Sammy Snake and Hairy Hat Man

Objective

To teach the digraph **sh** (as in the word **shop**).

What you need

☆ *Programme One Picture Code Cards*: **sh** and all the cards covered so far

☆ *Programme One Copymasters*: 11-13

☆ *Programme One Songs Cassette*

Introducing sh

The little word **she** is a very high usage word. It follows, therefore, that your children will need to be able to read, write and spell **she** long before it matters whether they have fully learnt the sound values of little used letters like **x** and **z**, for example. Experienced Letterland teachers do not hesitate to introduce the story explanation for **sh** early on, because it builds on the child's knowledge of **s** and **h** as single letters.

The following story has proved so effective, that large numbers of pre-schoolers now enter school knowing it, simply because older brothers and sisters have told them! Share the **sh** story with individual children (especially those with **sh** in their names) or with the whole class as soon as the need arises, presenting it along the following lines:

Which sound do we know that Sammy Snake usually says in words? Yes, 'sss...'

And what do we know that Hairy Hat Man hates? Yes, noise! So when Sammy Snake comes slithering and sliding up behind Hairy Hat Man in a word, do you think the Hat Man is going to put up with all that noise? [No!] So what does he do? He turns back and says 'sh...!' to hush Sammy up.

Show both sides of the **sh** *Picture Code Card*.

So whenever you see Sammy and the Hat Man side by side in a word, don't expect Sammy's usual 'sss...' sound or the Hat Man's usual 'hhh...' sound. Expect one big 'sh...!' instead.

Words containing sh

British	fresh*	shell	should*
brush	rush	shellfish	show*
bush	selfish	ship*	shut
dash	shall*	shoe*	sunshine
dish*	she*	shoot*	wash*
English*	shed*	shop*	wish*
finish*	sheep*	short*	
fish*	shelf	shot*	

* High usage words

Practising the sh digraph

Play-acting the sh story

By play-acting this story, it becomes fully memorable. Divide the class into Sammy Snakes and Hairy Hat Men. Each makes their single sound until you give them a special signal telling them to pair up. Immediately the children should fill the room with 'sh' sounds as the Hat Men use the hushing gesture to act out the new sound.

Word hunt

The most frequently used words in the English language containing **sh** are **she**, **should**, **wish**, **fish** and **shop**. You may like to set the children on a word hunt, seeking out the **sh** pattern wherever they can find it. They can write down all the words and then compare lists to see which ones turn up the most. You could also, for example, ask them to discover how many times the word **finish** turns up in *Programme One Workbook 1* (eight times: once with a capital **F**).

Word building with the sh digraph

Live spelling: dash, dish, fish and finish

Hand out the *Picture Code Cards* for **d**, **a**, **sh**, **i**, **f**, **n** and a second **i** card (use the plain side of the lower case Mr I). Give the **sh** card to two children to hold (and mime). Slow speak the word **dash**, getting the children to listen carefully and decide who is needed to form the word. Let them discover next which words they can make by replacing **a** with **i** (**dish**), **d** with **f** (**fish**) and finally by adding Naughty Nick and the second **i** to build the word **finish**. Children who know all their short vowel sounds and consonants could, in fact, build most of the words in the **sh** word list (see page 138).

Consolidation

Copymasters

Programme One Copymasters 11-13 provide practice in the **sh** digraph.

Cassette

Sing or listen to the **'Sh' Song** on the *Programme One Songs Cassette*. This song also works well as an assembly item, with some children miming as the others sing.

CONSONANT DIGRAPHS
Ticking Tess and Hairy Hat Man

Objective

To teach the two sounds of the digraph **th** (as in the words **this** and **thunder**).

What you need

☆ *Programme One Picture Code Cards*: **th** (both cards) and all the cards covered so far

☆ *Programme One Copymasters*: 14-17 and 20

☆ *Programme One Songs Cassette*

Words containing the voiced th (as in this)

although*	the*
another*	their*
brother*	them*
clothes*	then*
either*	there*
father*	these*
grandfather*	they*
grandmother*	this*
mother*	those*
other*	together*
rather*	weather*
than*	with*
that*	without*

*High usage words

Introducing th (both sounds)

The words **the**, **this**, **that**, **they**, **them**, **these**, **those**, **than** and **then** are extremely high usage words. Ideally, because they occur so often, inexperienced readers will acquire them as sight vocabulary through sheer repetition. However, to gain early proficiency in spelling them, children need to know what to write for the voiced **th** sound, as in the words **this** and **the**. They will also need to know what to write for the second sound of **th**, its whispered sound, as in the words **thunder**, **thick** and **thin**.

The following story covers both sounds.

Ticking Tess spends most of her time in Letterland sending messages in tiny little ticks like th is: 't..., t..., t...'. But have you ever noticed that Tess and Hairy Hat Man make a completely different sound whenever they meet each other in a word? Ticking Tess blames it on the weather. It is true, there is a lot of wind and rain in Letterland, and thunder storms as well!

By herself, Ticking Tess is afraid of the thunder, even though she knows it's only noise, and noise cannot hurt you. So Hairy Hat Man hurries to her side to make her feel safe whenever there is thunder in the air. Of course, he isn't afraid of the thunder, but do you think he likes it?

Elicit 'No!'

Whenever Ticking Tess and the Hat Man are together, Tess feels safe, but they both hate the thunder so much, that they stick out their tongues as they say, 'There's the thunder!'

This last phrase contains both sounds of **th**, voiced and unvoiced. Get everyone to say the first two words '**There's the**...' out loud, then to whisper the word '**thunder**'. Ask the children to place their tongues behind their upper front teeth, blowing at the same time and to pay special attention to this movement while they say these three key **th** words again. Help them to realise that the **th** sound appears in some words voiced (as in '**There's the**...') and in others as a whispered sound (as in '**thunder**').

Look out for children who pronounce **thunder** as 'funder', **thirsty** as 'firsty' or count 'one, two, free'. Children with English as a second language will often say 'dere' and 'dey' for **there** and **they**. Help such children as follows:

When Tess and the Hat Man put their thumbs to their mouths and say 'There's the thunder', their tongues wet their thumbs three times. You try wetting your thumb three times as you say 'There's the thunder'. If you don't stick out your tongue at least a little bit, watch out, you may be sounding like Dippy Duck or Fireman Fred, instead of Tess and the Hat Man!

Some useful phrases for practising the **th** sounds are: '**Th**ink of a **th**ing, **th**ink of **th**ree **th**ings, **th**ink of **th**ree **th**ousand **th**ings. **Th**anks for **the th**ought. Have you **th**ought it **th**rough? **Th**oroughly **th**ought **th**rough.'

To strengthen the difference between the 'fff...' and 'th...' sounds, you can say:

> When **F**ireman **F**red puts his **f**ingers to his **f**ace and says '**F**ireman **F**red', he can **f**eel his breath on his **f**ingers twice. You try saying '**F**ireman **F**red' with your **f**ingers to your **f**ace. Can you **f**eel your breath **f**lowing out twice as you say his name?

Practising the th digraph (both sounds)

Tess and the Hat Man in names

Children's names often have whispered **th**'s in them (e.g. Elizabe**th**, Ma**tth**ew and Ca**th**erine), but sometimes there is only a nice white cloud over Tess (e.g. **Th**omas and **Th**eresa)!

Word building with the th digraph (both sounds)

Live spelling: them, then, this, that, they and think, thing, thunder → tenth

Select four children to build the word **them**, with two children holding the **th** (**this**) *Picture Code Card*. When **them** has been built, everyone can read the word out loud. Next, ask who must take Munching Mike's place to spell **then**, and then build **this** and **that**. You could also introduce or revise Mr Mean-E, challenging the children not to be tricked just because he looks like an **e**, but says 'a' in the word **they**.

Next slow speak the words **think**, **thing**, **thunder** and **tenth** in a whisper to emphasise the unvoiced version of **th** in these words. After building the first three words (using the **th** (**thunder**) *Picture Code Card*), develop the words **sixth**, **seventh**, **ninth** and **tenth**.

Consolidation

Copymasters

Programme One Copymasters 14, 17 and 20 provide practice in the first **th** digraph (as in **this**) and *Copymaster* 15-17 and 20 in the second **th** digraph (as in **thunder**).

Cassette

Sing or listen to the **Thunder Song** on the *Programme One Songs Cassette*. You may like to include it (complete with a thunder cloud) as part of an assembly presentation on digraphs with **h**.

Words containing the whispered th (as in thunder)

anything*	tenth*
bath*	thank*
birthday*	thin*
both*	thing*
cloth*	think*
earth*	third*
everything*	thirsty
fifth*	thirteen*
fourth*	thirty*
month*	thought*
mouth*	thousand*
ninth*	three*
north*	through*
nothing*	throw*
sixth*	thunder
something*	Thursday*
south*	tooth*

*High usage words

CONSONANT DIGRAPHS
Wicked Water Witch and Hairy Hat Man

Objective

To teach the two sounds of the the digraph **wh** (as in the words **when** and **who**).

What you need

☆ *Programme One Picture Code Cards*: **wh** (both cards), **ch** and all the cards covered so far

☆ *Programme One Copymasters*: 18-20

☆ *Programme One Songs Cassette*

☆ *Programme One Flashcards*: 70

Words containing wh (as in when)

somewhere*	which*
whack	while*
whale	whip
what*	whiskers
wheat*	whisper
wheel	whistle
when*	white*
where*	why*

* High usage words

Introducing wh (as in when)

Proof that the Witch is a trouble maker is evident in a number of words. Moreover, six of them are among the 100 most used words in the English language: **when**, **what**, **where**, **which** and **why** (the first sound of **wh**) and **who** (the second sound).

Begin with the most common sound of **wh** by writing **when** very large on the board, using the side of a piece of chalk to achieve thick letters. Picture code just the **w** (with different coloured chalk if possible).

> *When the Wicked Water Witch goes into a word, she needs to be able to see ahead in the Reading Direction, just as everyone else does in Letterland. So just imagine how she feels **wh**en she finds a tall letter right next to her. Who is he?*

Elicit 'Hairy Hat Man', and draw on his head and feet.

> *On top of that, he's wearing a hat!*

Add his hat.

> *That makes it even harder for her to see ahead in the Reading Direction! So what does she do? She takes her broomstick and **wh**acks the Hat Man's hat off!*

Rub out the witch's broomstick and the Hat Man's hat and draw in the action.

> *The poor Hairy Hat Man is so startled that he cannot speak. That is **wh**y **wh**en you want to read this word, you will get it wrong if you try to sound it out like this: 'www-hhhen'. Instead, you have to remember that the Hairy Hat Man makes no sound at all in this word. And whose fault is that?*

Elicit 'The Wicked Water Witch'.

Warn the children that not only does the Witch whack the Hat Man's off in the word **when** (and several others too) to show the Hat Man how much she hates him being in her way. She also likes making reading and spelling difficult for anyone who is just learning how. She thinks that if she upsets the Hat Man so he can't say 'hhh...', she might make it harder for people to spell this word.

> *Wicked Water Witch also thinks that because you can't hear the Hat Man making his usual **wh**ispery 'hhh...' sound in the word **when**, you might forget to write his letter down **wh**en you go to spell it. Then she would be glad!*

*So are you going to let the Wicked Witch trick you in the word **when**?*

Elicit 'No!'

Well, we will hope not. But don't be too surprised if she does catch you out sometimes, at first, until you get used to her wicked ways.

Word building with the wh digraph (as in when)

Slow speak dictation

Bring **when** into the growing number of words in your sentence work. It will make combinations like the following possible:

Wicked Water Witch is wicked in **when**.
I can clap **when** I am sitting.
I can yell **when** I am kicking.

	sad	
When I am	glad	I like to . . .
	hot	

		lick ice cream.
I am glad **when** I can	yell.
		give Hairy Hat Man his hat.

Action sentences

Hand out the reverse side of *Flashcard* 70 to various pairs or groups of children, and ask them to read the card in silence and then to respond to it.

Introducing wh (as in who)

Choose your own timing to explain why it is that, although **h** is *usually* silent in the **wh** spelling pattern, occasionally **w** is silent instead. The best time may be when the word **who**, **whose**, **whom** or **whole** is needed in spelling. What follows is simply an extension of the first **wh** story:

*The Wicked Water Witch whacks off poor old Hairy Hat Man's hat as often as she can. We know that when that happens, the Hat Man is too startled to speak. You will find her whacking off his hat most often in the five question words **when, which, why, what** and **where**. But there is a sixth question word. When they meet in the word, **who**, the Hat Man has had enough. So he howls at her: 'Who do you think you are?', grabs her broomstick and hits her hat off instead. Now the Witch is too startled to speak.*

Who do you think you are?

Words containing wh (as in who)	
who*	whom
whole*	whose

* High usage words

Ask the children to keep an eye out for the three other words where the Hat Man turns the tables on the witch (see the word box on page 143). They are the only other common words with a silent **w** beside **h**.

Practising the wh digraph (both sounds)

Play-acting the wh story

If your Costume box includes a hairy hat, a witch's hat and a toy broomstick made with straw or soft foam strips for bristles, the children will enjoy acting out this story. Begin with two children only, holding separate **w** and **h** *Picture Code Cards*. Write just the question words with silent **h** on one list on the board (**what**, **when**, **where**, **which** and **why**) and the four silent **w** words (**who**, **whole**, **whom** and **whose**) on another. Ask the **w** and **h** children to act out what is happening in whichever word you call out. The other children can check if they are right by listening to their own pronunciation as they repeat the called out word.

Word building with the wh digraph (both sounds)

Live spelling: when, whack and whole

At this stage, the children will find it easier to build words from the first group of **wh** words (i.e. as in **when**), since the second group generally results in the **o** becoming an irregular sound (as in **who** and **whose**). However, once they have learnt the Silent Magic **e** concept (see page 161), they should easily be able to build the word **whole**.

In the meantime, let four children build the word **when**, with two children holding the **wh** *Picture Code Card*. They can then go on to build the more difficult word **whack**, remembering to use the **ck** card at the end.

Consolidation

Copymasters

Programme One Copymasters 18 and 20 provide practice in the first **wh** digraph (as in **when**) and *Copymasters* 19 and 20 in the second **wh** digraph (as in **who**).

Cassette

Sing or listen to the **'Wh' Song** on the *Programme One Songs Cassette.*

CONSONANT DIGRAPHS
Clever Cat and Hairy Hat Man

Objective

To teach the two sounds of the digraph **ch** (as in the words **cheese** and **school**).

What you need

☆ *Programme One Picture Code Cards*: **ch**, Clever Cat (**c**), silent **h** and all the cards covered so far

☆ *Programme One Copymasters*: 21-22 and 72

☆ *Programme One Songs Cassette*

Introducing ch (as in cheese)

Normally a child has to hold back knowledge gained about **c** and **h** as single sounds if it is not to interfere with learning the new **ch** sound. By contrast, your Letterland teaching enables you to build on their first knowledge of 'who's who'. The characters remain the same. Only the story moves on to explain new behaviour whenever they meet each other in a word.

Clever Cat belongs to Hairy Hat Man. He looks after her well and she loves him. But she has one problem. As soon as she finds herself next to him in a word, his hairy hat makes her nose tickle. So whenever they come together in a word, all you can hear is her sneeze, 'ch...'.

Explain that cats, like people, find it very difficult to keep their eyes open when they sneeze. So to picture code **ch**, the children will need to draw Clever Cat with her eyes closed and her paw politely raised to cover her sneeze. (To make any child prone to allergies feel in good company, you can extend the story. Hairy Hat Man also sneezes because he is allergic to Clever Cat's fur!)

Explain the new picture coding (Clever Cat's eyes closed and paw to nose) along these lines:

Have you ever noticed how difficult it is to keep your eyes open when you sneeze? Well, Clever Cat can't keep her eyes open at all when she sneezes! So when you draw the picture coding for her sneeze sound in words, make sure you draw her with eyes closed, and show her paw politely raised to cover her sneeze.

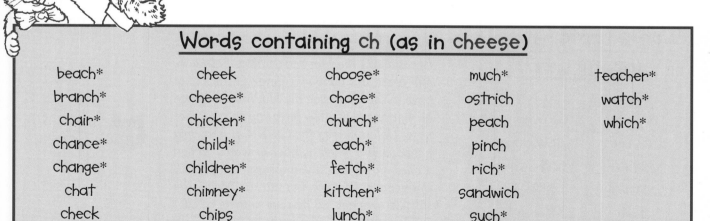

Words containing ch (as in cheese)

beach*	cheek	choose*	much*	teacher*
branch*	cheese*	chose*	ostrich	watch*
chair*	chicken*	church*	peach	which*
chance*	child*	each*	pinch	
change*	children*	fetch*	rich*	
chat	chimney*	kitchen*	sandwich	
check	chips	lunch*	such*	

* High usage words

Practising the ch digraph (as in cheese)

Play-acting the ch story (as in cheese)

You may like to divide the class into Clever Cats and Hairy Hat Men in the school hall or gym. The Clever Cats all make 'c..., c..., c...' sounds and the Hat Men make their sighing 'hhh...' sounds as they move about waiting for a signal from you. Then they form pairs, filling the room with sneezing sounds. Avoid 'aichoo' sounds. Remind the children that Clever Cat is very polite, so she keeps her sneezes as quiet as possible. In fact, she whispers them!

Word building with the ch digraph (as in cheese)

Live spelling: chat, chips, such/much/lunch and which

Let two children hold the **ch** *Picture Code Card*, with the **h** child wearing a hairy hat, if available. They can act out Clever Cat's sneeze and Hairy Hat Man's worried look as you direct them in forming and sounding out the words **chat**, **chips**, **such**, **much** and **lunch**. Do the same with the word **which**, as five children stand with the three cards for **wh** (as in **when**), **i** (Impy Ink) and **ch**, with two children acting out their roles at each end!

The less regular words in the first **ch** word box need to be studied, written down and then dictated to help teach their spelling. This also applies to the second word box, where you will want to give priority to the starred words.

Introducing ch (as in school)

If someone asked you to think of another way to spell the 'k...' sound, you would not immediately think of **ch**. Yet **school** and **chemist** are common enough words. Letterland logic accounts for this irregular sound of **ch** with an extension of the original **ch** story. Reserve it until it is relevant to reading or to learning to spell a particular word.

Occasionally the Hat Man's hairy hat blows off. When this happens, Clever Cat does not have to sneeze beside the Hat Man, because his hat has blown too far away to tickle her nose. Unfortunately for Clever Cat, this only happens in a small number of words. When it does, Clever Cat is very pleased to go back to saying 'c...' for cat. But the Hat Man is too startled to speak, so he says nothing at all.

Since this second **ch** sound is really just 'Clever Cat's' sound ('c...') followed by a silent **h**, you can use your Clever Cat *Picture Code Card* and your silent **h** card to build any of the words listed on the left.

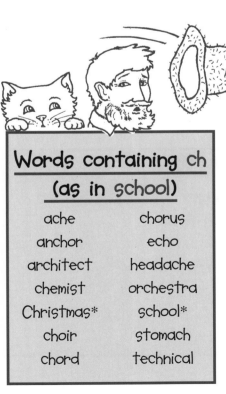

Words containing ch (as in school)

ache	chorus
anchor	echo
architect	headache
chemist	orchestra
Christmas*	school*
choir	stomach
chord	technical

* High usage words

Practising the ch digraph (as in school)

Play-acting the ch story (as in school)

Begin by reinforcing the usual sound for **ch** by letting two
children mime Clever Cat sneezing frequently beside the Hairy
Hat Man. Ask a third child to be the wind, rushing in from the
left, snatching off the Hat Man's hat (a pretend or real hat).
Immediately, Clever Cat stops sneezing and smiles happily, while
the Hat Man reaches out in the Reading Direction, looking too
startled to speak.

Consolidation

Copymasters

Programme One Copymasters 21-22 provide practice in the first **ch**
digraph (as in **cheese**) and *Copymaster* 72 in the second **ch** digraph
(as in **school**).

Cassette

Sing or listen to the **Clever Cat and the Hat Man Song** on the
Programme One Songs Cassette. Take care that no-one sings 'chuh' in
their enthusiasm. Like the **sh** song (see page 139), the **ch** song can
happily form part of an assembly event with the whole school joining
in at the end. To mime the song, the **c** child should approach the **h**
child from the left, moving in the Reading Direction. They can both
use the single letter cards, letting their actions illustrate first their
single letter sounds and then their joint sound as everybody sneezes!

CONSONANT DIGRAPHS
Ticking Tess finds Clever Cat's sneezes catching

Objective

To teach the trigraph -tch (as in the word **match**).

What you need

☆ *Programme One Picture Code Cards*: silent **t**, **ch**

☆ *Programme One Copymasters*: 24

Words containing -tch

batch	patch
catch*	pitch*
clutch	satchel
crutch	scratch*
ditch	sketch
Dutch	snatch
fetch*	stitches
hatch	stretch
hitch	switch
hutch	twitch
itch	watch*
kitchen*	witch
match*	wretched
notch	

Introducing -tch

The -**tch** sequence does not signal a new sound, because **t** has become a silent letter. Here is the Letterland explanation for this change in **t**'s behaviour.

*In some words you will see Ticking Tess wa**tch**ing Clever Cat sneeze beside Hairy Hat Man. Ticking Tess feels sorry for Clever Cat. Like the Hat Man, she does not know why Clever Cat sneezes, so she just stands there wishing she could help and wondering if Clever Cat's sneezes are ca**tch**ing. That is why when you see these three letters together, you only hear one big sneeze!*

Most *one-*syllable words with only one short-sounding vowel just before the 'ch' sound are, in fact, spelt with -**tch**. Exceptions to this -**tch** pattern are **much**, **which**, **such** and **rich**.

Practising the -tch trigraph

Live spelling or slow speak dictation

Use the high usage (starred) words on the list, saying them slowly. Help the children to notice that even though we cannot hear Tess, they need her, worrying away in these words. This provides a nice opportunity for a bit of miming. Point out how in **watch** Annie Apple is behaving differently, too. (Typically the Witch upsets her whenever she is next to Annie Apple, which is also easy to mime!)

Sentence-building

Write all the -**tch** words from the box on the left on the board and allow time for the children to put together quick stories using as many -**tch** words as possible.

Next let the children take turns to read their stories out loud. They will be learning to spell the -**tch** words as they use them, and will be clustering them in their minds as words of a kind.

Consolidation

Copymasters

Programme One Copymaster 24 provides practice in the -**tch** trigraph.

* High usage words

CONSONANT BLENDS
Introducing the blends

If a child has been taught the consonant sounds correctly, none of the consonant blends should cause difficulties in reading, and only a few should cause difficulties in spelling. Correct pronunciation means:

- never saying any of the nine unvoiced consonants (**c**, **f**, **h**, **k**, **p**, **q**, **s**, **t** and **x**) above a whisper.

- keeping an unwanted 'uh' sound to a minimum in pronouncing the 'b...', 'd...', 'g...', 'j...' and 'yyy...' sounds. This is best achieved by keeping the mouth almost closed and stopping quickly, immediately after making the sound.

- prolonging the following sounds: 'lll...', 'mmm...', 'nnn...', 'rrr...', 'vvv...', 'www...' and 'zzz...'. Again, keeping the mouth almost closed (completely closed for **m**) is a valuable tip, because as soon as the jaw opens wider, it causes an 'uh' sound which distorts the pure sound that the child should be saying. The 'uh', in turn, will distort any whole word a child tries to sound out, e.g. 'suh, luh, i, puh' becomes impossible to recognise as 'slip'. The same child, by whispering 'sss...', prolonging 'lll...', sounding out 'i..' but whispering 'p...' ('ssslllip') need never be stuck trying to read this word.

Therefore correct pronunciation of the single letter sounds is the secret to success with consonant blends in reading. It is also the secret to success in spelling these blends.

Teachers who have made good use of the 'slow speak' strategy, as described on page 19 of this guide, will have already given their classes a strong foundation for reading consonant blends. Further focus on them will then mainly be to expand spelling skills. For children entering the school with little skill in this area, you may like to start with any of the following: **fl**, **sl**, **fr**, **sm**, **sn** or **sw**, because in each case, both consonants are easy to prolong. Any uncertain child can see and hear from them how blending sounds works.

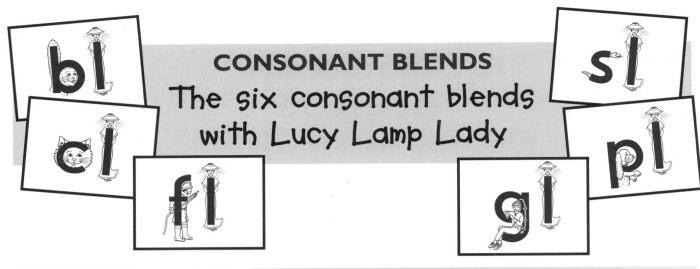

CONSONANT BLENDS
The six consonant blends with Lucy Lamp Lady

Objective

To teach the consonant blends **bl**, **cl**, **fl**, **gl**, **pl** and **sl** (as in the words **blue**, **clock**, **flat**, **glad**, **please** and **slip**).

What you need

☆ *Programme One Picture Code Cards*: Lucy Lamp Lady (**l**), Bouncy Ben (**b**), Clever Cat (**c**), Fireman Fred (**f**), Golden Girl (**g**), Poor Peter (**p**), Sammy Snake (**s**) and all the cards covered so far

☆ *Programme One Copymasters*: 25-28

☆ *Programme One Songs Cassette*

Introducing the blends with Lucy Lamp Lady

The first sound in any of these consonant-plus-**l** blends needs to be spoken quickly and without a pause, i.e. not 'puhluh', but a whispered 'p...' before 'lll...': 'plll...'. It is important to keep the tongue in contact with the roof of the mouth for the 'lll...' sound, and then to add the vowel sound without a pause, e.g. 'plllannn, **plan**'. Do the same with **bl**, **cl**, **fl**, **gl** and **sl**, e.g. 'blllock, **block**', 'clllip, **clip**', 'ffflllag, **flag**', 'ssslllide, **slide**', etc. Care in pronouncing these blends, and others to come, will bring confidence in spelling them.

Since there is no change in any of the consonants' sounds, there are no story explanations to accompany any of the consonant blends on the following pages.

Words beginning with bl, cl, fl, gl, pl and sl

bl	cl	fl	gl	pl	sl
black*	class*	flag*	glad*	place*	sleep*
blanket	clean*	flame	glass*	plan*	sleepy
blind	clear*	flash	glasses*	plant*	slide*
blister	climb*	flat*	glitter	plastic	slip
block*	clock*	flies*	gloomy	plate	slippers
blood*	close*	float	glove*	play*	slow*
bloom	clothes*	flood*	glue	playground	slowly*
blossom	clothing*	floor*		please*	
blow*	club*	flower*		plenty*	
blue*		fly*			

* High usage words

Practising the blends with Lucy Lamp Lady

Blends in stories

A good way to involve the children in reading and writing consonant blend words is for them to see how many they can link to the Letterlanders, e.g. 'Bouncy Ben and Lucy Lamp Lady get lost in a **bl**inding **bl**izzard and her light keeps on **bl**inking on and off. Ben is wrapped in a **bl**ue **bl**anket, but it **bl**ows off,' etc. As a group language activity, this is both popular and an excellent way to fully alert the children to the sound of each recurring blend in their own speech. That alertness will produce confidence in spelling. The word box on page 150 should provide you with some ideas for possible combinations.

Learning less regular words

Not all parts of words yield to sounding out, especially before the children have mastered the digraphs and spelling strategies in Programme Two. In the meantime, you may like to select from the starred, less regular words in the box on page 150. Write them on the board, and then read the words out together. The children can then copy the list and work in pairs to test each other in reading and (if appropriate) in spelling them.

Word building with the blends with Lucy Lamp Lady

Live spelling or slow speak dictation

Choose any of the following words to build in live spelling or to dictate: **plan**, **black**, **flat**, **clock**, **slip**, **cloth**, **block**, **flag**, **glad**, **plastic**, **flash** and **blanket**. Alternatively, give out these 12 words to 12 children to slow speak to the rest of the class for you. This will ensure practice in slow speaking words well themselves.

Consolidation

Copymasters

Programme One Copymasters 25-28 provide practice in the blends with Lucy Lamp Lady.

Cassette

Select the relevant song from the *Programme One Songs Cassette*: Bouncy Ben and Lamp Lady, Clever Cat and Lamp Lady, Fireman Fred and Lamp Lady, Golden Girl and Lamp Lady, Poor Peter and Lamp Lady, and Sammy Snake and Lamp Lady. The children can listen to it, picking out and writing down the blend words, or simply enjoy learning to sing the song.

CONSONANT BLENDS
The seven consonant blends with Robber Red

Objective

To teach the consonant blends **br**, **cr**, **dr**, **fr**, **gr**, **pr** and **tr** (as in the words **bread**, **cross**, **drum**, **frog**, **green**, **present** and **trip**).

What you need

☆ *Programme One Picture Code Cards*: Robber Red (**r**), Bouncy Ben (**b**), Clever Cat (**c**), Dippy Duck (**d**), Fireman Fred (**f**), Golden Girl (**g**), Poor Peter (**p**) and Ticking Tess (**t**)

☆ *Programme One Copymasters*: 29-32

☆ *Programme One Songs Cassette*

Introducing the blends with Robber Red

Just as in the consonant blends with **l**, the first sound needs to be spoken quickly, with no pause before rolling (prolonging) Robber Red's growling 'rrr...' sound. So avoid 'buhruh', 'cuhruh', etc. in favour of 'brrr...', 'crrr...', and so on.

Practising the blends with Robber Red

Blends in sentences

Draw children's attention to these blend sounds in their own speech, by helping them to combine and link words from the word box to the characters. They might think of sentences like, for example, **br**: 'Bouncy Ben and Robber Red both dropped **br**own **br**ushes off the **br**idge,' **cr**: 'Clever Cat is **cr**oss with Robber Red, because he made her **cr**y,' etc.

Consolidation

Copymasters

Programme One Copymasters 29-32 provide practice in the blends with Robber Red.

Cassette

Select the relevant song from the *Programme One Songs Cassette*: Bouncy Ben and Robber Red, Clever Cat and Robber Red, Dippy Duck and Robber Red, Fireman Fred and Robber Red, Golden Girl and Robber Red, Poor Peter and Robber Red, and Ticking Tom and Robber Red.

Words beginning with br, cr, dr, fr, gr, pr and tr

br	cr	dr	fr	gr	pr	tr
bread*	crash	draw*	friend*	grandma*	prince*	train*
bridge*	cross*	dress*	frog*	grass*	princess*	tree*
bring*	crowd	drink*	from*	green*	present*	trip*
brother*	cry	dry*	front*	grow*	pretty*	try*

* High usage words

CONSONANT BLENDS
The whispered blends with Sammy Snake

Objective

To teach the whispered blends **sc**, **sk**, **sp** and **st** (as in the words **scooter**, **skid**, **spell** and **stop**).

What you need

☆ *Programme One Picture Code Cards*: Sammy Snake (**s**), Clever Cat (**c**), Kicking King (**k**), Poor Peter (**p**) and Ticking Tess (**t**)

☆ *Programme One Copymasters*: 33-36

☆ *Programme One Songs Cassette*

Introducing the whispered blends with Sammy Snake

The key to pronouncing these blends correctly is to whisper them through an almost closed mouth. Avoid dropping the jaw open between sounds, as that creates a pause which breaks the flow, causing 'sssuhc...' instead of 'sssc...'. One problem is that both **sc** and **sk** sound identical, making it difficult for a child to know when to use each one in spelling. Fortunately, however, there are not many common words in either group. Once the children can correctly spell **skip**, **ski**, **skate**, **skid**, **skin**, **skirt** and **sky**, they can fairly safely assume that **sc** will be right for the start of a word. At the *end* of a word, however, they should choose **-sk**, because they know that the end is Kicking King's favourite spot for kicking.

Practising the whispered blends with Sammy Snake

Words with sp and sk

The **sp** blend is fun to learn if you let the children make up sentences containing as many **sp** words as possible. To begin with, write all the words from the **sp** list in the box below on the board. Each child should then try to combine them into meaningful sentences. They can then read out their sentences and compare their results.

Words containing sc, sk and sp

sc	sk	sk	sp
scared*	ask*	ski	especially*
school* **	basket*	skid	spell*
scooter	desk*	skin*	spelling*
score	disk	skip*	spend
scout	dusk	skipping*	spent*
	mask	skirt	spider
	risk	sky*	spin
	skate	whiskers	spoon*
	skeleton		spot

* High usage words ** See page 146

Words containing st

st–		–st–		–st		
stairs*	still*	downstairs*		against*	east*	lost*
stand*	stone*	dusty		almost*	fast*	most*
standing*	stood*	Easter*		artist	feast*	must*
star*	stop*	frosty		beast*	first*	nest*
start*	stopping*	instead*		best*	forest*	oldest*
starting*	store*	interested*		breakfast*	ghost*	past*
station*	story*	interesting*		coast*	highest*	rest
stay*	stove*	misty		cost*	largest*	trust
stick*		sister*		dentist*	last*	west*
		tasty		dust*	list	youngest
		thirsty				
		yesterday				

* High usage words

You could then do the same with the **sk** list. When the children have read out their results, you can give them the good news that from now on, almost any word that starts with this sound will be spelt with **sc**, because they have now learnt all the useful ones beginning with **sk**!

Consolidation

Copymasters

Programme One Copymasters 33-36 provide practice in the whispered blends with Sammy Snake.

Cassette

Select the relevant song from the *Programme One Songs Cassette*: Sammy Snake and Clever Cat, Sammy Snake and Kicking King, Sammy Snake and Poor Peter, and Sammy Snake and Ticking Tom. The children can listen to it, picking out and writing down the blend words, or simply enjoy learning to sing the song.

CONSONANT BLENDS
More blends with Sammy Snake

Objective

To teach the blends **sm**, **sn** and **sw** (as in the words **small**, **snack** and **sweet**).

What you need

★ *Programme One Picture Code Cards*: Sammy Snake (**s**), Munching Mike (**m**), Naughty Nick (**n**) and Wicked Water Witch (**w**)

★ *Programme One Copymasters*: 37-39

★ *Programme One Songs Cassette*

Introducing more blends with Sammy Snake

The **sm**, **sn** and **sw** blends all join a whispered sound, 'sss...', to a voiced one. Again a closed jaw position is helpful so that without a pause, the whispered hiss blends into the voiced sound of **m**, **n** or **w**.

Teach the children to say 'sssmmmelll', 'sssnnnifff' and 'ssswwwimmm', for example, so they can see how slowing down their speech can help their spelling. Their skill in blending these sounds will help them both to read and spell unfamiliar words.

Consolidation

Copymasters

Programme One Copymasters 37-39 provide practice in these other blends with Sammy Snake.

Cassette

Select the relevant song from the *Programme One Songs Cassette*: Sammy Snake and Munching Mike, Sammy Snake and Naughty Nick, and Sammy Snake and Wicked Water Witch. The children can listen to it, picking out and writing down the blend words, or simply enjoy learning to sing the song.

Words beginning with sm, sn and sw

sm	sn	sw
small*	snack	swan
smallest*	snail	sweep
smart	snake	sweet*
smell	snap	swell
smile	snatch	swift
smoke*	sneeze	swim*
smooth	sniff	swimming*
smash	ship	swing
	snow*	
	snowball	(but sword)
	snowing*	

* High usage words

CONSONANT BLENDS
The triple consonant blends

Objective

To teach the triple consonant blends **scr**, **spl**, **spr** and **str** (as in the words **scratch**, **splash**, **spring** and **string**).

What you need

☆ *Programme One Picture Code Cards*: Sammy Snake (**s**), Clever Cat (**c**), Robber Red (**r**), Poor Peter (**p**), Lucy Lamp Lady (**l**) and Ticking Tess (**t**)

☆ *Programme One Copymasters*: 40-42

☆ *Programme One Songs Cassette*

Introducing the triple consonant blends

These four triple consonant blends have in common the fact that they all start with two whispered sounds, leading on to a voiced sound: either **r** or **l**. Children seldom have a problem with the initial hiss, nor with blending it into the second whispered consonant in reading, so long as they have learned **p**, **c** and **t** as *whispered* sounds.

This tiny second sound ('p...', 'c...' or 't...') can, however, be easily overlooked and consequently left out in spelling unless the children have become fully alerted to the lip, tongue and teeth movements that they make as they start to pronounce words like **scratch**, **splash**, **spring** and **street**. Fortunately, there are not many triple consonant blend words among the high usage band of approximately 3,000 words. Give the starred words in the box priority in any live spelling and dictation.

Consolidation

Copymasters

Programme One Copymasters 40-42 provide practice in the triple consonant blends.

Cassette

Select the relevant song from the *Programme One Songs Cassette*: Sammy, Poor Peter and Lamp Lady, and Sammy, Tom and Robber Red. The children can listen to it, picking out and writing down the blend words, or simply enjoy learning to sing the song.

Words beginning with scr, spl, spr and str

scr	spl	spr	str	str
scramble	splash	sprain	straight*	strike
scrapbook	splendid	spray	strange*	string*
scrape	splinter	spread	straw*	strip
scratch	split	spring*	stream*	stroke
scream	splutter	sprinkle	street*	strong*
screen		sprint	strength*	struggle
screw		sprout	stretch	
scribble			strict	

* High usage words

CONSONANT BLENDS
Ticking Tess and Wicked Water Witch

Objective

To teach the blend **tw** (as in the word **twig**).

What you need

☆ *Programme One Picture Code Cards*: Ticking Tess (**t**) and Wicked Water Witch (**w**) and all the cards covered so far

☆ *Programme One Copymasters*: 43

☆ *Programme One Songs Cassette*

Preparation

☆ Write a large number 2 on a piece of card, using a thick black felt-tip pen.

Words beginning with tw

twelve*
twenty*
twice*
twig
twist
twinkle
twilight
twin
twitter

* High usage words

Introducing the tw blend

The most useful words containing the **tw** blend are numbers. There are not many others. You can explain them along these lines:

> *Ticking Tess is never comfortable being next to Wicked Water Witch, because she knows the Witch is a trouble-maker. Luckily the Witch does not manage to make trouble in these number words: **twelve**, **twenty**, **twelfth** and **twice**, but look what she does in the number **two**! She makes her sound disappear to see if she can trick you into reading and spelling the number **two** wrong. But here is a special way to remember it. Just say to yourself 'The number **two** always has the Witch's **two** swimming pools right in the middle of it.'*

The next most frequent place to find Tess and the Witch side by side is inside the word **between**. See the box below for other words beginning with **tw**.

Word building with the tw blend

Live spelling: twelve, twelfth and two

Let the children build **twelve** and **twelfth** by listening to you slow speaking these words.

Next, let two children build the little word **to** (using the plain side of an **o** *Picture Code Card*). By including the following bit of miming in your live spelling, you can ensure that no child need make the typical spelling error of **tow** for **two** or use **to** when they mean **two**.

Appoint a child to mime being the Wicked Water Witch. She will need to tiptoe across the room with fingers covering her lips and go round behind the two children building **to**. She will then need to separate the **t** and **o** children and enter the word. Finally, she can say, 'Ah ha, look what I have done to make a difficult new word for you: the number two!' and hold up your prepared big number two.

Consolidation

Copymasters

Programme One Copymaster 43 provides practice in the **tw** blend.

Cassette

Sing or listen to the **Ticking Tom and Wicked Water Witch Song** on the *Programme One Songs Cassette*.

LONG VOWELS
'Kind' words and 'old' words

Objective

To teach children to expect long vowels in words ending in **-ind** and **-old** (as in the words **kind** and **old**).

What you need

☆ *Programme One Picture Code Cards*: Mr I (lower case **i**), Naughty Nick (**n**), Dippy Duck (**d**), Mr O (**o**), Lucy Lamp Lady (**l**) and all the cards covered so far

☆ *Programme One Copymasters*: 44-46

Introducing -ind and -old

The **-ind** and **-old** spelling patterns occur fairly regularly in English, not because there are many words in either pattern, but because there are two or three among them that are often needed. In Letterland these are called 'kind' words and 'old' words.

*Mr I has a habit of saying his name in 'kind' words, because he is such a **kind** man. And Mr O has a habit of saying his name in 'old' words, because he is such an **old** man.*

Word building with 'kind' and 'old' words

Live spelling: kind, mind, remind, old and cold

Distribute the appropriate *Picture Code Cards* and also the five short vowel cards and let the children consider whether they need Vowel Men or not as you say **kind**, **mind** and **remind**, and then **old** and **cold**.

Slow speak dictation

Ask one or more children to take turns dictating any of the words in the boxes below for the others to write down. This is a good way to check if they are learning to pronounce words slowly and carefully when they are working on their own.

Consolidation

Copymasters

Programme One Copymasters 44-46 provide practice in the 'kind' and 'old' words.

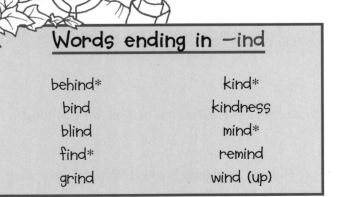

Words ending in –ind

behind*	kind*
bind	kindness
blind	mind*
find*	remind
grind	wind (up)

Words ending in –old

cold*	old*
fold	scold
gold*	sold
hold*	told*

* High usage words

LONG VOWELS
The Vowel Men
in other words

Objective

To teach children where to expect long vowels: in little high usage words (as in the words **he** and **she**) and on some signs (as in the word **danger**).

What you need

☆ *Programme One Picture Code Cards*: Mr A (ā), Mr E (ē), Mr I (lower and upper case ī), Mr O (ō) and Mr U (ū)

☆ *Programme One Songs Cassette*

Introducing the Vowel Men in other words

In sections on major teaching points to come (on the Magic **e**, and in Programme Two on Magic Endings, Vowels Out Walking (**ai**, **ea**, **ee**, etc.) and other vowel patterns) the emphasis will be on signals *built into words* which tell any uncertain reader when to expect the vowel to say its name. Before that stage, it is as well for the children to be fully familiar with the stick man picture coding and to have learnt to 'hear' the Vowel Man saying his name as they pronounce any already familiar long vowel words.

In this section the children will first be focusing on a few key words where there is *no* signal. They just need to learn that the Vowel Men have a habit of appearing and saying their names regularly in these particular words. By preparing the children to expect these appearances of long vowels in a few key common words, you are also encouraging a reading strategy of flexible response as they attempt any long vowel words not met so far. In other words, if pronouncing the vowel as short does not produce a meaningful word, they should try pronouncing it as long. Translated into Letterland terms, if the vowel sound does not make sense, try the Vowel Man saying his name!

Practising the Vowel Men in other words

The Vowel Men in little words

The box below provides many examples of short, common words, where the Vowel Men make an appearance.

The Vowel Men in little words

ā	ē	ī	ō	ū
a*	be*	I*	ago*	use
baby*	even	hi*	go	you*
	he*		most	
	me*		no*	
	she*		oh	
	the*		only	
	we*		open	
			over	
			so*	

* High usage words

The Vowel Men on signs

The children will inevitably come across Vowel Men saying their names on some signs. It is worth getting each child to make their own versions of the signs given below, drawing full pictures of the Vowel Men on them. They should be able to find other ideas for signs to make and picture code too.

Danger

Mr A says his name in **Danger**.

Beware

Mr E says his name in **Beware**.

Private

Mr I says his name in **Private**.

Notice

Mr O says his name in **Notice**.

Music Room

Mr U says his name in **Music Room**.

The children can also write out and picture code any little words that they already know. Remind them that the Vowel Men have a habit of saying their names at the end of very small words (see the box on page 159).

Consolidation

Cassette

Sing or listen to the **Vowel Men Song** on the *Programme One Songs Cassette*. This song works well as an assembly presentation with five children dressed as the five Vowel Men. The appropriate Vowel Man steps forward during his verse, reaches up with his right hand in greeting and shouts out the last line of the chorus alone.

THE SILENT MAGIC E

Objective

To teach the Silent Magic **e** concept (in words like **make** and **name**).

What you need

☆ *Programme One Picture Code Cards*: Magic **e**, Burnt-Out Magic **e**, Vase-Prop **e** and all the cards covered so far

☆ *Programme One Copymasters*: 47-62

☆ *Programme One Songs Cassette*

Preparation

☆ Prepare a wand made out of a rod with long yellow crepe paper strips attached to it.

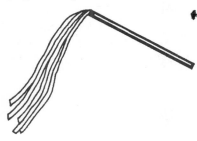

☆ Bring in an apron (if there isn't one already in the Costume box), a picture of a tap (or the real thing) and a tape measure.

Introducing the Silent Magic e

If you can teach children to predict the correct pronunciation of the vowels, you will have spared them much frustration in learning to read. Learning to spot final **e**'s is an important predictive strategy. Many children can parrot the rule that the Silent **e** makes the vowel before it say its name, but when they meet an unknown Silent **e** word, they fail to apply the principle. Use the Magic **e** story below to ensure that your children do apply it!

The Vowel Men work so hard behind the scenes, putting apples and oranges, elephants, ink bottles and umbrellas into words, that they seldom have the fun of appearing themselves in words. One day, Mr E decided that this would not do. He and his friends, the other Vowel Men, should have a chance to be in words more often. But how could he bring this about? He had to think up a new magic trick! Off he went to work on a very special new kind of e. When it was ready, he called Mr A, Mr I, Mr O and Mr U together, and with a flourish, he announced his new invention:

> *'Introducing the e you cannot hear,*
> *with power to make Vowel Men appear!'*

The brand new e was bright red and it had a top hat and a wand, just like Mr E himself.

Write the word **tap** twice on the board in very large letters. Fill both **a**'s with a red apple to picture code Annie Apple's sound. Read 'tap, tap' together. Ask a child to tiptoe up and very quietly write a big Silent Magic **e** with red chalk on the second version of **tap**. (Why quietly? Because Magic **e**'s are silent letters! They make no sound at all.)

Add a top hat and wand on to the child's red **e** and immediately draw a shower of magic sparks with yellow chalk, using several right to left strokes. Next, and with a flourish, wipe out Annie Apple's letter. Make Mr A appear by writing **a** again and adding a yellow stick man right through it (the magic trick!). Read and compare **tap** with the new word **tape**.

Ask another child to come up to the board. Guide him or her through the activity once again by talking along these lines:

> *Draw your top hat on the Silent Magic e, and Mr E's wand. And here's the yellow chalk for the sparks. Shoot them back from the tip of the wand up over exactly one letter so they land... Where? On Annie Apple! So make her disappear by rubbing her out. Who will take her place? Yes, Mr A himself appears and says his name!*

The child writes in a new **a** with a yellow stick man through it.

Notice that when you ask the children to draw the sparks firing back from the Magic **e**, you are asking their hands to do what their eyes and minds must do: take into account a word ending and use it to decide whether the preceding vowel will be short or long. Picture coding the 'event' helps to make this rather abstract concept more concrete and therefore manageable. (See also **The Magic e song** on page 165.)

When the children are confident about the Magic **e** concept in relation to **a**, use live spelling and slow speak dictation involving the other Vowel Men. The words listed in the boxes below are particularly useful examples, because they are all meaningful words with and without a Magic **e**.

Adding a Magic e to make a new word

at*	gap	mat	rat	tap
ate*	gape	mate	rate	tape
cap*	hat*	pan	Sam	van
cape	hate	pane	same	vane
fad	mad	plan	scrap	
fade	made*	plane	scrape	

bit*	quit	shin	spin	
bite	quite	shine	spine	trip
				tripe
fin	rid	slid	strip	
fine	ride	slide	stripe	
				win
kit	rip	slim	Tim	wine
kite	ripe	slime	time	

hop			cub	tub
hope			cube	tube
mop	rob		cut	us*
mope	robe		cute	use
not*			plum	human
note			plume	humane

* High usage words

162

Words containing the Silent Magic e

age	cake*	game*		
amaze	came	gate	name*	
ape	case	gave*	page	shake
awake	cave	grape	pale	skate
bake	crate	lake	place	space
base	date	lane	plate	state
behave	escape	late	race	take*
blame	fame	make*	safe	wake
brave	flame	male	sale	wave

	alive	five		
	arrive	glide		
	beside	hide	mine*	
	bike	inside	nine*	slide
complete	bite	invite	prize	smile
eve	describe	kite	quite	time*
these*	divide	life	ride	while
scene	drive	like*	shine	white*
Chinese	fine	line	side*	wide*
	fire	mile	size	wise

alone	froze			
bone	hole*			
broke	home*	phone	stroke	
choke	hope*	rope	suppose*	amuse	minute (tiny)
close*	joke	smoke*	those*	confuse	refuse
doze	nose*	stole	throne	excuse	tune
drove	note*	stone*	woke	huge	volume

* High usage words

Magic e before s

It is not enough for a young reader to be on the alert for Magic e's at the ends of words. They need to be alert to this spelling pattern even when it is obscured by the addition of an s to form a plural. Explore this point with the children using any of the words on the right in live spelling and in slow speak dictation.

ape → apes
cake → cakes
date → dates
flame → flames
game → games
grape → grapes
name → names
skate → skates

Burnt-Out Magic e words

done*	minute
gone*	one*
engine	promise
lettuce	purchase
machine	shone
manage	whose

* High usage words

gone
sure

Power failures: the Burnt-Out Magic e's

As soon as we try to teach the Magic **e** principle, exceptions seem to turn up everywhere! This is because 20 out of 60 of the most common Silent **e** words do not obey the rule. They are: **are**, **one**, **gone**, **done**, **come**, **some**, **more**, **before**, **here**, **where**, **there**, **were**, **sure**, **care**, **minute**, **have**, **give**, **love**, **live** and **above**. All are among the 200 most used words in the English language. Consequently they abound in most books and in children's free writing. There are many other slightly less common words, too (see left).

To deal with the exceptions as well as the rule, explain that, as with all kinds of power, occasionally Magic **e**'s power runs out. (Most children have experienced power cuts.) A child who notices, for example, that the **o** in **gone** is not saying its name can be congratulated for having discovered a Burnt-Out Magic **e**. The vowel in a Burnt-Out Magic **e** word either keeps its original sound (as in **gone**) or it becomes irregular as in **machine**.

Show everyone the pictogram side of the Burnt-out Magic **e** *Picture Code Card*. The children can illustrate these power failures themselves by drawing the top hat, wand and wisp of smoke on such **e**'s. Encourage them to start a special collection of these Burnt-Out Magic **e** words.

Only sometimes Magic: the Vase-Prop e

No English word ends in **v**. The Letterland explanation for why the uncertain speller must add a Silent **e** is as follows.

All the Vases of Violets in Letterland have little or no base, so the slightest breeze can blow them over! Because the winds in words always blow in the Reading Direction, the risk is always that a vase will tip over this way (→), unless it is propped up by a Vase-Prop **e**. The vases are safe from the wind inside words, but never safe at the end.

Vase in danger of falling over

Vase safe

When words end in **-ve**, the sound of the previous vowel is not always predictable. Occasionally the functions of a Vase-Prop **e** and a Magic **e** are combined, as in **behave** and **alive**.

have but behave

live but alive

Vase-Prop e words containing a short vowel or Oscar's Little Brother

active	(and the
expensive	many other
forgive	words ending
give*	in –tive)
have*	above*
live*	dove
olive	glove
	love*

* High usage words

Practising the Silent Magic e

The Magic e song

Sing or listen to the **Magic e song** on the *Programme One Songs Cassette*, while a child demonstrates how to picture code any Magic **e** word to strengthen the concept:

Draw your wand	[The child draws a wand]
Shoot every spark	
Jump back one letter	
To land on the mark.	[Adds sparks]
It's always the same.	[Adds stick figure of Vowel Man
The Vowel Man says his name.	through the vowel]
Whenever Magic lands on him	
The Vowel Man says his name.	

Magic e in names

If you happen to have a James, Jane or Kate in your class, you can congratulate them on having Magic **e**'s in their names. They can now picture code the **e** with a top hat and wand. Take care though, as names often include exceptions (see page 188 for examples). These may be caused by foreign pronunciation or by a 'power failure' (see page 164). Use a wiggly line if you need to, or top hat and smoking wand to show a Burnt-Out Magic **e**.

Magic e everywhere

Encourage the children to search for Silent Magic **e**'s everywhere. Shop signs often include Magic **e** words, such as **price**, **size**, **sale**, etc. Similarly they may find some on road signs and their own addresses, e.g. **Lane**, **Drive**, **Gate**, **Close**, **Grove**, **Place**, **-dale**. Children can also look for them among household items and in brand names such as washing powders, sweets, etc.

Instruction words

Many instruction words are also Magic **e** words (see right). They provide a very good reason for children to understand the Magic **e** principle, so they can access any of these words.

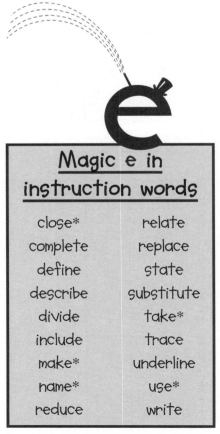

Magic e in instruction words	
close*	relate
complete	replace
define	state
describe	substitute
divide	take*
include	trace
make*	underline
name*	use*
reduce	write

Too many Magic e's?

All too often in the months following a focus on Silent Magic **e**'s, children will apply them liberally in their writing, where no **e** is needed! Let the child picture code the word, see what vowel the sparks land on and pronounce it with the Vowel Man saying his name. For example: 'I will win**e** that ra**c**e', 'Get rid**e** of it quickly' or 'My fishing rod**e** was bent'. Have a good laugh over it. The point will ride home on the laughter.

* High usage words

Word building with the Silent Magic e

Live spelling: tap/tape, plan/plane and cap/cape

Acting out this letter behaviour is the most effective way to make sure the children make the Magic **e** concept their own. Have an apron, picture of a tap and a real tape measure handy to emphasise how 'Magic' can transform a word's meaning as well as its sound.

Let three children build the word **tap**. Give your picture of a tap to the Poor Peter child to hold up, confirming the meaning of the word. Next place a Mr A child (wearing the apron) off to the left. Give a Magic **e** child your prepared wand (see **Preparation**). As he or she waves it over Poor Peter, he then hides his tap picture. When the wand's yellow strips land on Annie Apple, this is the signal for her to 'disappear' and for Mr A to dash in and take her place. As the children sound out the new word **tape**, give the tape measure to the Magic **e** child to hold up, confirming this new meaning.

Use the same approach (with or without props) with the word **plan**. Let the children discover what new word they have made when they have added Magic **e**, causing Mr A to appear (**plane**). Next, explore what must happen if the Magic **e** silently leaves the word. (Mr A leaves too and Annie Apple returns, making **plan** again!)

A further option is to let the children build **cap/cape**. Then slow speak the word **escape** for them to build.

> *What letters do we need now, to make the word **escape**? Listen, carefully, 'e...**sss**...**cape**'. Yes, Eddy Elephant and Sammy Snake.*

The children build **escape**.

> *So now we know that some longer words have a Magic **e** at the end. And now if you came across a word like **escape**, you will know, even before you try to sound out the letters, that Mr A must be in it, saying his name. How? Because you will see the Silent Magic **e** at the end!*

On another occasion, hand out all the consonant and vowel *Picture Code Cards*. Also include the Magic **e** card. Then call out any regular short vowel or Magic **e** word. The children will need to decide whether they are holding a relevant card to be in that word. Another time, also include the Burnt-Out Magic **e** and the Vase-Prop **e** cards.

Consolidation

Copymasters

Programme One Copymasters 47-62 provide practice in the Silent Magic **e** and the Burnt-Out Magic **e**. See if anyone notices two recurring Magic **e** words on all the copymasters: **Name** and **Date**! Let the children picture code them on all three sheets.

SECTION 4

The Handwriting Songs

By Lyn Wendon and Vivien Stone

These songs can be heard on the *Handwriting Songs Cassette*. Those teachers who wish to include exit strokes or 'flick-ups' at this stage, or a little later, can simply ask the children to chant the word 'Flick!' after the relevant verse (for the letters **a**, **d**, **h**, **i**, **k**, **l**, **m**, **n**, **q**, **t** and **u**).

Annie Apple

At the leaf begin.
Go round the apple this way.
Then add a line down,
so Annie won't roll away.

Bouncy Ben

Brush down Ben's big, long ears.
Go up and round his head
so his face appears!

Clever Cat

Curve round Clever Cat's face to begin.
Then gently tickle her under her chin.

Dippy Duck

Draw Dippy Duck's back.
Go round her tum.
Go up to her head.
Then down you come!

Eddy Elephant

Ed has a headband.
Draw it and then
stroke round his head
and his trunk to the end.

Fireman Fred

First draw Fred's helmet.
Then go down his clothes.
Give him some arms
so he can hold his hose.

Golden Girl

Go round Golden Girl's head.
Go down her golden hair.
Then curve to make her swing,
so she can sit there.

Hairy Hat Man

Hurry from the Hat Man's head
down to his heel on the ground.
Go up and bend his knee over,
so he'll hop while he makes his sound.

Impy Ink

Inside the ink bottle draw a line.
Add an inky dot. That's fine!

Jumping Jim

Just draw down Jim, bending his knees.
Then add the one ball
which everyone sees.

Kicking King

Kicking King's body is a straight stick.
Add his arm, then his leg, so he can kick!

Lucy Lamp Lady

Lamp Lady looks like one long line.
Go straight from head to foot
and she's ready to shine!

Munching Mike

Make Munching Mike's back leg first,
then his second leg, and third,
so he can go munch-munching in a word.

Naughty Nick

'Now bang my nail,' Naughty Nick said.
'Go up and over around my head.'

Oscar Orange

On Oscar Orange start at the top.
Go all the way round him, and... then stop.

Poor Peter

Pat Poor Peter properly.
First stroke down his ear,
then up and round his face
so he won't shed a tear.

Quarrelsome Queen

Quickly go round the Queen's cross face.
Then comb her beautiful hair into place.

Robber Red

Run down Robber Red's body.
Go up to his arm and his hand.
Then watch out for this robber
roaming round Letterland.

Sammy Snake

Start at Sam's head
where he can see.
Stroke down to his tail,
oh so care-ful-ly!

Ticking Tess

Tall as a tower make Ticking Tess stand.
Go from head to toe,
and then from hand to hand.

Uppy Umbrella

Under the umbrella
draw a shape like a cup.
Then draw a straight line
so it won't tip up.

Vase of Violets

Very neatly, start at the top.
Draw down your vase, then up and stop.

Wicked Water Witch

When you draw the Witch's wells,
where she works her wicked spells,
whizz down and up and then...,
whizz down and up again.

Max and Maxine

Fix two sticks, to look like this.
That's how to draw a little kiss.

Yo-yo Man

You first make the yo-yo sack
on the Yo-yo Man's back,
and then go down to his toes
so he can sell his yo-yos.

Zig Zag Zebra

Zip along Zig Zag's nose.
Stroke her neck...,
stroke her back...
Zzzoom! Away she goes.

The Alphabet Songs

These songs can be heard on the *Alphabet Songs Cassette*. They practise the sounds that need to be a child's first association with each alphabet letter. Make sure that the children drop into a whisper to pronounce each of the eight voiceless letters: **c**, **f**, **h**, **k**, **p**, **s**, **t** and **x**.

Annie Apple

(*To the tune of* **London bridge is falling down**)

Annie Apple, she says 'ă...'
She says 'ă...', she says 'ă...'
Annie Apple, she says 'ă...'
She belongs to Mr A.

Bouncy Ben

(*To the tune of* **Polly put the kettle on**)

Bouncy Ben says 'b...' in words,
Bouncy Ben says 'b...' in words,
Bouncy Ben says 'b...' in words,
before he bounces home.

Clever Cat

(*To the tune of* **Merrily we roll along**)

Clever Cat says 'c...' in words,
'c...' in words, 'c...' in words,
Clever Cat says 'c...' in words,
and cuddles close to me.

She also makes another sound,
another sound, another sound.
She also makes another sound.
Just you wait and see.*

Dippy Duck

(*To the tune of* **Hey, diddle diddle**)

Dippy Duck, Dippy Duck,
we never hear her quack.
She says 'd..., d...' instead.
The little duck dips
and dives about
as the water drips over her head.

Eddy Elephant

(*To the tune of* **Oh the grand old Duke of York**)

Here comes Eddy El-e-phant
to talk to you and me.
He just says 'ĕ...', he just says 'ĕ...'
He belongs to Mr E.

Fireman Fred

(*To the tune of* **Here we go round the mulberry bush**)

Fireman Fred goes 'fff..., fff..., fff...',
Fireman Fred, Fireman Fred;
Fireman Fred goes 'fff..., fff..., fff...',
fighting fires with foam.

* The soft **c** sound, which is explained in Programme Two.

Golden Girl

(*To the tune of **Merrily we roll along***)

Golden Girl says 'g...' in words,
'g...' in words, 'g...' in words.
Golden Girl says 'g...' in words,
giggling merrily.

Her girlfriend makes another sound,
another sound, another sound.
Her girlfriend makes another sound.
Just you wait and see.*

Hairy Hat Man

(*To the tune of **The wheels on the bus***)

The Hairy Hat Man whispers 'hhh...',
whispers 'hhh...', whispers 'hhh...'
The Hairy Hat Man whispers 'hhh...'
He never talks out loud.

Impy Ink

(*To the tune of **London Bridge is falling down***)

Impy Ink says 'ĭ...' in words,
'ĭ...' in words, 'ĭ...' in words.
Impy Ink says 'ĭ...' in words.
He belongs to Mr I.

Jumping Jim

(*To the tune of **Old MacDonald had a farm***)

Jumping Jim says 'j...' in words,
as he jumps along.
Jumping Jim says 'j...' in words,
as he jumps along.
With a 'j..., j...' here, and a 'j..., j...' there;
here a 'j...', there a 'j...',
everywhere a 'j..., j...'
Jumping Jim says 'j...' in words
as he jumps along.

Kicking King

(*To the tune of **Merrily we roll along***)

Kicking King says 'k...' in words,
'k...' in words, 'k...' in words,
Kicking King says 'k...' in words,
as he kicks along.

Lamp Lady

(*To the tune of **Twinkle, twinkle, little star***)

Look, look, look, that lovely light.
It's Lamp Lady's light so bright.
Listen, 'lll...' is what she'll say,
'lll...' for lamp, both night and day.
Look, look, look, that lovely light.
It's Lamp Lady's light so bright.

Munching Mike

(*To the tune of **Humpty Dumpty***)

'Mmm...', that monster Munching Mike.
My, he has an appetite.
'Mmm...', he hums contentedly,
munching mouthfuls merrily.

* The soft **g** sound, which is explained
in Programme Two.

Naughty Nick

(*To the tune of **Sing a song of sixpence***)

Naughty Nick is noisy,
banging all around.
But he's not a bad boy
when he makes his sound.
Listen, can you hear him,
'Nnn...' he says all day.
Even when he's banging nails,
that's what you'll hear him say.

Oscar Orange

(*To the tune of **Polly put the kettle on***)

Oscar Orange, he says 'ŏ...',
Oscar Orange, he says 'ŏ...',
Oscar Orange, he says 'ŏ...'
He belongs to Mr O.

Poor Peter

(*To the tune of **The wheels on the bus***)

Poor, poor Peter just says 'p...',
just says 'p...', just says 'p...',
Poor, poor Peter just says 'p...',
his poor ears droop.

Quarrelsome Queen

(*To the tune of **Here we go round the mulberry bush***)

Quarrelsome Queen says 'qu...' in words,
'qu...' in words, 'qu...' in words.
Quarrelsome Queen says 'qu...' in words.
She *must* have her umbrella.

Robber Red

(*To the tune of **Three blind mice***)

Rob-ber Red, Rob-ber Red.
See how he runs. See how he runs.
He rrreally makes a growling sound.
He's always heard, but he's never found.
Have you ever seen such a rascal around
'Rrr..., rrr..., rrr...'

Sammy Snake

(*To the tune of **Sing a song of sixpence***)

Sammy Snake says 'sss...' in words,
hissing all the time.
Sammy Snake says 'sss...' in words,
hissing all the time.
Hissing with a 'sss..., sss...',
hissing with a 'sss...'
Sammy Snake says 'sss...' in words,
he's hissing all the time.

Ticking Tess

(*To the tune of **Old MacDonald had a farm***)

Ticking Tess says 't...' in words,
ticking all the time.
Ticking Tess says 't...' in words,
ticking all the time.
With a 't..., t...' here and a 't..., t...' there;
here a 't...', there a 't...',
everywhere a 't..., t...'
Ticking Tess says 't...' in words,
ticking all the time.

Uppy Umbrella

(*To the tune of **Here we go round the mulberry bush***)

Uppy Umbrella says 'ŭ...' in words,
'ŭ...' in words, 'ŭ...' in words.
Uppy Umbrella says 'ŭ...' in words.
She belongs to Mr U.

Vase of Violets

(*To the tune of **London's burning***)

Vase of Violets, Vase of Violets.
Very pretty, very pretty.
'Vvv..., vvv...'; 'vvv..., vvv...';
Pour on water, pour on water.

Wicked Water Witch

(*To the tune of **Polly put the kettle on***)

Wicked Water Witch says 'www...',
Wicked Water Witch says 'www...',
Wicked Water Witch says 'www...'
in all her words.

Max and Maxine

(*To the tune of **Old MacDonald had a farm***)

Now let's whisper, whisper 'k-ss',
whisper, whisper 'k-ss'.
Now let's whisper, whisper 'k-ss',
whisper, whisper 'k-ss'.
With a 'k-ss', 'k-ss' here
and a 'k-ss', 'k-ss' there;
here a 'k-ss', there a 'k-ss',
everywhere a 'k-ss', 'k-ss'.
Now let's whisper, whisper 'k-ss',
whisper, whisper 'k-ss'.

Yo-yo Man

(*To the tune of **Baa, baa, black sheep***)

Yo-yo Man says 'yyy...' in words.
Yyyes sir, yes sir, 'yyy...' in words.
Yellow yo-yos he will sell,
and work for other men as well.

Zig Zag Zebra

(*To the tune of **Humpty Dumpty***)

Zig Zag Zebra is very shy.
Saying 'zzz...' while zzzipping by.
Zebras often seem to be shy,
but we'll never really know why.

The Traditional Alphabet Names Verses

My name's Annie Apple, but some people say
It's often quite handy to call me an 'a'.

My name's Bouncy Ben, as you can see,
But sometimes people call me 'bee'!

My name's Clever Cat, I know that's me,
But often people call me 'cee'!

My name's Dippy Duck, but I have to agree:
There are lots of people who call me 'dee'.

My name's Eddy Elephant, but someone told me
That quite a few people do call me an 'eee'.

My name's Fireman Fred, not Henry or Jeff,
But there are a few people who call me an 'ef'.

My name's Golden Girl, but goodness me,
I know many people who call me 'gee'!

My name's Hairy Hat Man but I've heard it said
That some people call me 'aitch' instead.

My name's Impy Ink: I'm not sure why,
But sometimes people call me 'i'.

My name's Jumping Jim, but I think it's OK
If people prefer just to call me 'jay'.

My name's Kicking King, but I've heard people say
They quite often choose to call me 'kay'.

My name's Lucy Lamp Lady, but I do know full well
That sometimes people call me an 'ell'.

My name's Munching Mike, but if you ask them,
People may say that they call me an 'em'.

My name's Naughty Nick, but now and then
I bump into people who call me an 'en'.

My name's Oscar Orange, but I happen to know
There are lots of people who *do* call me 'oh'.

My name's Poor Peter and I cannot see
Why anyone wants to call me a 'pea'!

My name's Quarrelsome Queen, but I know people do
Quite often decide to call me a 'queue'!

My name's Robber Red, but before you go far
You are bound to meet people who call me an 'are'.

My name's Sammy Snake, but I have to say "Yes,
There are lots of people who call me an 'ess'."

My name's Ticking Tess, as you can see,
But sometimes people call me a 'tea'.

My name's Uppy Umbrella, but I know it's true
There are lots of people who call me a 'you'.

My name's Vase of Violets, as sweet as can be,
But some people like to call me 'vee'.

My name's Wicked Water Witch, but some people do
Have a habit of calling me 'double-you'!

Our names are Max and Maxine, but what you'll learn next
Is that plenty of people may call us 'ex'.

My name's Yellow Yo-yo Man, yet hard as I try
I can't think why people call me a 'why'!

My name's Zig Zag Zebra, but please go ahead
And get in the habit of calling me 'zed'!

We're your Letterland friends, but you should now feel free
To start using our other names: 'aee', 'bee' and 'cee'!

TEACHER CHECKLIST (SECTION 2)

STEP	LETTERLAND CHARACTER(S)	PICTURE CODE CARDS	FLASHCARDS	CASSETTES	STORYBOOK
1	Clever Cat	Clever Cat (**c**)	1-4	*Handwriting Songs and Alphabet Songs Cassettes*	*Clever Cat and the Clown*
2a	Annie Apple	Annie Apple (**ă**)	5-7	*Handwriting Songs, Alphabet Songs and Programme One Songs Cassettes*	*Annie Apple's Adventure*
2b	Mr A, the Apron Man	Mr A (**ā**) and Annie Apple (**ă**)	8	*Programme One Songs Cassette*	*The Vowel Street Party*
3	Dippy Duck	Dippy Duck (**d**), Diana Duck (**d**) and Annie Apple (**ă**)	9-13	*Handwriting Songs and Alphabet Songs Cassettes*	*Dippy Duck Dresses up*
4	Hairy Hat Man	Hairy Hat Man (**h**), Annie Apple (**ă**), Dippy Duck (**d**) and Diana Duck (**d**)	14-16	*Handwriting Songs and Alphabet Songs Cassettes*	*The Hairy Hat Man's House*
5	Munching Mike	Munching Mike (**m**), Munching Maria (**m**) and all previous cards	17-19 and all previous character name cards	*Handwriting Songs and Alphabet Songs Cassettes*	*Munching Mike's Mistake*
6	Ticking Tess	Ticking Tess (**t**), Ticking Tom (**t**) and all previous cards	3, 15, 20-22 and all previous character name cards	*Handwriting Songs and Alphabet Songs Cassettes*	*Ticking Tess and the Tiger*
7	Sammy Snake	Sammy Snake (**s**), Sally Snake (**s**), Sammy and Sally Snake together (**ss**), Sleepy Sammy (**s**) and all previous cards	3, 6, 11, 15, 23-26 and all previous character name cards	*Handwriting Songs and Alphabet Songs Cassettes*	*Sammy Snake and the Snow*
	REVISION OF STEPS 1-7	All previous cards	All previous cards		
8a	Impy Ink	Impy Ink (**ĭ**) and all previous cards	27-28 and all previous character name cards	*Handwriting Songs, Alphabet Songs and Programme One Songs Cassettes*	*Impy Ink's Invisible Ink*
8b	Mr I, the Ice Cream Man	Mr I (capital and lower case **ī**) and Impy Ink (**ĭ**)	29-31 and all previous character and plural noun cards	*Programme One Songs Cassette*	*The Vowel Street Party*
9	Naughty Nick	Naughty Nick (**n**), Naughty Nicola (**n**) and all previous cards	28, 32-35 and all previous character name cards	*Handwriting Songs and Alphabet Songs Cassettes*	*Naughty Nick and the Nettle Nibbler*
10	Yellow Yo-yo Man	Yellow Yo-yo Man (**y**), Eddy Elephant (**ĕ**) and all previous cards	34, 36-39 and all previous character name cards	*Handwriting Songs and Alphabet Songs Cassettes*	*Zig Zag Zebra Saves the Day*
11	Golden Girl	Golden Girl (**g**), Golden Granny (**g**) and all previous cards	40-43 and all previous character name cards	*Handwriting Songs and Alphabet Songs Cassettes*	
12a	Oscar Orange	Oscar Orange (**ŏ**), Oscar's Bothersome Little Brother (**o**) and all previous cards	44-46 and all previous character name cards	*Handwriting Songs, Alphabet Songs and Programme One Songs Cassettes*	*Oscar Orange and the Octopus*
12b	Mr O, the Old Man	Mr O (**ō**), Golden Girl (**g**), Sammy Snake (**s**), Naughty Nick (**n**) and all previous cards	47	*Programme One Songs Cassette*	*The Vowel Street Party*
13	Fireman Fred	Fireman Fred (**f**), Fireman Frank (**f**), Fireman Fred and Frank together (**ff**), and all previous cards	48-51 and all previous character name cards	*Handwriting Songs and Alphabet Songs Cassettes*	*Eddy Elephant and the Forest Fire*

LINKS	IDEAS FOR SCIENCE AND TECHNOLOGY	SLOW SPEAK WORDS	LIVE SPELLING WORDS
	pages 16-17		
Group 1: Annie Apple (featuring short ă words) Group 2: I am… (featuring c and a, and short ă words)	pages 12-13		
Group 1: Five Vowel Men (focusing on the long vowels ā, ē, ī, ō and ū)	pages 12-13		
Group 2: Ducklings (featuring d words; 10-12 words a page)	pages 18-19		dad, add
Group 3: Harry's Hats (featuring h words; mostly 2 sentences per page)	pages 26-27		had, dad
Group 4: Munching Mike's Meal (for reading aloud)	pages 36-37		ham
Group 2: The Picnic (featuring c, a, d, h, m and t; story told in 30 words)	pages 50-51	hat, ham, mat, dad, add, cat, at	hat, cat, at, mat, had, has, hat, hats, cats
Group 2: Flat Hats (featuring c and s, and short ă words)	pages 48-49	sat, sad	sad, sat, mat, mats
Group 2: The Picnic (featuring c, a, d, h, m and t; story told in 30 words)		had, ham, hat, hats, mat, mats, sad, dad, cat, cats, has, add	All words built so far
Group 1: Impy Ink	pages 28-29	it, is, his, him	it, is, his, hiss, miss, him, hat, hit, hid, did
Group 1: Five Vowel Men (focusing on the long vowels ā, ē, ī, ō and ū)	pages 28-29	am, can	I am, I can, kind, find
Group 3: Noisy Nick (featuring n; recurring sentences and high usage words, e.g. said)	pages 38-39	man, ant, and, sand	an, can, man, and, hand, stand, handstand, in, tin
Group 4: Lost Yo-yos (for reading aloud; featuring y words; a book to come back to)	pages 60-61	yes, yet	yes, yet
Group 2: Help! Get the Hat (featuring c, f, g, h, m, y; mostly 2 sentences per page)	pages 24-25		gas, did, dig
Group 1: Oscar Orange (featuring short ŏ words; rhythm, rhyme and song) Group 1: Oscar's Brother	pages 40-41	not, hot, in, on	hot, hat, hit, in, on, cat, cot, dig, dog, dogs, dot, dots
Group 1: Five Vowel Men (focusing on the long vowels ā, ē, ī, ō and ū)	pages 40-41	no, so, old, sold	go, so, no, cold, told, gold, open
Group 3: Fred's Flippers (featuring f words; mostly 2 sentences per page) Group 2: Where are you? (featuring d, g, i, n, p, t, y; high usage words; rhythm, rhyme and song)	pages 22-23	fat cat, fat cats, on, off, I sat on his gift, if, fat, fit, fog	fit, fat, cat, cats, if, gift, gifts, it, is, off, sniff, stiff, staff, fantastic

TEACHER CHECKLIST (SECTION 2)

STEP	LETTERLAND CHARACTER(S)	PICTURE CODE CARDS	FLASHCARDS	CASSETTES	STORYBOO
14	Poor Peter	Poor Peter (**p**), Poor Patsy (**p**) and all previous cards	52-55 and all previous character name cards	*Handwriting Songs and Alphabet Songs Cassettes*	Poor Peter's Penguin Pals
15	Kicking King	Kicking King (**k**) and all previous cards	56-58 and all previous character name cards	*Handwriting Songs and Alphabet Songs Cassettes*	Kicking King Lost in Letterland
16a	Eddy Elephant	Eddy Elephant (**ĕ**), Silent **e**, Mr Mean-E (**e**) and all previous cards	59-61 and all previous character name cards	*Handwriting Songs, Alphabet Songs and Programme One Songs Cassettes*	Eddy Elephant and the Forest Fire
16b	Mr E, the Easy Magic Man	Mr E (**ē**) and Eddy Elephant (**ĕ**)	8, 29, 47 and 62	*Programme One Songs Cassette*	The Vowel Street Party
	REVISION OF STEPS 1-16	All previous cards	All previous cards		
17	Lucy Lamp Lady	Lucy Lamp Lady (**l**), Linda Lamp Lady (**l**), Lucy and Linda together (**ll**) and all previous cards	63-65 and all previous character name cards	*Handwriting Songs and Alphabet Songs Cassettes*	Kicking King Lost in Letterland
18	Vase of Violets	Vase of Violets (**v**), the Vase-Prop **e** (**-ve**) and all previous cards	66-68 and all previous character name cards	*Handwriting Songs and Alphabet Songs Cassettes*	Uppy Umbrella in Volcano Valley
19	Wicked Water Witch	Wicked Water Witch (**w**) and all previous cards	69-71 and all previous character name cards	*Handwriting Songs and Alphabet Songs Cassettes*	The Wicked Witch's Wish
20	Jumping Jim	Jumping Jim (**j**) and all previous cards	72-74 and all previous character name cards	*Handwriting Songs and Alphabet Songs Cassettes*	Impy Ink's Invisible (Jumping Jim in the Jungle)
21	Bouncy Ben	Bouncy Ben (**b**), Bouncy Barbara (**b**) and all previous cards	75-77 and all previous character name cards	*Handwriting Songs and Alphabet Songs Cassettes*	Bouncy Ben's Birthday
22a	Uppy Umbrella	Uppy Umbrella (**ŭ**) and all previous cards	78-81 and all previous cards	*Handwriting Songs, Alphabet Songs and Programme One Songs Cassettes*	Uppy Umbrella in Volcano Valley
22b	Mr U, the Uniform Man	Mr U, the Uniform Man (**ū**)	82-83	*Programme One Songs Cassette*	The Vowel Street Party
23	Quarrelsome Queen	Quarrelsome Queen (**q**), Quarrelsome Queen and the Royal Umbrella together (**qu**), and all previous cards	84-86 and all previous character name cards	*Handwriting Songs and Alphabet Songs Cassettes*	Quarrelsome Queen's Quiz
24	Robber Red	Robber Red (**r**) and all previous cards	87-89 and all previous character name cards	*Handwriting Songs and Alphabet Songs Cassettes*	Robber Red and the Robot
25	Max and Maxine	Max and Maxine (**x**) and all previous cards	90-92 and all previous character name cards	*Handwriting Songs and Alphabet Songs Cassettes*	Zig Zag Zebra Saves the Day
26	Zig Zag Zebra	Zig Zag Zebra (**z**), Zoe Zebra (**z**) and all previous cards	93-95 and all previous character name cards	*Handwriting Songs and Alphabet Songs Cassettes*	Zig Zag Zebra Saves the Day
	REVISION OF STEPS 1-26	All previous cards	All previous cards		

LINKS	IDEAS FOR SCIENCE AND TECHNOLOGY	SLOW SPEAK WORDS	LIVE SPELLING WORDS
Group 2: Peter's Pictures (featuring **p** *words, short vowel words; average of 3 sentences per page)*	pages 42-43	slip, hop	pat, pot, pots, stop, spot, spots, dots, pit, at, pin, pan, top, pig, dig, slip, pond, picnic clap
Group 4: King's Breakfast (featuring words beginning with **c** *or* **k** *and ending in* **-k** *or* **-c***)*	pages 32-33	kick, tick, stick, pick, pack, skip, skid, ink, sink, king, sing, song, kicking, singing, sinking	king, sing, song, kiss, milk
Group 1: Eddy Elephant (featuring short ĕ *words; rhythm, rhyme and songs)*	pages 20-21	dot, pot, pet, get, got, yes, end, send, spend, spent	ten, net, nets, nest, sent, tent, tents, man, men, miss, mess
Group 1: Five Vowel Men (focusing on long vowels ā, ē, ī, ō *and* ū*)*	pages 20-21	me, we, even	he, me, we, be, even
		Choose from words learnt so far	Choose from words built so far
Group 3: Lucy's List	pages 34-35	if, lift, fill, fell, yell, sell, lemon, leg, log, lost, lap, lips	if, gift, lift, cliff, fill, hill, fell, yell, sell, sells, spell, spelt, golden, lemon, leg, legs, log, logs, slip, spill, spilt, split, lot, lots, lips
	pages 54-55	velvet, five, seven	love, have, give, eleven
Group 3: What do you like to eat? (featuring high usage word **what***, recurring text and rhyming words)*	pages 56-57	get well, west wind, can swim, went back, will wish, wet windmill. We will get wet. We will miss him. The wind is from the west.	wind, mill, windmill
	pages 30-31	jog, jig, jug, just, jam, jet	jog, jig, jam, jet, jacket, Jim
Group 4: Bouncy Ben and the Black Thing	pages 14-15	bat, bet, best, bed, bend, bent, belt, bell, job, web, blob, big, bib, bit, bang	big, beg, bag, bags, blob, bells, black, begin, began
Group 1: Uppy Umbrella (featuring short ŭ *words)*	pages 52-53	us, sun, bud, big, beg, bag, bug, just, fun, fuss, huff, puff, mumps, lumps, mad, mud, mug	up, us, fun, sun, luck, stuck, bus, but, bet, bit, bun, buds, duck, dust, hum, cup, pup
Group 1: Five Vowel Men (focusing on long vowels ā, ē, ī, ō *and* ū*)*	pages 52-53		
	pages 44-45	quilt	queen, see, seen, keep, sleep, bee, been, kick, quick, liquid
Group 3: Really Ruined	pages 46-47	red, rip, rib, rub, rug, run, ran, rip, fog, frog, from, rob, robin	red, (read,) tree, three, green, grab, grass, trip, drip, drop, cross, dress, dresses
	pages 58-59	six, fix, mix, fox, wax, next, exit	six, fix, fox, box, next
	pages 62-63	zip, zap	zebra, zero, zoo, whiz, whizzing, buzz, buzzing
		Choose from words learnt so far	Choose from words built so far

Letterland Programme One Teacher's Guide Published by Collins Educational © Lyn Wendon 1997

TEACHER CHECKLIST (SECTION 3)

LETTERLAND CHARACTER(S)	PICTURE CODE CARDS	CASSETTES	SLOW-SPEAK WORDS	LIVE SPELLING WORDS
WORD ENDINGS				
Clever Cat and Kicking King (**-ck**)	**-ck** and all previous cards			**back, black, quick, tric** **lock, stick, rock, rocke** **thick, chick, chicken**
Shared sounds (**-ff**, **-ll** and **-ss**)	**-ff**, **-ll**, **-ss** and all previous cards		Any words from the word boxes, **will miss you, such a fuss, his address, shall sit still**	Any words from the wor boxes, **will miss you, such a fuss, his addres shall sit still**
Nick and a friend at the end (**-nd** and **nt**)	**-nd**, **-nt** and all previous cards			**and, band, bend, blen** **end, send, spend, frier**
Lucy Lamp Lady and a friend at the end (**-lk** and **-lt**)	**-lk**, **-lt** and all previous cards			**walk, talk, left, felt**
CONSONANT DIGRAPHS				
Nick and Golden Girl (**-ng**)	**-ng** and all previous cards	*Programme One Songs Cassette*	**king, sing, song, sting, string, strong, sang, singing, stinging**	**king, sing, song, sting, string, strong**
Nick and Kicking King (**-nk**)	**-nk**, **th** and all previous cards		**bank, bunk, ink, sink, think, thank, pink, drink, drank, blank, blanket**	**bank, bunk, ink, sink, think, thank, pink, drink, drank, blank, blanket**
Sammy Snake and Hairy Hat Man (**sh**)	**sh** and all previous cards	*Programme One Songs Cassette*		**dash, dish, fish, finish**
Ticking Tess and Hairy Hat Man (**th**)	**th** (both cards) and all previous cards	*Programme One Songs Cassette*		**them, then, this, that, they, think, thing, thunder, sixth, seventh ninth, tenth**
Wicked Water Witch and Hairy Hat Man (**wh**)	**wh** (both cards), **ch** and all previous cards	*Programme One Songs Cassette*	**when**	**when, whack, whole**
Clever Cat and Hairy Hat Man (**ch**)	**ch**, Clever Cat (**c**), silent **h** and all previous cards	*Programme One Songs Cassette*		**chat, chips, such, muc lunch, which**
Ticking Tess finds Clever Cat's sneezes catching (**-tch**)	silent **t**, **ch** and all previous cards		Any high usage words from the word box	Any high usage words from the word box
CONSONANT BLENDS				
The six consonant blends with Lucy Lamp Lady (**bl, cl, fl, gl, pl** and **sl**)	**l, b, c, f, g, p** and **s** and all previous cards	*Programme One Songs Cassette*	**plan, black, flat, clock, slip, cloth, block, flag, glad, plastic, flash, blanket**	**plan, black, flat, clock slip, cloth, block, flag, glad, plastic, flash, blanket**
The seven consonant blends with Robber Red (**br, cr, dr, fr, gr, pr** and **tr**)	**r, b, c, d, f, g, p** and **t**	*Programme One Songs Cassette*		
The whispered blends with Sammy Snake (**sc, sk, sp** and **st**)	**s, c, k, p** and **t**	*Programme One Songs Cassette*		
More blends with Sammy Snake (**sm, sn** and **sw**)	**s, m, n** and **w**	*Programme One Songs Cassette*		
The triple consonant blends (**scr, spr, spl** and **str**)	**s, c, r, p, l** and **t**	*Programme One Songs Cassette*		
Ticking Tess and Wicked Water Witch (**tw**)	**t** and **w** and all previous cards	*Programme One Songs Cassette*		**twelve, twelfth, two**
LONG VOWELS				
'Kind' words and 'old' words	$\bar{i}$, **n, d**, $\bar{o}$, **l** and all previous cards		Any high usage words from the word boxes	**kind, mind, remind, ol cold**
The Vowel Men in other words	$\bar{a}$, $\bar{e}$, $\bar{i}$, $\bar{l}$, $\bar{o}$, **u**	*Programme One Songs Cassette*		
The Silent Magic **e**	Magic **e**, Burnt-Out Magic **e**, **-ve**, all previous cards	*Programme One Songs Cassette*		**tap, tape, plan, plane, cap, cape**

STEP Section 2	LETTERLAND CHARACTER(S)	SHAPE	SOUND	WKBK NO.	WORKBOOK MAIN PAGES	REVISION PAGES	LISTEN AND WRITE COPYMASTERS	CODE SHEET COPYMASTERS
1	Clever Cat	cC	'c...'	1	2-3	18, 20, 22-24	1	1
2a	Annie Apple	aA	'ă...'	1	4-5, 7	18, 20-24	2	2
2b	Mr A, the Apron Man	aA	'ā...'	1	6-7	24		27
3	Dippy Duck	dD	'd...'	1	8-9	18, 20, 22, 24	3	3
4	Hairy Hat Man	hH	'hhh...'	1	10-11	19, 24	4	4
5	Munching Mike	mM	'mmm...'	1	12-13	19-21, 24	5	5
6	Ticking Tess	tT	't...'	1	14-15	19-20, 24	6/28	6
7	Sammy Snake	sS	'sss...'	1	16-17	19-20, 22, 24	7	7
8a	Impy Ink	iI	'ĭ...'	2	2-4	20, 22-24	8	8
8b	Mr I, the Ice Cream Man	iI	'ī...'	2	5	22-24		29
9	Naughty Nick	nN	'nnn...'	2	6-7	20, 24	9	9
10	Yellow Yo-yo Man	yY	'yyy...'	2	8-9	20, 24	10/29	10
11	Golden Girl	gG	'g...'	2	10-11	21, 24	11	11
12a	Oscar Orange	oO	'ŏ...'	2	12-14	21, 23-24	12	12
	Oscar's Bothersome Little Brother	oO	'o...'	2	15	24		35
12b	Mr O, the Old Man	oO	'ō...'	2	16-17	23-24		30
13	Fireman Fred	fF	'fff...'	2	18-19	21, 24	13	13
14	Poor Peter	pP	'p...'	3	2-3	18, 20, 24	14	14
15	Kicking King	kK	'k...'	3	4-5	18, 20, 24	15	15
16a	Eddy Elephant	eE	'ĕ...'	3	6-7, 9	18, 20-24	16	16
16b	Mr E, the Easy Magic Man	eE	'ē...'	3	8-9	24		28
17	Lucy Lamp Lady	lL	'lll...'	3	10-11	19-20, 24	17/27	17
18	Vase of Violets	vV	'vvv...'	3	12-13	19-20, 24	18	18
19	Wicked Water Witch	wW	'www...'	3	14-15	19-20, 24	19	19
20	Jumping Jim	jJ	'j...'	3	16-17	19-20, 24	20	20
21	Bouncy Ben	bB	'b...'	4	2-3	16, 18, 24	21	21
22a	Uppy Umbrella	uU	'ŭ...'	4	4-5, 7	16, 18-19, 21-24	22	22
22b	Mr U, the Uniform Man	uU	'ū...'	4	6-7	20-21, 24		31
23	Quarrelsome Queen	qQ	'qu...'	4	8-9	16, 18, 24	23	23
24	Robber Red	rR	'rrr...'	4	10-11	17-18, 24	24	24
25	Max and Maxine	xX	'k-ss'	4	12-13	17-18, 24	26	25
26	Zig Zag Zebra	zZ	'zzz...'	4	14-15	17-18, 24	25	26

Letterland Programme One Teacher's Guide Published by Collins Educational © Lyn Wendon 1997

LETTERLAND CHARACTER(S)	SHAPE	SOUND	CODE SHEET COPYMASTERS		PROGRAMME ONE COPYMASTERS	
WORD ENDINGS						
Clever Cat and Kicking King	-ck	as in **luck**			1, 3	
Shared sounds	-ff	as in **off**			2-3	
	-ll	as in **will**				
	-ss	as in **fuss**				
Nick and a friend at the end	-nd	as in **hand**			4, 6	
	-nt	as in **tent**			5-6	
Lucy Lamp Lady and a friend at the end	-lk	as in **milk**			7	
	-lt	as in **salt**				
CONSONANT DIGRAPHS						
Nick and Golden Girl	-ng	as in **sing**	33		8, 10	
Nick and Kicking King	-nk	as in **pink**			9-10	
Sammy Snake and Hairy Hat Man	sh	as in **shop**	32		11-13	
Ticking Tess and Hairy Hat Man	th	as in **this**			14, 17, 20	
		as in **thunder**			15-17, 20	
Wicked Water Witch and Hairy Hat Man	wh	as in **when**	34		18, 20	
		as in **who**			19-20	
Clever Cat and Hairy Hat Man	ch	as in **cheese**			21-23	
		as in **school**			72	
Ticking Tess finds Clever Cat's sneezes catching	-tch	as in **match**			24	
CONSONANT BLENDS						
The six consonant blends with Lucy Lamp Lady	bl	as in **blue**			25, 28	
	cl	as in **clock**			25, 28	
	fl	as in **flat**			26, 28	
	gl	as in **glad**			26, 28	
	pl	as in **please**			27-28	
	sl	as in **slip**			27-28	
The seven consonant blends with Robber Red	br	as in **bread**			29, 32	
	cr	as in **cross**			29, 32	
	dr	as in **drum**			30, 32	
	fr	as in **frog**			30, 32	
	gr	as in **green**			31-32	
	pr	as in **present**			31-32	
	tr	as in **trip**			31-32	
The whispered blends with Sammy Snake	sc	as in **scooter**			33, 36	
	sk	as in **skid**			34, 36	
	sp	as in **spell**			34, 36	
	st	as in **stop**			35-36	
More blends with Sammy Snake	sm	as in **small**			37, 39	
	sn	as in **snack**			37, 39	
	sw	as in **sweet**			38-39	
The triple consonant blends	scr	as in **scratch**			40, 42	
	spl	as in **splash**			40, 42	
	spr	as in **spring**			41-42	
	str	as in **string**			41-42	
Ticking Tess and Wicked Water Witch	tw	as in **twig**			43	
LONG VOWELS						
'Kind' words and 'old' words	-ind	as in **kind**			44, 46	
	-old	as in **old**			45-46	
The Vowel Men in other words	a, e, i, o, u	as in **he/she**				
		as in **danger**				
The Silent Magic e	a-e	as in **make**			47-50, 54	
	i-e	as in **like**			47, 51-54	
	o-e	as in **home**			47, 55-56, 58	
	u-e	as in **huge**			47, 57-58	

Flashcards and templates

picnic

ducks

cat

add

cats

hat

apple

hats

apples

monster

duck

telephone

snake	yes
snakes	you
in	yellow
I like	green
I am	going
no	lots
can	hot

Letterland Programme One Teacher's Guide Published by Collins Educational © Lyn Wendon 1997

if	everyone
of	live
puppy	I have
poor	very
kind	when
kangaroo	will
enjoys	jump

jumps

question

bounce

red

up

run

under

next

umbrella

box

use

zip

quick

Letterland Programme One Teacher's Guide Published by Collins Educational   © Lyn Wendon 1997

Page 38

add an apple

Page 64

it is

it is

Page 38

Page 41

Page 45

Page 58

Page 79

Picture-coded children's names

Alexander

Amy

Angharad

Ashish

Beatrice

Benjamin

Bethan

Charlotte

Christopher

Claire

David

Daniel

Dominic

Edward

Elizabeth

Elliot

Emily

Fiona

Gary

George

Gemma

Hannah

Harry

Hassan

Helen

Isobel

Isla

Jack

James

Jessica

Joshua

Katie

Kayleigh

Kimberley

Leila

Lauren

Lee

Louisa

Lucy

Martin

Matthew

Michael

Ming

Mohammed

Neil

Nicola

Oliver

Omar

Peter

Reece

Rachel

Rebecca

Richard

Sanjay

Sarah

Scott

Sophie

Tara

Thomas

Victoria

William

Yasmin

Yusef

Zoe

The Letterlanders

Annie Apple   Bouncy Ben   Clever Cat   Dippy Duck   Eddy Elephant   Fireman Fred

Golden Girl   Hairy Hat Man   Impy Ink   Jumping Jim   Kicking King   Lucy Lamp Lady

Munching Mike   Naughty Nick   Oscar Orange   Poor Peter   Quarrelsome Queen

Robber Red   Sammy Snake   Ticking Tess   Uppy Umbrella   Vase of Violets

Wicked Water Witch   Max and Maxine   Yellow Yo-yo Man   Zig Zag Zebra

Mr A   Mr E   Mr I   Mr O   Mr U

Letterland Programme One Teacher's Guide Published by Collins Educational © Lyn Wendon 1997

Letter to parents

Dear Parent/Guardian,

As part of our literacy teaching, we will be using *Letterland* to familiarise your child with the alphabet and to teach the letter combinations they will need to become confident readers and writers. *Letterland* is a well established and successful system for teaching children to read and write and meets the required curriculum guidelines.

Your child will learn about the characters which make up the *Letterland* alphabet. These characters help your child to know and understand letter shapes and sounds. Don't be surprised if your child comes home full of talk about Annie Apple, Clever Cat or Hairy Hat Man. Show an interest in the characters, even if you don't understand what your child is talking about just yet!

Once your child is familiar with the whole alphabet, he or she will be introduced to letter combinations, which is where *Letterland* really comes into its own. In ordinary teaching, children learn that **c** makes one sound and **h** makes another, but this does not help them to learn that **ch** together make a completely different sound. The *Letterland* explanation makes sense of this by using a story that will stick in children's minds. They will learn that whenever Clever Cat sits next to Hairy Hat Man, his hairy hat makes her nose tickle, and so she sneezes with a 'ch' sound. Children remember this story, because it engages their curiosity and captures their imagination.

As you will soon discover, once your child can understand how letters interact in words, they are on the road to becoming good writers and spellers. If you would like more information on using *Letterland* with your child, we will be happy to talk to you about it. You might also be interested to know that a *Letterland Parent's Guide* is available in the shops.

We are looking forward to introducing your child to the world of *Letterland* and we hope you will join in the fun and learning with your child at home.

Thank you for your help.

Letterland Programme One Teacher's Guide Published by Collins Educational © Lyn Wendon 1997

Index